A Treatise On A Section Of The Strata, From Newcastle-upon-tyne, To The Mountain Of Cross Fell, In Cumberland: With Remarks On Mineral Veins In General. Also, Tables Of The Strata, In Yorkshire, Derbyshire, &c. To Which Is Added A Treatise On The...

Westgarth Forster

A TREATISE

ON A

SECTION

OF

THE STRATA,

From Newcastle-upon-Tyne,

TO

The Mountain of Cross Fell, in Cumberland;

WITH REMARKS

ON MINERAL VEINS IN GENERAL.

ALSO,

TABLES OF THE STRATA,

In Yorkshire, Derbyshire, &c.

To which is added,

*A Treatise on the Discovery, the Opening, and the
Working of Lead Mines;*

WITH THE

DRESSING AND SMELTING OF LEAD ORES.

Second Edition, greatly enlarged,

BY WESTGARTH FORSTER.

Printed, for the Author, at the Geological Press, and Sold
by John Pattinson, Alston, Cumberland:
Sold also, by W. Baynes and Son, Paternoster-row, London;
and by Thomas Bell, Newcastle-upon-Tyne.

1821.

TO THE COMMISSIONERS AND GOVERNORS OF
THE ROYAL HOSPITAL FOR SEAMEN, AT
GREENWICH, IN THE COUNTY OF KENT.

My Lords and Gentlemen,

I return you my most sincere thanks, for the honour and great favour you have pleased to confer upon me, in your having granted me permission to Dedicate to you, a new edition of my Treatise on a Section of the Strata, from Newcastle-upon-Tyne to Cross Fell, in Cumberland. You, my Lords and Gentlemen, undoubtedly, of all others, have the best claim to a work of this nature, who are most justly looked up to as the encouragers of the industrious miner. and whose judicious system, generosity, and benevolence, have been so conspicuous in promoting the welfare and good of the mining districts under your direction.

There are many who can bear testimony to the truth of these sentiments, but no one with more unfeigned respect, than, my Lords and Gentlemen,

Your most devoted,
much obliged,
and most obedient servant,

WESTGARTH FORSTER.

PREFACE.

SINCE the First Edition of this Work was offered to the public, the Science of Geology has been more assiduously cultivated in this country, than at any former period; and the exertions of many of our most eminent modern Philosophers, have caused it to assume a highly imposing appearance. The Science itself is intrinsically of a nature to excite the greatest interest in inquiring minds. All the different branches of human knowledge, tend to make us better acquainted with the objects around us: the Astronomer directs our attention to the heavenly bodies, the Chemist investigates the changes that take place in the molecules of matter, and the

Natural Historian arranges, classifies, and describes, the objects on the surface of our globe. The Philosophical Cultivator of these Branches, is amply repaid for his labour, not only by the refined and delicate pleasure he experiences in his investigations, but by the consciousness, that he is extending the boundaries of human knowledge, eliciting new objects of inquiry, and displaying new topics for discussion.— These inducements to the prosecution of research, are not wanting when applied to the Science of Geology. As far as regards the extension of our knowledge, its importance is sufficiently established. It makes us acquainted with the internal structure of our globe, displays the peculiar organization of the planet we inhabit, and has enabled us partially to explain some of the most recondite and tremendous natural phenomena.

The Geologist, in the course of his inquiries, is frequently led to contemplate appearances, which inspire him with the most sublime and interesting ideas. To him the rugged mountain or the trackless desert, are alike objects of importance; and amidst apparent chaos and confusion, he surveys the world in primeval ages. He traces vestiges of many tremendous convulsions which our globe has, at different periods, undergone; he distinguishes in these relics of devastation, the marks of awful omnipotence; and his mind is alternately overwhelmed with wonder or filled with admiration.

But the mere extension of our knowledge is comparatively of little importance, however sublime the truths developed, or however hidden the secrets disclosed, except they promote the comforts, or convenience, or happiness of mankind. The Philosopher, who, after a life spent in refined speculation, sinks into the grave without leaving a monument of his utility, deserves but little gratitude from his surviving fellow creatures.

The Science of Geology is not, however, recommended only by the sublimity of the facts which it brings under our observation, but it is of the greatest utility to mankind in a civilized state; affording him the means of more readily procuring many of those substances, without which polished society could not exist. This position is so completely substantiated in the following pages, that it is useless here to insist upon it at greater length.

The district, which it is the object of this Treatise to describe, does not possess that sublimity of external appearance, which characterizes many other portions of the globe; but in rich and valuable deposits of Lead Ore, the world cannot, at present, produce its parallel. It has for ages individually produced more of this valuable substance, than all other parts of the kingdom taken together, and invariably excites the astonishment of those Mineralogists, who have visited the reputed rich Lead Mines of more celebrated countries. It has, however, been strangely neglected by scientific men. ~~Before the publi-~~

Before the publication of the First Edition of this Work, little had been written upon it to excite attention. That Edition was therefore received with considerable avidity; and has, for some time, been confined to the libraries of original subscribers. More recently, Dr. Thompson and Mr. Winch have separately written upon the subject; and, although, each essay contains valuable information, yet, in what are denominated the Lead Measures, they have made many mistakes, for want of a correct local knowledge of the country. Under these circumstances it is presumed that the present Edition of this Work, cannot be unacceptable to the Geological world; and, that the additions it has experienced, are of a nature to render it still more worthy of their patronage. In making these additions, I have availed myself of several modern works, particularly of the paper, before alluded to, written by Mr. WINCH. I have also received information from Messrs. JOHN and THOMAS DICKINSON, of *Lowbyer*, near *Alston;* Mr. ISAAC HORNSBY, *Nenthead;* Mr. THOMAS FENWICK, of

b

Dipton; and Mr. ROBERT HAYTON, of *Grassfield,*
near *Alston.* I am indebted to Mr. JAMES MULCASTER,
of *Langley* Mill, one of the ablest Metallurgists in
the kingdom, for much valuable information in the
Smelting department ; and to Mr. H. L. PATTINSON,
late of *Alston,* but now of *Newcastle,* for a revision
of a great part of the work, and for several detached
portions of original matter.   To all these gentlemen,
and to some others, whom I cannot enumerate, I beg
leave to return my thanks for their friendly assistance.

With regard to the manner in which I have exe-
cuted my task, as an author, a very few observations
may suffice.   I have not used that polished language
which distinguish some elegant authors, who embellish
with the beauties of composition whatever they describe.   But, if I have not written the language of
elegance, I have at least confined myself to the
language of truth.   I have been more solicitous to
give plain, substantial, and solid practical informa-

tion, than to indulge in flights of fancy, or excursions of imagination. Theory has hitherto been the bane of Geological Science, it has cramped the efforts of inquiry, and paralized the exertions of research. Geologists have been too apt to spurn the drudgery of patient investigation; but it is the road that leads to truth, and the road which I have undeviatingly pursued.

Some Practical Miners have censured the former Edition of this Work, because each individual Stratum did not occur, and agree in thickness, with those in the Mining Field where they were concerned. It may be observed, however, that it is impossible to make a single Section correspond with every Mining Field, as differences occur in the thickness of each Stratum, in a very short distance; when local accuracy is therefore required, the Mine-master, or Agent, would do well to construct, from actual admeasurement, a Section for himself.

In preparing for the publication of this Edition, I have met with the most liberal patronage from many gentlemen engaged in subterranean researches; and, in returning them my most grateful acknowledgments, I may be allowed to express a hope, that their endeavours will be finally crowned with success.

Garrigill Gate, June 26, 1821.

Directions to the Binder.

Plates 3 and 4, to face page 210.

Signature 4 A to follow signature 3 I.
Table of Superposition at the end of Appendix.

INTRODUCTION.

NATURAL History is the name given to that branch of human knowledge, which has for its object, the examination of the bodies that constitute our globe. This Science comprehends all terrestrial phenomena, from the meteoric changes of the Atmosphere, to the mutations to which the interior parts of the globe are subject. The whole is full of grandeur and sublimity, and its parts are immense. The surface of the earth; its seas, lakes, rivers, mountains, vallies, plains, caverns, ruptures, and dislocations; the animated and organized beings, which, heretofore, have dwelt, and now dwell thereon, and the inanimate matter of which they are composed, occupy alternately the attention of the Natural Historian. The philosophy, or natural history of the superficies of the globe, is a subject highly interesting to mankind. Many of the neces-

saries, and most of the conveniences, of life, are found
either upon, or a little within, the surface of the earth,
being the productions of the mineral kingdom; and
we are, in a considerable degree, obliged to certain of
the strata, for the plenty and excellence of our food.
Lime is of great use to meliorate the soil, and to sti-
mulate or excite vegetation; and the gradual decay
and decomposition of the superficies of many other
strata, has the effect of restoring and increasing the
soil, which may have been, in part, exhausted, or carried away by rains and inundations. The extensive
utility of the metals, affords also an ample and irrefrag-
able proof, of the great advantage we derive from the
mineral kingdom; and, indeed, we can survey no article, either upon our habitations, or within them,
without being sensible how much we are indebted, to
that invaluable department of the works of nature.

Earths and stones form the greatest part of our
globe, and are easily distinguished from salts, and in-
flammable bodies, by their insolubility, and unchange-
ableness in the fire. Their arrangement in beds, or

successive strata, constitutes mountains or hills, and plains. In the former, they are either in apparently shapeless masses, or in strata generally much inclined to the horizon. In the plain, they are more horizontally disposed, and covered with a bed of mould, fit for the vegetation of plants, which is produced by the decomposition and mixture of the strata, with the organized bodies, that are formed and decay on the surface of the earth. The several kinds of earth are frequently found in regular crystalline forms, distributed in clefts or subterraneous cavities, and water, which seems to have been present and assisted in their formation, continually attenuates them, transporting them from one place to another, and generally producing in them considerable changes.

The aggregation of the parts which compose stones, is so various, that lithologists have advantageously made use of it, to distinguish them from each other. Some have a cohesion* so strong, and are consequent-

---

* Cohesion is that attractive power in fossils, by which their integrant particles cohere together, and by which they more or less resist the force applied to separate them According to the coherence of the molecules of fossils, they are said to be solid, friable, or fluid.

ly so hard, that steel of the highest temper makes no impression upon them ; such are the precious stones, or gems. Others yield, but with difficulty, to the action of instruments : such are quartz, flints, agate, hard sand-stone, porphyry, and granite. All these, when struck against a piece of steel, produce a number of sparks ; which circumstance has occasioned them to be called *scintallant*, or sparkling. The sparks arise from small portions of the steel, which are struck off by the stone, and inflamed by the great heat excited in the percussion. This heat is so considerable, that the particles are melted, and when collected on white paper, and observed with a good magnifier, they are found reduced to a kind of semi-vitrified oxide. In stones that give fire from steel, the quantity of sparks varies in proportion to their different degrees of cohesion, and this law holds in all cases, from the hardest gem or rock-crystal, to the tender sand-stone, or siliceous breccias of modern formation.

There are many stones whose aggregation is so inconsiderable, as to prevent their giving fire with steel.

Some of these stones are sufficiently hard to break, with different degrees of facility, when struck with a hard tool, while others, are soft enough, to be cut and formed by steel instruments. The difference of consistence in these stones, which do not give fire with steel, is observable in their other properties. Some, as marble and alabaster, receive a good and uniform polish. Others, as most of the calcareous stones, are only capable of an inferior or false polish, and have always a dull and greasy appearance. Some judgment may be formed of the kind of polish which stones are capable of receiving by the appearance they exhibit when wetted; the moisture producing the effect of a polish while it lasts.

It is to be noted, that many stones may afford sparks from steel, though they are not really of the class of scintallant stones. This anomally is occasioned by their being of a mixed kind, and containing, in their substance, small fragments of other stones, sufficiently hard to produce sparks. Thus it is, that several kinds of calcareous marble emit sparks, when

struck with steel, in consequence of the quartz spar,
or flinty particles, intermixed with their calcareous
paste.

Mineralogists are in the habit of distinguishing the
different species of stones, by other means, as well as
those we have enumerated. In their investigations,
acids are frequently employed, but many stones are
not at all acted upon, or changed, by certain of the
acids. Others, upon a drop of diluted nitric, sulphuric, or muriatic acid, being applied to their surface,
by means of a glass tube, present an appearance resembling ebullition. This phenomenon is called effer-
vescence, and is occasioned by the escape of an aeriform matter, separated from the substance by the action of the acid. This elastic fluid, is itself a peculiar aeriform acid, and is called, in chemical language, fixed air, or carbonic acid gas. All calcareous
stones, which contain fixed air, or carbonic acid gas,
effervesce by the contact of these acids, especially
that of nitre, which is usually employed in those assays. This disengagement of an aeriform fluid,

shews, in reality, that the matter from which it escapes, is a saline combination ; but as it possesses neither taste nor solubility in water, in any obvious degree, and as it forms, besides, a great part of the external crust of the globe, naturalists have always regarded it as a species of stone. All stones may therefore be distinguished, into effervescent and non-effervescent. A small phial of nitric acid becomes, of course, a necessary article in excursions made with the intention of collecting, or examining stones. A phial of this sort, a magnifier, a steel, a pocket knife, and a hammer are the principal instruments used by the lithologist.

Bergman recommended the examination of stones by fire, with the assistance of the blow-pipe, and they are now frequently so assayed, with the addition of a little mineral alkali, borax, or black flux, to promote their fusion.

The mineral kingdom, comprehends all those substances which have been formed under the surface of

our earth, whether at the creation, or at any other
time subsequent to that period. There is great reason
to believe, that these substances are still daily produced, in small quantities, where circumstances are
favourable to their formation. This is generally the
case in fissures, or rents in the strata, in caverns, or
where certain mineral springs issue, and deposit the
particles with which they are surcharged. The mineral substances produced *under the surface of the earth,*
differ, in this circumstance, from the subjects of the
vegetable kingdom, to which, in other respects, they
have some resemblance. Many venigenous fossils *
seem to grow nearly in the same manner as vegetables;
the clefts, fissures and veins, in the strata, answering
to the tubes in plants, and water is the vehicle of nutri-
ment common to both. Fire, of the nature of which
we still know so little, may perhaps be an auxiliary,
equally necessary to all the three kingdoms of nature.

On the other hand, we know, with a kind of cer-

---

* These are such as do not form strata, but line or coat
the surfaces of fissures or rents across the strata, which fissures when lined or filled with ores of metals, are called mineral veins.

tainty, that the mineral kingdom has existed before the other two, and, in part, furnished them with materials for their existence, although itself deprived of those wonderful and incomprehensible qualities of life, and the production of seeds, which are the distinguishing properties of the animal, and vegetable kingdoms.

Many observations and experiments must yet be made, before we can expect to determine, whether mineral bodies are at the present time formed, in that large elaboratory the earth, by the very same process as the stratified or full grown minerals seem to have required.

The author of this treatise, has; in the course of his subterraneous surveys, often observed, in the old workings which had not been touched for several years, white crystals of Lead Ore, like so many fine needles, shooting from the cheeks or sides of mineral veins; and he remembers once observing, in an old working at *Wolfcleugh*, in the county of Durham, which had not been opened for twenty years, white lead ore projecting from the sides of the vein, to the length of two inches or upwards.

On quitting this important subject, it may not be improper to advise beginners not too hastily to conclude, that one mineral body is produced by another, merely because those bodies are situated near each other, if it cannot, at the same time, be demonstrated by analysis, or rendered probable by artificial mutation ; nor to content themselves, with making observations on collections of minerals, or heaps of ores, but to visit the mines, quarries, and diggings in the strata, and thus prosecute their studies, in the very workshop of nature herself.

A TREATISE, &c.

PART I.

OF THE STRATIFICATION OF COAL, &c.

THE terms *Stratum*, (singular) and *Strata* (plural,)
in Geology or Mineral Geography, signify one or
more of the several beds or layers of stone, or other
substances, whereof the solid parts of the earth are
composed. These Strata consist of various kinds of
matter; as freestone, limestone, indurated clay, coal,
&c. (to be specified in the sequel) which are disposed
in beds or layers, the under surface of one, bearing
against, or lying upon, the upper surface of the inferior Stratum, which last lies upon or bears against the
next below, in a similar manner.

These Strata are generally found nearly uniform in
their thickness, throughout their whole extent, but in
this point they differ, considerably from each other.

c 2

Some of them are from sixty, to upwards of one hundred, feet from their upper to their under surface, while others are so thin, as scarcely to be discernible, except by a narrow inspection.

The Strata are divided or *parted* from each other, by nearly horizontal smooth separations, with, occasionally, a thin laminæ of soft dusty matter between them, called the *parting*, which renders them easy to disunite; at other times, the two contiguous surfaces, are closely conjoined together, without any visible matter interposed, though the respective substance of each stratum is quite distinct. In the latter case, they are exceedingly difficult to separate, and are technically said to have a *bad parting*. Besides their principal divisions, or nearly horizontal partings, there are, in some Strata, secondary divisions or partings, separating, or approaching towards a separation, of the same Stratum into parts of different thickness, nearly parallel to each other, in the same manner as the principal partings divide the different Strata from each other. But these secondary partings are not so strong nor visible to the eye, nor make so effectual a parting as the principal ones. They are only met with in the Strata that are not of an uniform hardness, texture, or colour from their upper to their under surface.

There are other divisions or joints, called *backs* or *slines*, in almost every Stratum, which cross the former horizontal ones transversely, and cut the whole Stratum through its two surfaces, into long rhomboidal masses. These, again, are crossed by others, called *cutters* or *end joints*, running either in an oblique or perpendicular direction to the before-mentioned *backs*, and also cutting the Stratum across through its two surfaces. Both these kinds of joints, the *backs* and cutters, generally extend from the upper or superior Stratum, down through several of the lower ones; so that, together with the horizontal partings, they divide measures of the strata, into innumerable nearly cubical, prismatical, or rhomboidal figures, according to the thickness of the Stratum, and the position and number of the joints. These joints have, sometimes, a kind of soft dusty matter within them, and sometimes none, like the first-mentioned horizontal partings; and the softer Strata have generally more backs and cutters, than those that are harder, which do not extend or penetrate through the others. Limestone Strata have usually the most open vertical joints, of any other; freestone of the siliceous or sandstone kind, have also many open joints in some situations.

A seam, or bed of coal, is a real Stratum, which is found to be quite as regular, as any of the comitant

Strata found in the coal field, lying above, or below the coal; or, indeed, as any other of the various Strata, which compose the external crust of our globe.

There are, sometimes, in many coal countries, and many coal fields, a considerable number of Strata or beds of coal, of various quality and thickness, placed *Stratum super Stratum*, with a variety of other Strata interposed between them; and sometimes different Strata, or seams of coal, are so near to one another, that, two, three, or more of them, are cut through and worked in one pit.

Every Stratum of coal has some degree of declivity or slope, together with a longitudinal or horizontal bearing; and it stretches as far every way as the Strata which accompany it. The conclusion, therefore, appears reasonable, that coal is not an adventitious recent production, but that every Stratum of it, bears its proportion in composing the superficies of our globe, and that the Strata of coal are coeval with the other Strata which accompany them.

The Strata are seldom found to lie in a truly horizontal position, but generally have an inclination or descent called the *dip*, to some particular part of the ho-

rizon. If this inclination be to the eastward, it is called an *east dip*, and a *west rise*, and according to the
point of the compass to which the dip inclines the fast-
est or most rapidly, is the denomination. The ascent
or rise is, of course, to the contrary point. This inclination or dip of the Strata, is found to hold almost
every where. In some places it varies very little from
the level; in others, very considerably, and in some
so much as to be nearly vertical. But whatever degree
of inclination the Strata have to the horizon, they are
always found to dip in the same regular and uniform
manner throughout their whole extent, if not inter-
cepted by a *ridge* or a *trough*, or disordered by *dykes,
hitches,* or *troubles.* If the Strata have an *east dip,*
they may, by the intervention of a *dyke* or a *trough,*
have on the other side an *east rise,* which is a *west dip;*
and any considerable alteration in the dip is never met
with, unless occasioned by the circumstances last mentioned.

Every Stratum, in a whole range, or coal field, is
spread out to a vast extent, in an inclining plane, suppose of a mile, or of several miles square, like an inclining field or face of a country. A dead level line
drawn across or upon this inclining plane, is called the
bearing of the Strata; and another line, drawn at right

angles to the dead level line or bearing, is called the *declivity of the Strata*, or the dip and rise of the Strata. In general we can see, on the surface, but a very little way from the rise to the dip, or along the line of declivity of the Strata; because they soon dip down out of our sight, and, generally, a great number of other Strata come on above them. But, on the contrary, we can sometimes trace the same individual Stratum, or number of Strata, along the surface or dead level line, for several miles;* and, therefore, we may properly call this the *longitudinal line of bearing*.

It very frequently happens, perhaps, that the Strata stretch or spread as far, upon the latitudinal line of declivity, as they do upon the longitudinal line of bearing, although we are unable to trace them, in this direction, to any great distance. We often see the edges of the Strata, in different places upon the line of bearings, bursting out and appearing to the day, in rivers, rivulets, rocks, cliffs or scars, &c. and we frequently work quarries, and especially beds of coal, to a considerable length upon the stretch of this line.

---

* Mr. Wm. Smith, of Milford, near Bath, was the first to extensively verify and apply this very important Geological fact; by having, prior to the year 1795, actually traced and mapped the course of the beds of several of the thicker Strata of the south-east of England, across the Island, from the west to the east Sea, in his Geological Map of England, sold by Carey, London.

From these observations, it appears that every individual Stratum, in the whole section, keeps its station where it is placed; and that, in general, it spreads as wide, and stretches as far, as any of those that are placed above or below it, which may, perhaps, be for several miles in every direction. Now a seam of coal being a regular Stratum, when the crop or outburst is once discovered, we may take it for granted that it will spread as wide every way, as any of the other Strata which are found to accompany it, above or below.

The Stratum which is placed immediately above the seam of coal, is properly called the roof of the coal; and the Stratum which is placed immediately below a seam of coal, is, with equal propriety, called the pavement, or floor of the coal. Now these three, that is the seam of coal, its roof, and its pavement, with the other concomitant Strata lying above and below them, almost always preserve their parallelism and stations with respect to each other, that is, they are all stretched out and spread one above another, upon the same inclining plane, and they have the same lines of bearing and declivity.

It is here proper to give an account of the several

D

Strata of stone and other matters, which are usually
connected with coal, and are generally found to occur
along with it. For the sake of distinction we shall ar-
range them in six principal classes, which will include
all the varieties of Strata that have been found to accompany coal, in every district, both in England and
Scotland, where it abounds.

—⁓◦⁓—

I.—OF WHINSTONE.

The Strata of what is denominated whinstone are
the hardest of all others. The angular pieces will
sometimes cut glass. It is often of a very coarse texture, and, when broke across the grain, exhibits the
appearance of large particles of sand, in a semi-vitrified
state. Each Stratum is commonly homogeneous in
substance and colour, and is often cracked in the rock
from the surface downwards to a great depth. The
common colours of these Strata, are black and dark
blue; yet there are others of an ash colour and light
brown. Their thickness, in all the coal countries, is
but inconsiderable, varying from five or six feet, down
to a few inches, and it is only in a few places, that
they are found to attain the maximum we have stated.

In the air whinstone, decays a little, leaving a brown powder; and in the fire it cracks and turns a reddish brown.

———∽∾∽∾∽———

II.—LIMESTONE.

Limestone, or what is called bastard limestone, is sometimes, though rarely, met with in collieries. It is a well known stone; but from its resemblance in hardness and colour, it is often mistaken for a kind of whin.

———∽∾●∾∿———

III.—POSTSTONE OR GRITSTONE.

This is a freestone of the firmest kind, and next to the limestone in hardness and solidity. It is of a very fine texture; and, when broken, appears as if composed of the finest sand. It is commonly found in a homogeneous mass, though variegated in colour; and, from its hardness, is not liable to perish on being exposed to the weather. Of this kind of stone there are four varieties, which may be distinguished by their colour.

D 2

The most common is white post, which is sometimes variegated with streaks or spots, of brown, red, or black.

Grey post is also very common: it appears like a mixture of fine black and white sand, and is often variegated with brown and black streaks, which resemble small clouds. These spots are sometimes composed of particles of coal.

Brown or yellow post is often met with of different degrees of colour, most commonly of light ochre or yellow sand. It is as hard as the rest, and is also variegated occasionally with white and black streaks. Red post is generally of a dull red colour. It is rarely met with in collieries and is often streaked with white or black.

All these lie in Strata of different thickness, but they are commonly thicker than any other Strata. They are separated from each other, and from other Strata, by partings of plate or shiver, coal, sand, or soft matter of various colours.

IV.—SANDSTONE OR STONEBIND.

This is an imperfect freestone of a coarser texture than post, and not so hard. Its pores are so open as to render it easily pervious to water. When broken, it is apparently of a coarse, friable substance, mouldering to sand when exposed to the wind and rain. It has frequently white shining spangles, *pebbles* or *nodules*, and other small stones, inclosed in its mass.

This sandstone is most generally found in Strata of considerable thickness, without many secondary partings, but where these do occur, they are commonly sandy or soft. It is also occasionally found subdivided into layers, as thin as grey slate.

There are two varieties of this Stratum commonly met with, distinguished by their colours, grey and brown, which are of different shades, lighter or darker, in proportion to the colouring matter contained in the stone.

V.—OF METALSTONE, BIND OR CLUNCH.

This is a tolerably hard Stratum, being, in point of hardness, next to sandstone, generally solid, compact, of considerable weight, and of an argillaceous substance, containing, in many places, nodules or balls of iron ore, and sometimes yellow or white pyrites. The partings, or those surfaces that are horizontally in contact, are hard, polished, and frequently smooth as glass. It is internally of a fine texture, and when broken has a dull dusky appearance, like hard dried clay mixed with particles of coal. It is hard in the mine or quarry, but when exposed to the fresh air, it falls into very small pieces, and at length into clay. The most usual colour of this stone is blackish; but there are several other lighter colours, down to light brown, or grey. It is easily distinguished from freestone by its texture and colour, as well as by its other characteristics. It lies in Strata of various thickness, though seldom so thick as the two last-mentioned kinds of stone.

VI.—OF SHIVER, SHALE OR PLATE.

This Stratum is more frequently met with in collieries than any other. There are many varieties of it, which differ from each other both in hardness and colour, but they all agree in their principal characteristics.

The black colour is by far the most common, and is called by the miners *black shiver, black metal,* or *bleas.* It is softer than metal stone, and in the mine, is rather a tough than a hard substance. It is not however of a solid or compact matter, but seems to be a sort of indurated clay, which is easily separable by the multitude of its partings, into very thin pieces or laminæ, of unequal thickness. These laminæ break again into irregular rhomboidal fragments when struck with a slight force, and they have the property of rapidly absorbing water.

Each of these small pieces has a polished glassy surface, and when broke across the grain, appears of a dry leafy or laminated texture, like exceedingly fine clay.

It is very friable, feels to the touch like an unctuous substance, and dissolves in air or water to a fine, pinguid, black clay. There are very often found inclosed in it, lumps or nodules of iron ore, commonly called *catheads.*

An accurate knowledge of the Strata in a coal field, is indispensibly necessary to the coal master; and to obtain this knowledge, he should himself enter the

pits, mines, or levels sunk or drove in the coal field.
In these he will see a great number of the different
Strata of stone, and of the other coal metals,* thick
and thin, hard and soft. An accurate coal master will
make himself well acquainted with the quality, colour,
and thickness of each of these, and how far each of
them is above or below such and such a seam of coal.
He will carefully consider the order of the different
Strata, as they lie *Stratum super Stratum*, with respect
to one another; so that when he sees any one of them,
he will know what others are to be found next to it,
either above or below. Now this knowledge is often
of singular use to him; as, for instance, when the
coal is thrown either up or down, by one of those
faults or slips, which will be presently described. In
this case the coal appears to be lost.—Well what is he
to do in this difficulty ? The coal is of too much consequence to be given up.—What method then is to be
adopted in order to recover it ? That he cannot properly resolve upon, until he first knows how far it is
thrown out of its course, up or down.—The readiest
way to be master of this interesting point, is to pierce

* By coal metals, or coal measures, in treating of coal,
are meant such Strata as are commonly found accompanying
coal, without reference to metallic fossils.

the stone, or rather the Stratum, which faces the workmen where the coal is cut off and lost, and if he knows it with certainty he is encouraged to proceed, as he is thereby made tolerably sure how far the coal is thrown off its ordinary level, either up or down; and he can then judge which is the most proper method to recover it, with the least expenditure of time and money. The coal is sometimes thrown a great way out of its former course by *faults*, *dykes*,* or *slips*, which frequently makes it necessary to search for it on the other side of such *trouble;* and many accidents happen, which occasionally render it prudent to quit the former station altogether, and to sink new pits. When this is the case an intimate acquaintance with the Strata, which, in that particular district, accompany the coal, becomes indispensably necessary; the want of it making many to grope in the dark, and often to commit serious blunders, at much unnecessary expense, and loss of time.

An expert coal master will therefore be careful to observe the order, disposition, and appearance of each

---

* A dyke is a natural crack, fissure, or chasm, in the Strata, which chasm, is commonly filled up with heterogeneous matter.

E

Stratum, wherever it is seen cropping out, or baset-
ting, in the edges of rivulets, or other places; he will
examine, investigate, and compare, all that he sees
from time to time, and by this means, he will ulti-
mately become acquainted with the nature and internal position of the Strata, in the district or coal field
to which his operations are confined.

It is difficult to explain all the phenomena of every
particular *fault* or *slip*, which may be met with in
working coal, because they all differ from one another
in some manner or degree. All the *faults* or *slips*
found in the coal Strata, are called by naturalists *perpendicular fissures*, and by miners *rake veins*. As the
matter filling these veins is softer or harder, and as
the sides are wider and closer, so are the slips.—But
this subject will be more fully explained in Part II.

'The different coal seams, with their concomitants
near Newcastle-upon-Tyne, rise and crop out regularly, one after another, upon the general rise or
aclivity of the Strata, considerably to the east of the
river *Derwent*, or indeed east of *Healy-field* lead
mine.

27

EXPLANATION OF THE SECTION.

PART I.

COAL MEASURES.

The first part of the section commences with the highest Stratum sunk through at St. Anthon's colliery, about two miles east of Newcastle-upon-Tyne. Before we proceed to describe it in detail, it may be proper to observe, that although it is presumed to commence with the uppermost Stratum, which occurs in the coal measures, yet the Stratum with which it commences, is supposed, in order of super-position, to be overlaid by the magnesian limestone, which bounds the eastern extremity of this part of our island. Mr. Winch has described the position and extent of this limestone, with great accuracy, in the transactions of the Geological Society, *vol. 4, page 3*, from which we extract the following account. In the south-eastern part of the county of Durham, a fine-grained red sandstone is stated to predominate, after describing which, Mr. Winch proceeds, as follows :—

"To the north-west of the red sandstone, the magnesian or Sunderland limestone is found. In the cliffs

B 2

at Cullercoats, in Northumberland, a dyke, well
known by the name of the *Ninety Fathom Dyke*, is
seen dislocating the coal measures, and passing into
the sea. Here is the northern extremity, of the western boundary, of the magnesian limestone. A few
masses again occur, among the rocks of sandstone
and slate clay, upon which Tynemouth-castle stands;
but it is on the coast, in the neighbourhood of South
Shields, in the county of Durham, that this formation first becomes extensive. From this point it swells
into a range of low round-topped hills, and is seen
stretching towards the south-west, protending into the
coal-field, and forming an undulating line, by Clea-
don, Boldon, Clacksheugh, upon the Wear near Hil-
ton-castle, Painshaw, Houghton-le-Spring, Sherburn,
Coxhoe, Ferry-hill, on the turnpike road leading from
Durham to Darlington, Merrington, Eldon, Brussle-
ton, Morton, Langton, and Sellaby, till it reaches
the Tees below Whinston-bridge, thirty miles west-
south-west of that river's junction with the sea, and
forty-four miles from the Tyne at South Shields. The
sea coast forms its eastern boundary for twenty-seven
miles and a half, from the Tyne to the rocks of Hartlepool, and the red sandstone already mentioned,
from Hartlepool to the termination of that rock west
of Croft-bridge. The same bed is afterwards continu-

ed through Yorkshire, Derbyshire, and Nottingham-
shire, to the neighbourhood of Nottingham, where it
suddenly terminates. The quarry at Whitley near
Cullercoats, affords the geologist an opportunity,
of ascertaining that the magnesian limestone, overlies the coal measures, and that the latter were consolidated before the limestone was deposited upon them.
I shall therefore describe that curious spot. A hollow
space, formed like a bason or trough, is filled with the
limestone. The length of this, from east to west, is
about a mile, the breadth, from north to south, four
hundred yards, the depth seventy feet. The beds pass
over the *Ninety Fathom Dyke, which has occasioned in
them no confusion or dislocation, so that there can be
little hazard in stating, that the beds of the magnesian
limestone belong to a more recent formation than those of
the coal field.* The limestone has been quarried across
its whole breadth, and a numerous set of thin Strata
are thus exhibited to view. At the surface loose blocks
of blueish grey coralloid limestone, the produce of the
lead mine district, are found imbedded in the soil.
Three or four of the uppermost Strata of the quarry,
are of white slaty limestone, which, being nearly
free from iron, burns into a pure white lime. Below
these, an ash-grey fine-grained Stratum is met with,
which strongly resembles a sandstone, and seems to

contain nearly as much iron, as the ferri-calcite of Kir-
wan, becoming magnetic by the action of the blow-
pipe : it produces a brownish yellow lime, less esteemed for agricultural purposes than the former.   The
beds next in succession, are of an ash-grey colour,
compact in texture, and conchoidal in fracture : these
afford a buff-coloured lime, which sells for nearly the
same price as the white.   Near the bottom of the
quarry the limestone alternates with shale, the whole
rests upon a Stratum of shale upon the southern side,
and upon a thick bed of sandstone upon the northern.
The shale has been cut through to a considerable distance from the kilns, in the direction of North Shields,
for the purpose of laying a rail-way to the Tyne.   The
thickness of the limestone Strata, varies from three or
four inches to as many feet.   Small strings of galena
have been found here, and, in one of the Strata that
was walled up when I visited the quarry, a few organic
remains have been noticed.

It is well ascertained that the magnesian limestone
of this district, as is the case with that of Derbyshire
and Yorkshire, rests upon the coal measures.   No coal
mine has yet been won, in Northumberland or Durham,
by sinking a shaft through the limestone, although the
workings of collieries, situated on its western bound-

ary, have been carried underneath it. It is therefore
a matter of great importance, to those who have roy-
alties within its limits, to know under what thickness
of limestone the coal measures are buried, whether,
after passing under the limestone, they continue to
dip at the same angle as before, and whether the quality or thickness of the coal seam is then altered.

Along the coast of Durham, from Shields to Hartlepool, the limestone Strata dip to the south-east.
At Chapter Main, near South Shields, the coal measures, although approaching the limestone, rise towards the sea, in conformity to their direction on the
north side of the Tyne; but at Painshaw, Newbottle,
Rainton, &c. they dip to the south-east, the limestone
being there protuded into the coal field beyond the
prolongation of that line, from which the coal measures, that are without covering, begin to rise in an
eastern direction. It appears, therefore, that their
dip is not affected by the limestone. It is a circumstance, however, too well ascertained to admit of a
doubt, though difficult to be accounted for, that the
coal is deteriorated in quality, when covered by the
limestone."

The facts which Mr. Winch here states, are of a
very interesting nature, and afford great room for Geo-

logical speculation. His observations prove, in the most decisive manner, the position of the magnesian limestone, but, as the section commences, as we have before stated, merely with the uppermost Stratum of the *coal measures*, we have not thought proper to insert it.

————

We have before given a general description of whinstone, bastard limestone, poststone, sandstone, metalstone, &c. all of which, with their several varieties, may be seen in the first part of the section. It would be tedious and unnecessary to describe all the different alternations in succession, as many of them intimately resemble each other, and, perhaps, the whole comprized in the varieties we have enumerated.

Of the coal itself three distinct kinds are found, the common or slate coal, cannel coal, called *splint*, or *parrot coal*, and *coarse* coal, also called splint.

The texture of fine splint is compact, the cross fracture conchoidal, and the fragments are cubical. Coarse coal is slaty in its texture, and it seems to be intermediate between common and cannel coal.

These varieties are not found to occupy separate
and peculiar seams of the coal formation, but alternate irregularly with one another, as layers of the
same bed.

Though the *same kinds of Strata* are found to occur,
in almost every colliery or district affording coal, yet
they frequently differ considerably in thickness. They
are also irregular in their other qualities. In some
places they are most of the hard kinds, in others, most
of the softer, and it rarely happens, that in any one
district, all the various kinds are found. Some may
perhaps occur once or twice only, while others are met
with ten or twenty times, before we reach the principal
Stratum of coal. Hence, in forming an individual
Section of an extensive district, it is impossible to enumerate all the irregularities, that are found at different
places, or to define the precise thickness of each Stratum, for any considerable distance, either on the aclivity of the Strata, or the horizontal line of bearing.
Anomalies of this nature also frequently occur in the
lead measures, for which it is impossible to account, but
these individual differences, are not of much consequence in a geological point of view, as they do not
generally affect the aggregate depth of the Strata, the

F

deficiency in thickness of one Stratum, being supplied by the redundancy of another.

The order, position, and thickness of the Strata, alters so considerably at different parts of the Northumberland coal field, that it is sometimes very difficult to identify *even the various coal seams*, which are objects of the greatest attention. Sometimes two of the coal seams on the river Tyne, form only one on the river Wear, as particularly mentioned in the section.

The first eight small seams, and the high main coal, on the river Tyne, are scarcely noticed on the river Wear. The next below, called the Metal coal on Tyne, makes part of the Five-quarters on Wear; and again, the Stone coal on Tyne, makes part of the Five quarters on Wear; then the next called the Yard coal on Tyne, forms the High main coal on Wear, six feet thick. A seam six inches thick, together with the Bensham seam on Tyne, three feet three inches thick, from the Maudling seam on Wear, four feet thick. The next below is a coal called the Six-quarter coal on Tyne, three feet six inches thick, which unites with the Five-quarter coal on Tyne, three feet two inches thick, to form the Low main coal on Wear. Underneath is a small seam nine inches thick, below which we find the Low main coal on Tyne, six feet six inches thick, which forms the Hutton seam on Wear, four feet three inches thick. We then find five small seams (as will appear by the section) when we come to the Hervey seam, three feet thick on Wear, identical with the Whickham stone coal on Tyne, six feet thick. The lowest seam which occurs, is the Brockwell seam. It has not been much worked on the river Tyne, and is totally unknown on the river Wear, where it has never yet been sunk to.

The basset of the Whickham stone coal (numbered 88 in the section) to the westward is near Conset, in the county of Durham, and it is visible on that part of the Stanhope road, leading down from Carr-house, to Stannyford dam. The basset of the Brockwell seam, which lies a few fathoms under the Whickham stone coal, has not been discovered, and, it is therefore very probable, that it is split in pieces on approaching the surface, and by that means never discovers itself through the clay.

Mr. Winch's paper, in the Geological transactions, to which we have before alluded, contains so much valuable information, on the Newcastle coal field, and elucidates in so clear a manner, what we have already stated, that we beg to present the following extract to our readers :—

"The coal seams and the rocky Strata, which together constitute the coal formation of Newcastle and Sunderland, are, in part, covered by the magnesian limestone, and rest upon the lead mine measures. They occupy a hollow or trough, of which the extreme length, from the *Aklington* colliery near the *Coquet,* in the north, to *Cockfield* in the neighbourhood of *West Auckland,* is 58 miles; and the breadth from *Bywell* on the Tyne, to the sea shore, is 24 miles.— This formation first makes its appearance on the south bank of the Coquet, near that river's junction with the sea, and bounds the coast of Northumberland, in a south-south-eastern direction for twenty-three miles. It then crosses the mouth of the Tyne, after which the magnesian limestone begins to cover a part of it, and continues to intrude, more and more, upon it, until both approach the Tees, The distance from South Shields to Cockfield, is thirty-two miles, in a south-westerly direction. The western side of this district cannot be so easily defined, since many of the lead mine measures strongly resemble those of the coal field, but when the *millstone grit* (a coarse-grained sandstone so called) and the *Blue Enerinal Limestone* (or *Fell top limestone*, numbered in the section 121) are seen cropping out, one may then be sure that the boundary of the coal formation is passed. However, if a line be drawn from the vicinity of Aklington on the Coquet, to cross the Tyne at Bywell, the Derwent near *Allensford*, and the Wear below *Wolsingham*, and to terminate at Cockfield, a tolerably correct idea may be formed of its western limits.

This district is characterized by low round-topped hills, which rise gently from the sea, and increase in height towards the west. *Pontop-pike*, situated on the Derwent, not far from the western boundary of the coal Field, is reckoned by Mr. Fenwick, of Dipton, to be one thousand feet high, and by Colon el Mudge, one thousand and eighteen; and a pit sunk near the summit, proves that it cannot be much less. That part of Newcastle leases which lies close to Spring Gardens, and the western turnpike-gate, is ascertained to be one hundred and ninety feet above the level of the Tyne, and two hundred and five above the sea. Benwell Hills to the west, and Gateshead Fell to the south, are somewhat higher.

The inequality of the surface does not affect the dip

or inclination of the coal measures, and when they are interrupted, or cut off, by the intervention of a valley, they will be found on the sides of the opposite hills, at the same levels as if the beds had been continuous. Thus the *grindstone bed* may be seen on *Byker Hill, Gateshead Fell,* and *Whickham Banks,* though no where in the vales of the *Tyne* and the *Team,* which severally intersect those elevated portions of land. The conclusion is obvious, that the present irregularity of hill and dale, has been occasioned by the partial destruction and dispersion of the uppermost rocky masses, which constitute the coal formation.

That part of the trough in which the greatest thickness of the coal measures is found, seems to lie in the vicinity of *Jarrow,* and from this point, the beds appear to rise to some considerable distance, on each side; particularly in a western direction. The average dip of the coal measures is one inch in twenty, but this inclination is by no means uniform in every part of the district. Thus, that seam of coal called the high main, which lies buried at Jarrow under one hundred and sixty fathoms of beds of stone, soon rises to the day in a north-east direction, and bassets out in the cliffs, between Cullercoats and Tynemouth. In its north-westerly range it reaches Benwell Hills, and at *Pontop*, nearly eighteen miles due west of the sea shore at Sunderland, it is met with at thirty-eight fathoms and a half from the surface. In a southerly direction, it is found at fifty-two fathoms on Gateshead Fell, but bassets out before it reaches the Wear.

The principal substances, besides coal, which constitute the coal formation, are shale and sandstone, which, as they vary in hardness or colour, receive different provincial names from the miners. It is not possible to discover in the coal measures, any regular order of succession, which will apply to the whole coal field, and it is even with difficulty that, in limited portions of it, the continuity of particular seams can be traced. This arises from the variable thickness, and the rapid enlargement and contraction of the different beds, that which in one section is scarcely perceptible, having attained, in a neighbouring pit, the thickness of several fathoms. It is thus that the Five-quarter coal seam of the mines on the Wear, is divided into the Metal and Stone coal seams of Sheriff Hill, and that the Low main seam of the Wear, becomes the Five-quarter and Six-quarter seams of the Tyne and Gateshead Fell. Thus also in Brandling and Hebburn collieries, a parting of stone first divides, and after-

wards usurps the place of the High main coal seam;
and thus the two upper coal seams that are well worth
working (see the section of Montague colliery north)
at *Kenton*, are no longer so in the neighbouring colliery
of *Killingworth*.

The following is an account of a similar occurrence
in Montague colliery, abridged from an unpublished
memoir by Mr. Thomas, of Denton, on the dykes
found in that mine:—Within the Newbiggen Stone
coal seam, at twenty inches from the floor, there is a
band of soft clayey substance one inch and a half thick,
but the band increasing in thickness towards the east,
the coal is divided into two distinct seams, whose aggregate thickness is less than that of the original seam.
At the distances of one thousand yards to the east,
and three hundred yards north of the main dyke (the
ninety fathom dyke described before) the band is
twenty-four feet thick, the upper coal seam six inches,
and the lower sixteen inches. The band decreases towards the north, at the rate of something more than
one inch per yard, and the coal at the same time increasing, the upper and lower parts are so nearly united, at the distance of one hundred and sixty yards, as
to form again a workable seam. The upper coal then
measures twenty-one inches, the lower twenty-four,
and the band fifteen.

It is useless therefore to attempt any general section
of the coal formation, and it will be seen in the sections subjoined to this paper, how difficult it is, from
want of uniformity in the beds, to identify the coal
seams in the vicinity of Newcastle. I refer to the sections of *Hebburn* and *Sheriff-Hill*, as exhibiting, when
taken in succession, a series of coal measures of the
thickness of about two hundred and seventy fathoms.
In the former colliery, are the beds which lie above
the High main coal, in the latter, principally those
which lie beneath it, together they present the entire order of the coal seams, that are best understood
in the Newcastle district: but it will be seen, even in
these two examples, what want of agreement there is
in the beds, which lie in the two sections above the
High main coal.

The most valuable seam in the whole coal field, in
point of thickness and quality, is that called the *High
Main,* of the mines, situated between Newcastle and
Shields. It there averages above six feet from the
roof to the floor, contains a large proportion of bitumen, and is sufficiently hard to bear carriage without
breaking into very small fragments. I have already
described, in part, the basseting of this coal seam,
along the course of an oval line, of which Jarrow is the

centre, from which some idea may be formed of the
extent of country which it underlies, south of the
Ninety Fathom Dyke. At a land-sale pit, a little
above the *Ouse-burn Bridge*, near Newcastle, this
seam was found at fourteen fathoms, but on the Town
Moor, from the numerous vestiges of ancient pits, it
appears to be exhausted.

The lower seams under the same lands are, without
doubt, untouched. Wallis, in the history of Northumberland, gives an account of a fire happening in
the High main coal, about a hundred and forty years
ago, on the Town Moor and Fenham estates, which
continued to burn for thirty years. It began at Benwell, about a quarter of a mile north of the Tyne,
and at last extended itself northward into the grounds
of Fenham, nearly a mile from where it first appear-
ed. There were eruptions at Fenham in nearly twenty places, sulphur and sal-ammoniac being sublimed
from the apertures, but no stones of magnitude
ejected. Red ashes and burnt clay, the relics of this
pseudo volcano, are still to be seen on the western declivity of Benwell-hill, and it is credibly reported,
that the soil, in some parts of the Fenham estate, has
been rendered unproductive by the action of the
fire.

At Byker St. Anthony's, and at an adjoining colliery, the Low main coal is found at fifty-nine fathoms below the High main, but though the seam proved to be six feet and a half thick, the workings of it were abandoned as unprofitable, the coal being extremely fragile, and the mines very subject to the fire-damp. On the south side of the Tyne at Felling, Tyne-main, and Gateshead Fell, the quality of this coal is very much improved, and, under the name of the Hutton main, it forms one of the most valuable seams on the Wear."

SECTION OF THE STRATA,

AT

MONTAGUE MAIN COLLIERY,

On the North side of the Ninety Fathom Dyke.

	Fth.	Yds.	Ft.	In.
Soil and Clay	1	0	1	6
Grey Metal Stone	3	1	0	0
Strong grey Post	1	1	0	0
Grey Metal Stone with girdles .	4	0	1	6
Grey Post with Metal partings .	6	0	2	6
* Whin	0	0	0	9
Blue Metal Stone	5	1	2	0
1. —COAL, waste of the Seven-quarter coal or Kenton main worked out in 1690	0	0	0	9
Blue grey Metal	0	0	1	0
Carried forward,	23	0	1	0

* The author of the article Mine in Brewster's Encyclopedia, says, in the sections which have been made of the Newcastle coal field, the term *Whin* is applied to many of the Strata; these Strata, so named, are however not *Whin*, but are sandstones of the hardest kind. The mis-application of the name *Whin*, (or Greenstone) has led mineralogists to wrong conclusions as to the coal formation of that district.

	Fth.	Yds.	Ft.	In.
Brought forward,	23	0	1	0
Grey Metal Stone	2	0	2	0
Grey Post	1	1	0	0
Grey Metal Stone with girdles .	2	0	1	0
White Post	3	0	0	6
Metal Stone	1	1	2	0
Blue grey Metal	0	0	2	6
2. { Stone Coal . . . } Two Five-quarter or Newbiggen {	0	0	0	3
Black Metal Stone .	0	0	0	2
Coal	0	0	1	9
Black Metal Stone .	0	0	0	2
Coal	0	0	2	1
Grey Metal Stone	0	1	1	0
Strong white Post	1	1	1	0
Strong grey Metal Stone . . .	0	1	1	0
Strong white Post	0	0	2	0
Grey Metal Stone	2	1	0	0
3. —Coal	0	0	0	6
Grey Stone with Post girdles . .	3	0	1	6
Mixture Whin	0	0	1	3
Grey Post	1	0	0	0
Grey Metal Stone	0	1	2	10
4. —Coal	0	0	0	6
Carried forward,	46	1	1	0

	Fth.	Yds.	Ft.	In.
Brought forward,	46	1	1	0
Grey Metal Stone	0	0	0	2
5. — COAL	0	0	0	8
Grey Metal Stone	1	0	0	0
Strong white Post	1	0	0	4
6. — COAL	0	0	0	8
Grey Metal Stone	0	0	1	0
Grey Post	0	0	1	6
Strong white Post	1	0	0	0
Dark grey Metal	0	0	1	11
7. — COAL	0	0	0	4
Grey Metal Stone	2	1	1	4
8. — COAL	0	0	0	4
Grey Metal Stone	0	0	1	3
Black slaty Metal mixed with COAL	0	0	1	0
Strong grey Metal Stone . . .	5	0	2	11
Strong white Post with Whin . .	12	1	0	0
Grey Metal Stone with black } skamy partings . . . . . }	2	1	2	0
Strong white Post	1	1	0	0
9. — COAL	0	0	1	0
Grey Metal Stone	0	0	2	0
Grey Metal Stone with girdles .	2	0	0	0
Carried forward,	78	1	1	5

		Fth.	Yds.	Ft.	In.
Brought forward,		78	1	1	5
Strong white Post with Whin girdles and skamy partings . .		5	0	1	7
10. { Coal . . . . } Benwell {	.	0	0	2	5
{ Black slaty Metal } main {	.	0	0	0	3
{ Coal (foul) . .) coal {	.	0	0	1	0
Grey Metal	.	1	1	0	0
Strong white Post	.	5	0	0	9
Black grey Stone	.	2	0	0	0
11.—Coal	.	0	0	0	9
Blue grey Metal	.	0	0	0	5
12.—Coal	.	0	0	0	4
Blue grey Metal	.	0	1	0	6
Strong white Post	.	0	1	1	7
Grey Metal Stone with girdles	.	0	1	1	8
Grey Metal with skames of coal	.	0	0	1	3
Grey Metal Stone	.	3	1	0	0
Grey Metal with a mixture of Coal		0	0	2	0
Grey Metal Stone	.	1	1	0	6
Grey Metal with Whin . . .	.	0	0	1	6
Grey Metal Stone	.	0	0	2	2
13.—Coal	.	0	0	0	10
Grey Metal	.	0	0	0	6
Carried forward,		102	0	0	5

	Fath.	Yds.	Ft.	In.
Brought forward,	102	0	0	5
White Post	0	0	1	6
Grey Metal . . . . . · . . .	0	0	2	6
Whin	0	0	0	4
Strong white Post with partings .	0	1	0	0
Whin	0	0	1	0
Strong white Post	0	0	2	0
Grey Metal Stone with girdles and partings . . . . }	1	1	0	6
14.—COAL	0	0	0	8
Grey Metal Stone	0	0	0	4
Strong grey and white Post . .	0	0	1	6
Grey Metal Stone with hard girdles	0	1	2	6
Strong white Post	0	1	2	0
Whin . . . . . . · . .	0	1	1	2
Strong white Post mixed with Whin	1	0	2	6
Blue Metal	0	1	0	0
Mixed Whin, girdles, or lumps .	0	0	0	4
Blue Metal	0	0	0	10
15.—COAL, Beaumout seam . . .	0	1	0	10
Grey Metal Stone	1	0	0	0
Strong Post with Whin	2	1	1	0
Whin	0	0	0	8

Carried forward, 114 1 1 7

	Fth.	Yds.	Ft.	In.
Brought forward,	114	1	1	7
16.—COAL	0	0	0	6
Black Slate with Coal	0	0	1	2
Grey Metal	0	0	1	6
Strong white Post	0	0	2	6
Grey skamy Post	0	0	2	0
Strong white Post with Whin . .	2	0	1	10
17.—COAL	0	0	0	10
Grey Metal Stone	0	0	1	1
	118	1	1	0

SECTION OF THE STRATA,

AT

MONTAGUE MAIN COLLIERY,

South of the Dyke.

	Fth.	Yds.	Ft.	In.
Soil	0	0	1	0
Clay	2	0	2	0
White Post	0	0	2	6
1. —COAL	0	0	0	4
Carried forward,	2	1	2	10

H

		Fth.	Yds.	Ft.	In.
Brought forward,		2	1	2	10
Black Stone		0	1	0	2
Grey Post		1	1	2	0
Blue Metal Stone		2	1	1	0
Grey Post		2	0	0	0
Strong white Post		2	1	0	0
Grey Post		0	1	2	0
Strong white Post with black Metal partings		5	0	0	0
Grey Post		0	0	1	4
Brown Post with Coal Pipes		0	1	1	8
White Post		2	1	0	0
Strong white Post with Whin		0	1	0	0
2. —COAL		0	0	0	6
Black Stone		4	1	0	0
Grey Metal Stone		4	0	2	0
Brown Post with Metal partings		0	1	1	0
3. —COAL		0	0	0	9
Grey Metal Stone		1	1	2	10
4. —COAL	Benwell main	0	0	1	0
Black Metal Band		0	0	0	9
Coal		0	1	0	6
Grey Metal		1	1	0	0
Strong white Post		2	1	1	0
Carried forward,		39	0	0	4

	Fth.	Yds.	Ft.	In.
Brought forward,	39	0	0	4
Whin	0	0	2	0
White Post	1	0	2	0
5. — COAL	0	0	1	0
Black Metal Stone	1	1	0	8
White Post	3	0	0	0
Black Metal Stone	4	1	0	0
Grey Metal	5	0	2	4
Grey Post with Whin girdles . .	2	1	0	0
Strong white Post	6	0	2	0
Grey Metal Stone	3	0	2	0
6. — COAL	0	0	0	8
Post girdles	0	0	2	0
Grey Metal Stone	1	0	1	0
7. — COAL, Beaumont seam . . .	0	1	0	4
Strong white Thil	0	1	0	7
Strong white Post	2	0	0	4
8. — COAL	0	0	1	6
Black Thil	0	0	2	4
Grey Metal Stone	0	0	1	2
Grey Post	0	0	2	0
Grey Metal Stone	0	0	2	10
Grey Metal Post	0	1	0	4
Carried forward,	74	1	0	5

52

	Fth.	Yds.	Ft.	In.
Brought forward,	74	1	0	5
9. — COAL	0	0	1	3
Black Stone	1	0	2	4
White Post	0	0	1	8
Blue Metal Stone with Post girdles	1	0	0	0
Strong white Post with Whin girdles	2	0	1	9
Black Stone	0	0	1	5
Grey Post	0	0	1	2
Blue Metal Stone	0	1	0	0
Strong white Post	0	0	1	3
Blue Metal Stone	1	0	2	1
10.— COAL	0	0	0	8
Black Thil	0	1	0	4
Blue Metal Stone with Post girdles	1	0	1	0
Grey Post	0	1	0	0
Strong white Post	3	1	2	7
11.— COAL, Low Main	0	0	2	11
Grey Metal Stone	4	1	0	0
White Post	2	1	0	0
Grey Metal Stone with Post girdles	1	0	0	0
White Post with Whin girdles .	3	0	1	6
Grey Metal with Post girdles . .	0	1	1	0
12.— COAL, Low Low Main	0	0	2	10
Carried forward,	101	0	2	2

	Fth.	Yds.	Ft.	In.
Brought forward,	101	0	2	2
Grey Metal Stone	0	1	2	0
White Post	0	0	2	0
Grey Metal . , ...	0	0	1	8
Black Stone	0	0	0	10
Grey Metal Stone	1	0	2	6
Grey Post	1	0	0	6
Strong white Post with Whin girdles	3	1	1	8
Grey Metal Stone	3	0	2	6
Grey Post	0	0	2	0
White Post	0	1	2	0
Grey Metal Stone	0	0	1	0
13.— COAL	0	0	0	6
Grey Metal	0	0	1	0
Grey Metal Stone with Post girdles	3	0	2	2
14.— COAL	0	0	0	5
Grey Metal Stone	0	0	0	4
Grey Post	1	0	0	3
Strong white Post with Whin . .	2	1	0	4
Grey Metal Stone	0	1	0	0
15.— COAL	—	—	—	—
Grey Metal Stone with Post girdles	1	0	0	0
Strong white Post with Whin girdles	0	1	0	5
	123	0	2	3

STRATA

SUNK THROUGH IN THE B PIT,

HEBBURN COLLIERY.

	Fths.	Ft.	In.
Clay	9	5	0
Grey Metal Stone	1	1	0
Post with Metal partings	8	4	0
Blue Metal	0	2	0
1. — Coal *	0	3	0
Blue Metal	1	2	0
Grey Metal Stone	2	3	0
Post with Metal partings	1	4	0
Blue Metal Stone	0	5	6
Grey Metal with Post girdles . . .	2	4	6
Blue Metal Stone	1	5	0
Grey Metal with Post girdles . . .	5	2	0
Hard white Post	1	4	0
Grey Metal with Post girdles . . .	4	4	0
Grey Metal with open partings . .	0	3	0
Blue Metal	6	5	6
Carried forward,	50	3	6

* This seam lies all through Hebburn and Jarrow collieries.

	Fths.	Ft.	In.
Brought forward,	50	3	6
Black and blue Metal	1	1	6
2. —COAL	0	0	$1\frac{1}{2}$
Black Metal	0	0	6
White Thil	0	4	$10\frac{1}{2}$
White Post	0	2	5
Blue Metal	0	0	1
Grey Post	0	0	6
Grey Metal mixed with Post . . .	0	1	0
Strong white Post	2	3	6
White Post with grey Metal partings	0	4	6
Strong white Post	8	0	0
3. —COAL	0	0	$1\frac{1}{4}$
Grey Thil	0	3	$10\frac{1}{4}$
Grey Metal mixed with Thil . . .	1	5	0
Grey Metal	0	1	0
Post with Metal partings	0	3	0
Strong white Post mixed with Whin	0	3	0
Grey and blue Metal	0	4	0
Black Stone	0	3	0
4. —COAL	0	0	4
Black Stone	0	1	4
5. —COAL	0	1	0
Carried forward,	70	0	2

	Fths.	Ft.	In.
Brought forward,	70	0	2
Strong grey Thil	0	2	6
Strong grey Post	0	0	10
White Post girdles with Metal part- ings	1	3	0
White Post	0	3	0
Thin Post girdles with Metal part- ings	0	1	0
Whin	0	3	0
White Post with Metal partings . .	0	5	6
Grey Metal	0	1	0
White Post	0	4	9
Blue and grey Metal	4	5	9
White Post	0	4	0
Blue and grey Metal	2	3	6
6. —COAL	0	0	5½
Blue and grey Metal	2	5	6
7. —COAL	0	0	2
Grey Thil	0	2	4
Blue and grey Metal	8	1	2
8. —COAL (called the 70 fathom coal) .	0	1	2
Grey Thil	0	4	6
9. —COAL	0	0	2
Carried forward,	90	5	5¼

	Fths.	Ft.	In.
Brought forward,	90	5	5½
Grey Metal and Post girdles . . .	2	0	0
Black and grey Metal	2	5	6
Post	1	1	2
10.— COAL	0	0	4
Grey Thil	1	0	0
Blue and grey Metal with Post girdles	3	0	6
Strong white Post	4	4	6
Brown Post with blue Metal partings	1	1	10
Strong white Post	4	2	2
Blue Metal	1	0	0
Post	0	1	6
Black Stone	0	5	0
White Post	0	2	6
Blue and grey Metal	1	5	0
Black Stone	2	0	0
11.— COAL	0	0	6
Grey Thil	0	4	0
Blue and grey Metal	0	5	0
Post	10	2	0
12.— HIGH MAIN COAL	1	0	0
White Thil	0	1	8
Carried forward,	131	0	7½

I

		Fths.	Ft.	In.
Brought forward,		131	0	7½
13.— Slaty COAL		0	2	4
Blue Metal		0	1	0
		131	3	11½

SECTION

OF THE

STRATA, AT SHERIFF HILL,

On Gateshead Fell.

	Fth.	Yds.	Ft.	In.
Shiver and blue Slate Sill . . .	3	0	0	0
White Flag Post	2	0	0	0
Grindstone Sill	11	0	0	0
White Post Plate	1	1	0	0
Blue Plate	1	0	0	0
Grey Post Plate	1	1	0	0
Carried forward,	20	0	0	0

	Fth.	Yds.	Ft.	In.
Brought forward,	20	0	0	0
Blue Plate	1	0	0	0
Whin Plate	1	1	0	0
Blue Sill	1	0	0	0
White Post Sill	3	1	0	0
1. — Three-quarter COAL	0	0	2	3
White Post Sill	5	1	0	0
Grey Post	1	0	0	0
Dun Post Sill	6	0	0	0
Blue Plate	1	0	0	9
Eleven Fathoms white Post . .	11	0	0	0
2. — High Main COAL *	1	0	0	0
Grey Post Sill	6	0	0	0
Metal Plate	1	0	0	0
3. — Metal COAL	0	0	1	2
White Post	4	0	1	10
4. — Stone COAL †	0	1	0	0
Black Stone Sill	1	1	0	0
5. — Bandy COAL Seam	0	0	0	6
Carried forward,	66	1	0	6

* This seam does not extend to the mines on the Wear.

† This and the Metal Coal form the Five-quarter Coal on the Wear.

	Fth.	Yds.	Ft.	In.
Brought forward,	66	1	0	6
White Post Sill	4	1	0	6
Blue Plate	2	1	0	0
Black Plate	0	0	1	6
6. — Little COAL Seam	0	0	0	6
Grey Sill	2	0	0	0
7. — Yard COAL	0	1	0	0
White Post Sill	11	1	0	0
8. — Bensham Seam *	0	1	0	3
Blue Plate	2	0	0	0
9. — Bandy COAL Seam	0	0	0	9
White Post Sill	5	0	2	0
Blue Plate	0	1	0	0
10.— Six-quarter COAL	1	0	0	3
Grey Whin Post	1	1	2	7
11.— Five-quarter COAL †	0	1	0	2
Grey Post	1	1	2	3
12.— Bandy COAL Seam	0	0	0	9
White Post	5	0	0	0
13.— Low Main COAL ‡	1	0	0	6
Carried forward,	108	0	0	6

* Maudlin seam on the Wear.

† The Six-quarter and Five-quarter Coal seams form the Low Main Coal on the Wear.

‡ Hutton seam on the Wear.

	Fth.	Yds.	Ft.	In.
Brought forward,	108	0	0	6
Dark white Sill	0	0	1	0
White Post	3	1	2	6
14.—Two-quarter COAL	0	0	1	6
White Post Sill	21	0	0	6
15.—Harvey's Main COAL, or Whickham Stone Coal .	0	1	0	0
	134	0	0	0

To the Brockwell, the lowest seam; which crops out at Basty Bank, near Conset Park, Durham.

	Fth.	Yds.	Ft.	In.
Grey Metal and Metal Stone . .	5	0	2	10
Brockwell Seam	0	1	0	2
	6	0	0	0

* I have stated, (page 35) on the authority of Mr. Fenwick, of Dipton, that the Whickham Stone Coal bassets near Conset, in the county of Durham, and that the Brockwell seam does not appear. I am inclined to believe Mr. Fenwick's statement correct, and that the above is a mistake, which might easily occur, from the trifling distance between the two seams.

STRATA,

AT PONTOP PIKE COLLIERY,

Situated on Lanchester Common.

	Fths.	Ft.	In.
Soil and Clay	1	0	0
Brown Post	1	5	9
Grey Metal Stone	3	3	0
1. — COAL	0	0	10
Grey Metal Stone	2	4	0
2. — COAL	0	2	0
Grey Metal Stone mixed	8	1	6
3. — COAL	0	0	8
Grey Metal Stone mixed with Coal .	0	4	9
Grey Metal Stone	2	0	0
Grey Post	1	0	6
Grey Metal Stone the top mixed with girdles . . . . . . }	4	0	3
White Post, ShieldRow Post (the Main Post) . . . . . . }	13	0	10
4. — Shield Row COAL (High Main at Sheriff Hill) . . . . . }	0	5	3

Carried forward, 39 5 4

	Fths.	Ft.	In.
Brought forward,	39	5	4
Whitish grey Metal Stone with Post girdles . . . . . . }	6	3	0
Grey Post	2	3	5
Grey Metal Stone	0	3	0
White Post	1	3	0
Grey Metal Stone	3	2	0
Black grey Metal Stone	0	1	4
5. — COAL, the Hard Coal Seam (Stone Coal, at Sheriff Hill) . }	0	4	9
Dark grey Metal Stone mixed with Coal	0	1	9
6. — COAL, the Brass Coal Seam, (Yard Coal, at Sheriff Hill) . }	0	5	3
White Post	1	2	2
Grey Metal Stone with girdles . . .	0	4	0
Black grey Metal Stone	0	1	3
Grey Metal Stone with Post girdles .	3	0	2
Dark grey Metal Stone with Post girdles	4	1	0
Brown Post	0	3	0
Grey Metal Stone	0	3	2
Brown Post	0	3	1
Grey Post	0	3	1
White Post	1	5	2
Carried forward,	69	4	11

	Fth.	Ft.	In.
Brought forward,	69	4	11
Black Metal Stone	0	1	3
Strong white Post	3	0	6
Grey Metal Stone	0	4	6
Strong grey Post	1	3	7
Whin	0	3	0
Strong grey Post	2	1	6
Whin	0	3	8
Grey and white Post mixed with Whin	6	5	6
Blue grey Metal Stone with Whin girdles	1	1	0
7. — COAL, Hutton Seam, Five-quarter and Six-quarter Coal, at Sheriff Hill	1	1	0
White Post	0	5	10
8. — COAL, twenty-inch seam	0	1	8
Blue Metal Stone	1	3	9
Grey Post mixed with Whin . . .	3	0	0
Blue Metal Stone	1	5	0
9. — Main COAL, Low Main, at Sheriff Hill	0	3	6
	96	2	2

SECTION

OF THE COAL STRATA,

ON THE WEAR.

	Fth.	Yds.	Ft.	In.
Soil and Clay	9	0	0	0
Brown Stone	2	0	0	0
Grey Metal Stone	4	0	0	0
Brown Stone	2	0	0	0
White Post	7	0	0	0
Blue Stone	1	1	0	0
Grey Post	5	0	0	0
Blue Slaty Stone	2	0	0	0
Grey Stone	1	1	0	0
White Post	3	1	0	0
Black Slaty Stone	2	1	0	0
Whin	0	1	0	0
Grey Post	1	1	0	0
White Post	2	0	0	0
Blue Stone	1	1	2	3
Carried forward,	45	1	2	3

K

	Fth.	Yds.	Ft.	In.
Brought forward,	45	1	2	3
1. — Five-quarter COAL *	0	1	0	9
Blue Metal	1	1	1	0
Grey Post	5	0	2	0
Grey Metal Stone	3	1	0	0
Whin	0	1	1	0
White Post	4	0	0	0
Blue Stone	0	0	2	0
2. — High Main COAL	1	0	0	0
Blue grey Stone	2	1	0	0
White Post	2	1	0	0
Grey Stone with partings	2	1	1	0
Brown Post	4	0	2	0
Whin	1	0	0	0
3. — Maudlin COAL	1	0	0	0
Blue Stone	1	1	0	0
White Post	3	1	0	0
Grey Metal Stone	3	0	0	0
Blue Post	2	0	0	0
Blue Stone	1	0	0	0
Carried forward,	86	0	0	0

* Forms the Metal and Stone Coal seams on Sheriff Hill.

	Fth.	Yds.	Ft.	In.
Brought forward,	86	0	0	0
4. — Low Main COAL *	0	1	0	0
Blue Stone	1	0	0	0
White Post	2	1	0	0
Whin	0	1	2	0
Grey Post	1	0	0	0
Blue Metal	1	1	0	0
5. — COAL, Hutton seam †	1	0	1	0
	94	1	0	0

---

* Forms the Six-quarter and Five-quarter seams on Sheriff Hill, and on the Tyne.

† The Low Main on Sheriff Hill, and on the Tyne.

SEAMS OF COAL,

AT WALBOTTLE COLLIERY,

AT THE

NEWBURN WINNING.

			Ft.	In.	
Engine seam,	at 50 fathoms,		3	8	thick.
Main Coal,	„ 69	„	3	2	„
Splint Coal,	„ 85	„	4	0	„

The last seam consists of 3 feet 4 inches of clean Coal, and about 8 inches of Splint, next the Thil.

SEAMS OF COAL,

AT THROCKLEY COLLIERY.

			Ft.	In.	
Engine seam,	at 54 fathoms,		3	8	thick.
Main Coal,	„ 70	„	3	0	„
Splint Coal,	„ 86	„	3	3	„

SEAMS OF COAL,

AT

WYLAM COLLIERY.

			Ft.	In.	
High Main,	at 6 fathoms,	5	7	thick.
Five-quarter Coal,	,, 21 ,,	3	4½	,,
Six-quarter Coal,	,, 26 ,,	3	4	,,
Yard Coal,	,, 32 ,,	1	2	,,
Horsley Wood seam,	,, 38 ,,	0	11½	,,

SECTION OF THE STRATA,

AT STUBLICK,

Five miles and a half south-west of Hexham.

	Fth.	Yds.	Ft.	In.
Soil and Romble	1	1	1	0
Grey Metal Stone with girdles and water . . . . }	3	0	2	0
Carried forward,	5	0	0	0

	Fth.	Yds.	Ft.	In.
Brought forward,	5	0	0	0
White and grey gullety Post, which sets away the water	3	1	2	0
1. — COAL, with water	0	0	2	4
Grey Metal with girdles	1	0	0	0
Grey Metal	1	0	0	0
2. — COAL	0	0	1	1
Grey Metal	0	0	2	0
3. { COAL	0	0	0	7
{ Foul Coal	0	0	0	3
Grey Metal	0	0	0	9
4. — COAL, with white Spar	0	0	0	5
Grey Metal	0	0	2	0
Whitish grey Post	1	0	1	1
Blue grey Metal	0	0	2	0
White Post mixed with Whin	0	0	1	0
Soft Sandy white Post	1	0	1	0
Dark grey Metal	0	1	2	6
5. — COAL, with white Scares	0	0	0	2
	16	0	1	2

SECTION OF THE STRATA,

IN

Birtley Colliery.

	Fths.	Ft.	In.
Brown Post			
Grey Metal Stone			
Brown Stone			
White Post	32	0	0
Blue Metal Stone			
Grey Post			
Blue and grey Metal Stone . .			
Five-quarter COAL	0	3	9
Grey Post			
Grey Metal Stone with Whin girdles	10	2	3
Main COAL	0	5	6
White and brown Post			
Grey Metal Stone with Whin near the bottom	11	0	6
Maudlin COAL seam	0	4	6
Blue Post			
Blue and grey Metal Stone . .	12	1	6

Carried forward, 68 0 0

		Fths.	Ft.	In.
Brought forward,		68	0	0
Low Main COAL		0	3	3
Blue Metal Stone				
White Post and Whin . . .	}	7	2	9
Hutton COAL seam		0	4	6
		76	4	6

— ::::::::::::::::: :: —

SECTION OF THE STRATA,

AT

HARTLEY BURN COLLIERY,

On the North Side of the Great Stublick Dyke, *

And Nine Miles North-west of the Town of Alston.

	Fths.	Ft.	In.
Moss and Clay	8	0	0
Plate	1	4	0
Carried forward,	9	4	0

* The Great Stublick Dyke, here mentioned, runs in a direction nearly east and west, and may be traced for a considerable distance on its line of bearing, viz —from Stublick syke, westward to Cupola bridge, where it crosses the Allen Water, from thence over Whitfield ridge, to the river Tyne, a little below Eals bridge, thence to the south of Hartley

	Fths.	Ft.	In.
Brought forward,	9	4	0
Coal	0	2	0
Grey Beds	1	0	0
Hazle Sill	0	3	0
Grey Beds	1	0	0
Hazle Sill	0	4	0
Plate	1	8	0
Coal (workable seam)	0	4	0
Hazle Sill	2	0	0
Grey Beds and Plate	2	0	0
Coal (workable at Blackshield Boggs)	0	2	4
	19	4	4

Burn and Tindale Fell collieries. It has an immense throw
down to the northward, but the precise distance cannot be
exactly ascertained; it must however be very considerable,
as it throws down the lower part of the Newcastle Coal series
in the districts through which it passes There is some
reason to suppose it identical with the Ninety Fathom Dyke,
which dislocates the Coal measures near Tynemouth-castle.
(See page 28.)

L

THE FOLLOWING ARE

THE DEPTHS OF PITS,

As mentioned by William Casson, in his Plan of the Collieries of Tyne and Wear,

Published March, 1801.

THOSE MARKED THUS * ARE WEAR COALS.

	Fathoms.
Ryton Moor	30
Whitefield	45
Bladon Main	25
Thornley	25
Pontop	80
Windsors	80
Marley Hill	36
Tanfield Moor	50
South Moor	45
Stanley	45
*Beamish South Moor	46
*Twizle, or Bedford Main	48
*Pelton Moor	42
Team	60
Ayton Moor	90
Sheriff Hill	80

	Fathoms.
Tyne Main	65
Brandling Main	70
Hebburn	132
*Usworth Main	77
*Washington	80
*Birtley Moor	70
*Warwick	60
*Lee Field	63
*Peareth's Main	60
*Harraton	70
*Lambton's Main	60
*Painshaw	82
*Wharton Main	84
*Eden Main	60
*Biddick	80
*Burn Moor	63
*Newbottle	52
*Lumley	90
*Primrose Moor	60
*Oxclose	70
*Wentworth	70
*Rainton	55
Wylam	32
Greenwich Moor	35
Holywell Main	36

	Fathoms.
Walbottle	51
Baker's Main	25
Montague Main	60
Kenton	70
Lawson's Main	137
Heaton Main	72
Bigg's Main	90
St. Anthon's	135¼
Walker	100
Wall's End	105
Long Benton	105
Willington	121
Flatworth	86
Shire Moor	45
Murton Main	45
Plessey	58
Cowpen	80
Hartley	40

The Sections which are here inserted, it is hoped will be found exceedingly useful, in giving a general view of the Northumberland Coal Field.

I have before observed the impossibility of giving in one Section, all the information that might be required, and, indeed, it is only by a comparison of the stratification in different parts of the district, that a correct idea of its conformation can be obtained. The discrepances which will be found by comparing one Section with another, will appear, in many instances, very difficult to reconcile, yet, it will be perceived, that the general order and disposition of the Strata, still remain the same, over the whole tract of country, where the coal formation occurs.

Before proceeding to describe that part of the Section which comprizes the Lead measures, it will not be improper to insert tables of the Strata, which are found to accompany Coal, in other parts of the kingdom; as information of this sort is sometimes particularly valuable to practical men.

The three following, with the accompanying remarks, are from Dr. Miller's edition of Williams's Mineral Kingdom.

TABLE I.

ACCOUNT OF THE

STRATA AT CROFT PIT,

AT

PRESTON HOWS;

About a mile and a half to the south-west of Whitehaven;

The Depth of 108 Fathoms.

	Ft.	In.
Soil	1	3
Soil and Clay mixed	4	9
Black Soil	1	0
1. Brown soft Limestone, resembling stone marl in irregular Strata	9	0
2. Dark-coloured Limestone, harder	6	0
3. Yellowish Limestone, mixed with Spar	4	0
4. Reddish hard Limestone	2	0
5. Reddish hard Limestone, but with finer particles	1	6
6. Hard dark-coloured Limestone	1	4
7. Yellowish Limestone, mixed with Spar	4	0
8. Soft brown Limestone	4	2
9. Soft brown and yellow Limestone, mixed with Freestone	2	6
10. Limestone, mixed with yellow Freestone	2	0
11. Reddish soft Freestone	1	6

		Ft.	In.
12.	Red Slate, striated with Freestone in thin layers	2	6
13.	Red Freestone	42	6
14.	Soft red Slate	0	6
15.	Red Slate, striated with red Freestone, in thin layers	25	0
16.	Red Slate, striated with Freestone	27	0
17.	Strong red Freestone, rather greyish	29	9
18.	Lumpy red Freestone, speckled with white Freestone	0	9
19.	Blue Argillaceous Schistus, speckled with Coal	0	9
20.	Red soapy Slate	13	0
21.	Black Slate, with a small appearance of Coal under it	1	0
22.	Ash-coloured friable Argillaceous Schistus	4	0
23.	Purple-coloured Slate, striated with Freestone	23	3
24.	The same, and under it black Slate	4	0
25.	COAL—1.	1	0
26.	Soft whitish Freestone	10	2
27.	Blackish Slate, a little inclined to brown	4	11
28.	COAL—2.	1	10
29.	Blackish Shale, intermixed with Coal	2	6
30.	Whitish Freestone	8	6
31.	Strong blueish Slate, mixed with grey Freestone	3	0

		Ft.	In.
32.	White iron Stone	1	0
33.	Freestone, striated with blue Slate . . .	1	8
34.	Freestone, striated with Slate in thin layers	9	3
35.	Dark blue Slate	13	6
36.	COAL—3.	0	9
37.	Dark grey Slate	15	8
38.	COAL—4. with Slate, one inch thick .	2	0
39.	Grey Freestone, mixed with iron Stone .	8	0
40.	Hard white Freestone	15	6
41.	COAL—5.	1	0
42.	Shale, mixed with Freestone . .	8	0
43.	Olive-coloured Slate, adhering to black	2	4
44.	COAL—6.	1	1
45.	Black Shale, mixed with Freestone .	8	8
46.	White Freestone, mixed with Slate .	8	0
47.	Dark blue Slate	22	4
48.	COAL—7.	1	3
49.	Black Shale, mixed with Freestone .	7	6
50.	Strong white Freestone . . .	6	0
51.	Brown iron Stone	3	0
52.	Dark grey Slate	6	0
53.	Dark grey Shale, with an intermixture of COAL—8. about five inches thick	5	6
54.	Light-coloured Slate, mixed with Freestone	5	6
55.	Blue Slate, striated with Freestone . . .	10	0

		Ft.	In.
56.	Strong white Freestone, a little tinged with iron	2	6
57.	Very black shivery Slate	10	3
58.	COAL—9. strong, and of a good quality	0	4
59.	Soft grey Slate	0	3
60.	COAL—10. very black, burns well	0	8
61.	Hard black Shale	1	7
62.	COAL—11. mixed with pyrites	1	2
63.	Argillaceous Schistus, grey and brittle	3	0
64.	Blue rough Argillaceous Schistus	4	6
65.	Fine blue Slate	3	0
66.	Freestone, mixed with iron Stone	3	0
67.	Black shivery Slate	6	0
68.	Dark blue Slate, very fine	5	6
69.	Dark blue Slate, very brittle	0	6
70.	COAL—12.	2	6
71.	Soft grey Argillaceous Schistus	0	6
72.	Argillaceous Schistus, mixed with Freestone	2	0
73.	White Freestone, with fine particles	7	0
74.	Blue Slate, striated with white Freestone	4	7
75.	Light-blue Slate, very fine	3	0
76.	Blue Slate, a little mixed with iron Stone	12	0
77.	Black shivery Slate	1	0
78.	COAL—13.	0	6
79.	Brownish hard Slate	9	0

		Ft.	In.
80.	Strong blue Slate, tinged with iron Stone	28	6
81	Dark blue Slate, rather inclined to brown, and brittle	1	6
82	Blue soft brittle Slate	0	6
83.	COAL—14.	1	0
84.	Lightish grey Argillaceous Schistus, brittle and soapy	4	0
85.	Freestone, striated with blue Slate . . .	7	0
86.	Fine blue Argillaceous Schistus, striated with white Freestone	4	0
87.	Black Slate, with hard, sharp, and fine particles	3	0
88.	Blue Slate, light and fine	27	0
89.	COAL—15.	5	4
90.	Soft grey Argillaceous Schistus	4	3
91.	Black shivery Slate	2	2
92.	COAL—16.	1	3
93.	Strong lightish-coloured Shale	3	4
94.	Blue Slate, striated with white Freestone	3	4
95.	Iron Stone	0	4
96.	Grey Slate	3	9
97.	Strong white Freestone	5	6
98.	Freestone striated with blue Slate . . .	0	10
99.	White Freestone	1	3

	Ft.	In.
100. Freestone, striated with blue Slate	3	11
101. Black Slate	0	5
102. Freestone, striated with blue Slate	1	$4\frac{1}{2}$
103. Strong white Freestone	0	4
104. Freestone, mixed with blue Slate, in thin layers	2	4
105. Strong white Freestone	0	5
106. Greyish Slate, of a shivery nature	6	0
107. Freestone, mixed with blue Slate, in thin layers	4	0
108. Very strong, with Freestone	5	3
109. Fine blue Slate	2	3
110. White Freestone, striated with blue Slate	0	$7\frac{1}{2}$
111. Fine blue Slate	0	4
112. White Freestone, striated with blue Slate	2	1
113. Freestone, striated with blue Slate, in fine particles	0	10
114. White Freestone, in thin layers	0	4
115. The same, but more friable	0	5
116. Fine blue Slate	2	1
117. Coal—17.	7	10

TABLE II.

EXHIBITS THE STRATA,

MET WITH

IN SINKING A PIT,

*At Ilkeston, in Derbyshire, thirty-one Fathoms
and a quarter.*

		Ft.	In.
1.	Soil and yellow Clay	6	6
2.	Black Shale	4	0
3.	Iron Stone	1	6
4.	Coal—1.	1	3
5.	Clunch	6	6
6.	Grey Stone	9	0
7.	Blue Stone	7	0
8.	Black Shale	1	6
9.	Brown iron Stone	1	0
10.	Black Shale	6	0
11.	Light blue Bind	6	6
12.	Burning Shale	2	6
13.	Light blue Clunch	4	0
14.	Light blue Stone	9	0
15.	Blue Bind	2	3
16.	Coal—2.	1	6
17.	Black Clunch	0	4

		Ft.	In.
18.	Black Jet, a kind of Cannel Coal . . .	0	9
19.	Lightish blue Clunch	2	5
20.	Broad Bind	7	6
21.	Light-coloured Stone	4	0
22.	Greyish blue Cank (a hard substance) . .	6	6
23.	Very light-coloured Stone	14	0
24.	Strong broad Bind	4	0
25.	Grey Stone	7	0
26.	Blue Bind	4	0
27.	COAL—3. soft quality	2	6
28.	Black Bind	6	6
29.	COAL—4. soft	4	0
30.	Black Clunch	3	0
31.	Light-coloured Clunch . . . . : . .	3	0
32.	Broad Bind	11	6
33.	Black Clunch	3	0
34.	Clunch and Bind	25	6
35	COAL—5.	6	3
36.	Clunch	3	9

TABLE III.

SHOWS THE STRATA,

DISCOVERED

IN BORLAND PIT,

AT DYSART, IN SCOTLAND,

Which was sunk in 1788 and 1789, to the depth of 46 fathoms.

	Ft.	In.
1. A coarse Freestone	27	0
2. COAL—1. called Sandwell Coal	4	0
3. Blaes, the pavement of the Coal . . .	4	0
4. Hard Freestone	14	0
5. Blaes	9	0
6. COAL—2.	0	9
7. Hard Freestone	20	0
8. Blaes	5	0
9. Hard Freestone	4	0
10. Blaes . . . . :	18	0
11. Hard Stone	2	0
12. Grey feaks or bands, a *Sandstone* of a lamellated structure, with a mixture of clay, and streaks of coaly matter . .	9	0
13. COAL—3.	0	9

	Ft.	In.
14. Kirkstone, a porous Freestone, with balls of iron Stone	54	0
15. Blaes	4	0
16. COAL—4.	0	9
17. Blaes	4	0
18. Grey Feaks	7	0
19. Hard Freestone	2	0
20. Grey Feaks	2	0
21. Hard Freestone	2	6
22. Grey Feaks	12	0
23. White hard Bands	6	0
24. Blaes	3	0
25. Pier Stone, a very hard Freestone . .	11	0
26. Blaes	26	3
27. COAL—5. the Main Coal	24	0

" In the preceding tables the local names are retained. Many of these, it must be acknowledged, are extremely arbitrary; but it will not be difficult to understand them by a comparison of the Strata in the different tables. It may be just noticed, that the grey Stone and blue Stone of Table 2. are Sand

Row, on the banks of the Frith of Forth, where the highest of these Strata occurs) and the commencement of the Basiltic rocks, forming the general floor and border of this important Coal-field. These Strata lie internally in the form of a lengthened bason, or *Strata trough*, and consist of Sand-stone, Shale, (or Blae) Fire-clay, Coal, Lime-stone, Iron-stone, &c.

In the general Section containing the above-mentioned particulars, which Mr. Farey prepared for the late Duke of Buccleugh, sixty-six seams of Coal (without reckoning double or treble Coals at more than one each) and seven Lime-stones, are seen separated by seventy-two assemblages of barren or stone sinkings, forming an aggregate thickness of above five thousand feet.

In all, eighty-four seams of Coal, and eight intervening Lime-stones, appear in this general section of the Midlothian Coal measures; showing a greater number of such Strata, than Geological writers have hitherto admitted any where to exist together.

PART II

LEAD MEASURES.

The Strata, which I shall now endeavour to describe, is that part of the series which occurs in the Lead district; comprising, Derwent, East Allendale, and West Allendale, in the county of Northumberland; Weardale and Teesdale, in the county of Durham; and Alston-moor, in the county of Cumberland.— There are, in this district, two places where three counties meet in one point, viz :—Rampgill-head, one mile south-west of Coal-cleugh, and Caldron-snout, a Waterfall, on the river Tees. At the former of these places, the counties of Northumberland, Cumberland, and Durham, form a union; and at the latter, the counties of Durham, Yorkshire, and Westmorland.

This tract of country differs considerably in external appearance, from that in which Coal occurs so plentifully. The easy and natural undulations of the sur-

N 2

face in the neighbourhood of Newcastle, become exchanged for more rugged and alpine elevations; the fertile valleys of the *Tees*, the *Wear*, and the *Tyne*, are greatly contracted in breadth, and separated by steril and desolate mountains, whose summits, for a great part of the year, are covered with snow.

Among these mountains are distributed, the various valuable Lead Mines, which constitute so large a part of the mineral treasures of Great Britain, and equal, if not excel, in productiveness, any yet discovered in the world.

The Stratification of this part of our island has been ascertained with the greatest precision, as the multitude of shafts and workings of the Lead Mines, together with the numerous bassets of the Strata on the side of the mountains, afford such ample means for observation over an extensive district; and, it must be observed, that, although some irregularities, in order and thickness, are found to occur, yet, the general agreement of sections from different mining fields, is much more striking, than in that part of the series I have just described. In working the Lead Mines, each individual bed, is anticipated and calculated upon with the greatest confidence, by practical miners, by whom it is received as a general rule, that what is lost in thickness in one Stratum, is, very often, gained in another; that is to say, what is lost in the Plate beds or indurated Argillaceous earths, is generally gained in the Lime-stones and Hazles, or the Calcareous and Siliceous parts of the Strata; so that the same thickness is produced throughout the section, by the Siliceous, Calcareous, and Argillaceous earths, taken together.

I have observed, in page 26, that the different Coal Strata, rise and crop out or basset to the east of Healy-field Lead Mine, and, in the same manner, the uppermost Strata of the Lead measures, are presumed to basset from beneath the lower Coal seams. It must be confessed, that the continuity of any individual bed, has never yet been actually traced below the lower series of Coal measures, in such a manner as to connect the Lead measures accurately with them, and, it is therefore probable, that a few thin beds may intervene between the Brockwell Coal seam (No. 90, in the section) and the Slate sill (No. 91) but they are too inconsiderable to deserve much notice, and do not at all affect the general accuracy of the section.

Before proceeding to notice, in detail, the different alternations of the Strata, it will be necessary to give an account of their general rise or aclivity, which is pretty well known to be, in this part of our island, to the south-west, and the dip or declivity to the north-east; which, in Crossgill-burn, in Alston-moor, Cumberland, makes 2 degrees 15 minutes with the horizon, or nearly a yard in twenty-seven; the bearing with the true meridian S. 35 W. which is about the full rise, or aclivity of the Strata.

GREY BEDS.

The Strata, to which this term is applied, are several thin beds of Free-stone, or *Hazle*, of a Siliceous kind, seldom above an inch in thickness, which alternate with other thin beds of Plate, Shiver, or Argillaceous Schistus.

They occur pretty frequently in the Lead measures, and are numbered in the section 99, 100, 101, 102, 103, 107, 115, 116, 189, and 205.

SLATE SILLS.

These Strata are of a Siliceous kind, will strike fire with steel, and frequently contain small particles of mica. Some of the Slate sills are so thinly laminated or stratified, that they are frequently wrought in quarries, for the purpose of covering houses, and are commonly called grey Slate.

These Strata are numbered in the section 91, 129, and 131.

— · : : : : : 0 : : : : : · —

GIRDLE BEDS.

These are harder Strata than grey Slate, of a closer texture in stronger posts, and strike fire plentifully with steel.

They are numbered in the section 93, 141, 236.

FREE-STONES.

These Strata are numbered in the section 95, 108, 219, 222, 224, 226, 228, 231, 235, and 237.

They are of a softer nature than the last-mentioned, being more porous and open, but harder than the

Sand-stone, described in page 21. They are generally divided into posts, with partings between them, and will strike fire with steel, but not so plentifully as the Strata called Grey Beds.

MILL-STONE GRIT, OR GREY MILL-STONE.

This Stratum (No. 104, in the section) is of a coarser grain, and considerably more porous, than Free-stone. In some places it is quarried for Mill-stones, for grinding corn, and is commonly called the GreyStone. Mr. Farey supposes that the famous Peak Mill-stones, of Derbyshire, are of a similar kind of stone. This Stratum may be seen upon the mountains between *Stanhope* and *Wolsingham*, in the county of Durham.

COARSE HAZLE, OR RIBONY BIND.

The Stone to which this term is applied, occurs very frequently in the section, and its different Strata are numbered 96, 106, 110, 112, 114, 119, 123, 125, 127, 133, 143, 157, 161, 164, 167, 171, 174, 176, 178, 180, 182, 184, 194, 196, 198, 206, 209, 212, and 215. It is harder than Free-stone, but not so hard as Girdle Bed, and will, only with difficulty, emit fire with steel.

GRIND-STONE SILL.

This Stratum, numbered in the section 117, is less porous and harder than the Mill-stone Grit. It is in some places hewn into Grind-stones, from which circumstance it has derived its name. It is the uppermost Stratum in the rich mining fields of *Allenheads* and *Coal-cleugh*, in the county of Northumberland, and at *Rampgill-head*, near *Nenthead*, in the county of Cumberland. It is also nearly the uppermost Stratum upon the summit of the mountain, Cross-Fell, as will be seen by referring to that part of the section marked D.

Immediately below the Grind-stone Sill is a pretty thick Plate Bed, No. 118, and below the Plate Bed a Stratum of Hazle, No. 119, (see page 96). Underneath the Hazle we find another Plate Bed, No. 120, which overlies a thin Stratum of Lime-stone, commonly called the *fell-top* Lime-stone. This is the first Lime-

stone that occurs in the Lead measures,* and the uppermost that we find either in *Weardale*, *Allendale*,
Derwent-dale, or *Alston-moor*.

Underneath the fell-top Lime-stone, is a thin Coal
seam, about six or eight inches thick. It is of that
species of Coal, called by the country people Crow
Coal, and emits, while burning, effluvia of a suffocat-
ing and sulphureous nature. In Alston-moor it is
mixed up with clay, and formed into round balls, commonly called *cats*, for fuel. All the other Coal seams
in this part of the section, are of this species.

The next Stratum below is a Hazle, No. 123, about
four yards thick, commonly called *the upper Coal Sill.*
It is a kind of Free-stone, and has been more generally, described in page 96.

Below the Stratum of Plate, which underlies the
upper Coal Sill, is a Hazle, No. 125, rather of a sandy
nature, but of a pretty close texture. It is sometimes used for sharpening scythes, &c. and has from
thence been called the Whet-stone Sill.

---

* See page 37.

Underneath this is a Plate Bed, and again another Hazle, or Whet-stone Bed, of a similar nature; No. 127.

We now arrive at the upper Slate Sill, eight yards, and the lower Slate Sill, seven yards, thick; divided from each other, by the Stratum of Plate, No. 130.

These sills have been very productive of Lead Ore at *Coal-cleugh*, and *Rampgill* Lead Mines, to which we have before referred, and, indeed, in most of the mines in *Allendale*, *Weardale*, and *Alston-moor*, where they occur. Underneath the lower Slate Sill, we meet with a Hazle or hard dry Slate, which is occasionally found united to the lower Slate Sill, without the intervening Stratum of Plate, No. 132, forming with it a thick continuous Stratum, which is then called *The Low Great Sill.*

Below the Plate Bed, No. 134, we meet with a thin bed of sulphureous Coal, No. 135, (similar to that we have already mentioned) which overlies the Stratum of Iron-stone, No. 136, so called from its containing a quantity of Iron, in its composition. This is a close hard stone, varying much in thickness in different places; for at *Coal-cleugh*, it is only about a foot thick, while at *Middle-cleugh Moss*, near *Nenthead*, it is above a yard in thickness, and in other places scarcely perceptible.

FIRE-STONE SILL.

This Stratum, No. 137, is of various thickness in different Mining Fields; at *Allenheads*, it is about six fathoms, and at *Coal-cleugh* only about three. At *Wolf-cleugh*, in *Rookhope*, in the county of Durham, the *white tuft* or *white sill*, No. 139, and the *fire-stone*, form nearly one Stratum; it strikes fire with steel plentifully, is micaceous, and is sometimes used as hearthstones for fire-places, whence, probably, its name.

The Plate Bed, No. 140, Girdle Bed, No. 141, and Plate Bed, No. 142, in some places form one Stratum of Shiver, Plate, or Indurated Argillaceous Schistus, commonly called the *Eleven Fathom Shiver*.

PATTINSON'S SILL.

This Stratum, No. 143, is a Hazle, four yards thick,

called *Pattinson's Sill*, from the person who first sunk
in it at *Rampgill Vein*, before-mentioned. It has been
very productive of Lead Ore in several Mining Fields,
and is described generally in page 96, which see.

LITTLE LIME-STONE,

Is the next Stratum of Lime-stone, No. 145, under
the fell-top Lime-stone, and the second which occurs
in the Lead measures. It is tolerably hard, and has
been very productive of Lead Ore, in *Alston-moor*,
and other places.

From the last-mentioned Lime-stone, downwards,
we have a Plate Bed, which immediately overlies the
High Coal, No. 147, which is sulphureous, as before
described. This Coal seam rests upon the High Coal
Sill, which, with the Low Coal Sill, have been already referred to, in the general description of Hazles,
page 96. Upon the Low Coal Sill, rests another Seam
of sulphureous Coal, numbered in the section 150.
In some places we find three Coal Sills, all of which

are tolerably hard, and emit sparks freely with steel.*

The Plate Bed, No. 152, beneath the lower Coal Sill, rests upon the top of the Tumbler Beds, which constitute part of the Great Lime-stone. This Plate is tolerably hard, and frequently contains a number of balls, or nodules, of iron pyrites, commonly called *Cat-heads.* Some of these are very curious when cut and polished, being veined and streaked all through, in different forms. This Plate Bed frequently bursts down in large masses, after a current of atmospherical air has circulated freely through levels drove in it, and it then requires a great deal of timber, or *grove-wood,* to secure the roofs or sides of these workings.

TUMBLER BEDS AND GREAT LIME-STONE.

This is the most predominant Stratum of Lime-stone that we find throughout the whole section, and

* At Cross-Fell Lead Mine, the Plate Bed, under the little Lime-stone, is about five feet thick, then a Coal about six inches thick, underneath is a white Hazle, three and a half fathoms thick. There is a *Famp* Bed, about a foot thick, six or seven feet from the bottom of the Hazle.

has been nearly as productive of Lead Ore, as all the
other Strata taken together, in the extensive mines in
Weardale and *Teesdale*, in the county of Durham,
East and *West Allendales*, in the county of Northumberland, and *Alston-moor* and *Cross-fell*, in the
county of Cumberland. About sixteen feet of the
upper part of this Stratum is called the *Tumbler
Beds*, which, in some places, contain entroche and
other organic remains. Between the Tumbler Beds
and body of the Lime-stone, is a soft, argillaceous
substance, about a foot thick, commonly called the
Black Bed. From the Black Bed to the high flat
vein, is generally about four feet, and from thence to
the middle flat vein, ten feet, or thereabouts; from the
middle flat vein to the low flat vein, about thirteen
feet. What are here called flat veins, will be more
fully explained in Part II, where the subject of dilated
veins is discussed. This Stratum keeps, in general,
pretty regular in its thickness, yet it varies a little in
some places.

It bassets a little to the south of *Dun-fell* Lead
Mine, and occurs also upon *Meldon-fell*, in the county
of Westmorland. It is the uppermost Stratum at
Hartside Cross, on the Penrith and Alston road.—
There is an occurrence of a thin seam of *CrowCoal*, un-

der it, about one mile south of *Cross-fell* mines, where it bassets on the north bank of the river Tees, and at Meldon-fell, in like manner.

It may be seen too dipping below the bed of the river Wear, between *Wolsingham* and *Frosterly*, in the county of Durham, where it has been quarried, for marble, by Mr. Jopling, of Newcastle.

TUFT, OR WATER SILL.

This Stratum, No. 154, is a tender, irregular Grit-stone, considerably softer than most of the Hazles, before described. It has a sandy appearance, will strike fire with steel, and is pervious to water, in several places: it lies close to the bottom of the Great Lime-stone, and has been very productive of Lead Ore, in many mining fields.

Underneath the Tuft or Water Sill is a Plate Bed, or strong Indurated Argillaceous Schistus, which divides it from the

QUARRY HAZLE.

This Stratum, No. 157, is of various thickness; in

some places, about 6 fathoms, in others only about 3 or four, and it is sometimes divided into two, with a *famp* bed between them.   Its upper part is occasionally rather of a calcareous nature, and is then called the *Lime-stone Post*, numbered in the section 156.— The Quarry Hazle is commonly called in *Weardale,* *Hewitson's Sill;* it strikes fire with steel pretty freely, and has been very productive of Lead Ore in the mines at *Allenheads.*   It is underlaid by a Plate bed, No. 158, which is a strongly Indurated Argillaceous earth.   The lower part of this Plate is considerably harder than the upper, and rather of a cherty * nature, in most cases forming a distinct Stratum called the Till bed, No. 159.

FOUR FATHOM LIME-STONE.

This is a strong close Stratum of Lime-stone,

---

* Chert is a production of the Lime stone Strata in Derbyshire.   It is of a flinty substance, in nodulous forms, as flint in chalk, though sometimes a little stratified.   Some of it plentifully abounds with the impressions of *entrochi,* which have manifestly been inclosed in the solid substance of the *chert,* though not the least fragment of them is now remaining.   Its colour is similar to that of other flints, but when stratified it is generally a good black.   It is sometimes so like, in colour, to the Lime-stone in which it is inclosed, as to be only distinguished by its not effervescing with acid.

P

No. 160, keeping pretty regular in its thickness, wherever it has been sunk through. Below this Lime-stone, at *Nattriss Gill*, in *Alston-moor*, there occurs a thin seam of Coal, which is worked for sale, near the top of *Hartside*, at *Lugill-head*, where it is much in-creased in thickness. It may be observed that Lime-stones, in general, are more regular in their thick-ness, than any other Stratum throughout the section.

NATTRISS GILL HAZLE.

This Stratum, No. 161, frequently lies close to the bottom of the four fathom Lime-stone, at other places there will be found a thin Coal seam, as at *Nattriss Gill*, before mentioned, and occasionally about two feet or a yard of Plate between them, as at the Lead Mine called *Grass-field*, in *Alston-moor*.

This Hazle is rather of a coarser nature than seve-ral others, and strikes fire with steel as usual.

THE THREE YARDS LIME-STONE,

Is the next Stratum of Lime-stone, as will appear by

the section, it varies a little in its thickness in different places; sometimes we find it only about a fathom.

SIX FATHOM HAZLE.

This Stratum, No. 164, is commonly called, in *Alston-moor, Arthur's Pit Hazle.* It is a Siliceous substance, pretty hard, strikes fire with steel like most of the other Hazles, and lays close to the bottom of the last-mentioned Lime-stone.

....

THE FIVE YARDS LIME-STONE.

This is the next Lime-stone that we find under the three yards Lime-stone. It is in some places underlaid by a small Coal seam, of a sulphureous nature.

SLATY HAZLE.

This Stratum, No. 167, lays close to the bottom of

the last-mentioned Lime-stone, in all cases where the Seam of sulphureous Coal does not occur. It is of a close texture, and strikes fire with steel, like most of the other Hazles.

--- --- --- --- --- ---

SCAR LIME-STONE.

This Lime-stone is next to the Great Lime-stone in thickness, and has three flat or famp beds in it in the same manner, called the high, middle, and low flats. The great acqueduct Level, called Nent-force Level, which is now driving by the Commissioners and Governors of Greenwich Hospital, commences under this Limestone, near the town of Alston, in Cumberland. At the same place the river *Nent* is precipitated over the basset of this Stratum, forming a romantic waterfall several yards in height, called *Nent-force*. The stupendous Level of Nent-force was begun in the year 1776, for the double purpose of discovering metallic veins, and draining several rich mines in the neighbourhood of Nenthead. It has now proceeded upwards of three miles, and, as it is drove in the direction of the rise or aclivity of the Strata, it will reach a great depth before its termination. Its fore-head, at present, stands in the upper part of the Tyne-bottom Plate, number 189 in the section.

Underneath the Scar Limestone are several thin Strata of Hazle, Plate, &c. (as will appear by the section) until we arrive at a Lime-stone, commonly called the *Cockle-shell Lime-stone.* It has *entrochi, anomia, ostrea,* and other organic remains imbedded in it; which may be observed in *Garrigill, Eshgill,* and *Cross-gill Burns,* in *Alston-moor,* Cumberland.

Below the Cockle-shell Lime-stone are two thin Plate beds, and two small Hazles, and then the single Post, or Garrigill Burn, Lime-stone. From thence to the Tyne-bottom Lime-stone, we find a considerable thickness of Plate, alternating with Grey Beds, No. 189, which is so very hard and compact, that it can scarcely be wrought without blasting with gunpowder; in some places it may be raised so thin, that it is frequently used as slates, for roofs, &c. This Stratum is generally distinguished by the term *Tyne-bottom Plate.*

TYNE-BOTTOM LIME-STONE.

This is the lowest Stratum of Lime-stone in *Alston-*

moor. The river South Tyne, runs nearly all the way
from Tyne-head to Garrigill-gate upon it, a distance
of about four miles; the Strata rising as fast to the
south or south-west, as the river falls to the north or
north-east. It is the uppermost Stratum at *Dufton-
fell*, in the county of Westmorland. It has three flat
or famp beds in it, similar to the *Great* and *Scar* Lime-
stones,* which, in this Stratum, always occur, whether there are flat or dilated veins or not, but this circumstance will be discussed more fully, when treating
of dilated veins in general. The Tyne-bottom Lime-
stone may be traced from the Smelting-house at Tyne-
head to the southward over to the banks of the river
Tees, in the county of Westmorland, and from thence
to the Lead Mines at Nether-hurth and Dun-fell.
We next observe it in the same direction at Birdall,
near Maze-beck, (a rivulet which divides the counties
of Westmorland and Yorkshire) and up the said beck

	Ft.	In.
*From the top of the Lime-stone, to the high flat .	2	6
From Ditto, to the sole	4	6
From Ditto, to the middle flat	5	0
From the middle flat to the sole	4	0
To the bottom of the Lime-stone	5	0
Total . . .	21	0

to High-Cup Nick, from whence it may be traced to Lune-head, in the county of Yorkshire.

WHET-STONE BED.

This is a thin soft Stratum of Argillaceous earth, commonly called the Whet-stone bed, No. 191, underneath it is a very hard Post of Basalt, called the *Whin Post;* it is so very difficult to sink through, that it blunts the workmen's tools, almost as fast as they can get them sharpened: it strikes fire with steel abundantly.

GREAT WHIN SILL.

This Stratum, No. 192, is of various thickness in different places. At *Caldron-snout,* a waterfall on the river Tees, it is nearly thirty fathoms; at *Dufton-fell,* before-mentioned, we find it only about seven or eight fathoms, and at Hilton, (a lead mine, in Westmorland) it is little more than four fathoms in thickness. This Stratum occurs at the Smelting-house, near *Tyne-head,* and also at *Kesh Burn Force,* a waterfall in *Alston-moor*. It may be traced down the river Tees to *Caldron-snout*, and up *Maze-beck* to *High-Cup Nick*, where it bassets. It again occurs in *Lune-head*, in the county of Yorkshire, and to the north of *Lune*, at *Hollwick*, in the same county. At *Tyne-bottom Mine*, near *Garrigill*, the same Stratum is sunk into near twenty fathoms; and at *Settling-stones Lead Mine*, two miles and a half north-east of Haydon-bridge, in Northumberland, it occurs at the surface, and is penetrated to the depth of twenty-two fathoms; it also bassets at *Sewn-shields Crag*, a little north of the Great Picts Wall, in the same neighbourhood; and forms the bed of the river Wear, at *Unthank-bridge*, near Stanhope, in the county of Durham. It is a very hard Stratum, of a brown or reddish brown colour, emits fire with steel, and, except in one instance, which will be afterwards mentioned, has not been productive of metallic ores, in several veins where it has been tried.

According to modern Geologists, the *Great Whin Sill*, is *Basaltic Green-stone*, similar to that which occurs at Salisbury Crags, near Edinburgh, Catham Hill, in the vicinity of Glasgow, and at the celebrated

Giant's Causeway, in the county of Antrim, in Ireland.[*]

Underneath the Great Whin Sill, we find four Plate Beds and three Hazles, when we come to a Lime-stone, commonly called *the Jew Lime-stone*, which is the next Stratum of Lime-stone under the Tyne-bottom Lime-stone, and has never been sunk to in Alston-moor, but crops out in descending the mountains on the west side of *Cross-fell*, or at Dufton-fell, before-mentioned. At Hilton Lead Mine, this Lime-stone lays close to the bottom of the *Great Whin Sill*, and is about *eighteen* fathoms in thickness.

Below the Jew Lime-stone, we have two Plate Beds and a Hazle, when we come to another blue and hard Lime-stone, No. 204, commonly called *the Little Lime*, by the miners at Dufton, below which, there

---

[*] Mr. Winch says the Great Whin Sill of the Lead Mine district does not consist of the Whin of the colliery sinkers, but is really Basalt, coarse-grained in texture, and composed of white Feltspar and black Horn-blende, the latter Mineral predominating, and giving to the rock a dark greenish grey colour.—*See Geological Transactions, vol.* 4, *p.* 73.

Q

is a Plate Bed about three fathoms thick. Underneath we find a Hazle Sjll, No. 206, and again another Plate Bed, which overlies a Lime-stone, called *the Smiddy Lime-stone.*

Below the Smiddy Lime-stone there is a Hazle, about three fathoms thick; and then another Lime-stone, under which we find two thin Plate Beds, and a Hazle; when we come to a Lime-stone, commonly called *Robinson's Lime;* from thence there is a thin Hazle, with Grey Beds, upon the top of a very thick Lime-stone, called

THE GREAT RUNDLE BECK,
OR
MELMERBY SCAR LIME-STONE.

This Stratum of Lime-stone is blue and hard; it is the thickest that we find throughout the section, and may be seen bursting out at Melmerby Scar, in the county of Cumberland, from which it has derived its name. It may also be traced along the bearing of the Strata to the south, above *Dufton,* and other places in Westmorland, still keeping pretty regular in its thickness.

Below the above Lime-stone there is a Plate Bed, about three fathoms in thickness, which overlies the Free-stone, No. 219. Underneath is another Plate Bed, and again another Lime-stone, below which we find a thick Free-stone, and several thin Plate Beds, as will appear by the section, until we arrive at a thick Plate Bed, No. 232, with a Coal seam in it, about seven inches thick. This Coal seam is considerably thicker, where it occurs, and is worked for sale, on Renwick Fell, five miles east of Kirkoswald, in the county of Cumberland.

Below the Plate Bed, No. 234, we find a Free-stone about six fathoms thick, and then a Girdle Bed, below which is another Lime-stone, No. 237, the lowest cal-careous Stratum that the section contains. Below the above Stratum of Lime-stone is a very white Free-stone, rather of a sandy nature, and more porous and open than several of the other Free-stones; it is of a siliceous nature, striking fire with steel, but not freely.

— ·::::::::·—◆—·::::::::·—

GREAT RED SAND-STONE.

In the last edition of this Work, the Great Red

Sand-stone which occurs in the vicinity of Penrith, and covers so large a portion of the county of Cumberland, was represented as regularly under-lying the series of Strata already described. Since the publication of that edition, this part of our island has received considerable attention from modern Geologists, and the opinion stated above, has been combated by some, and supported by others. This controversy the author will not presume to decide, but on a recent examination of the district, he is induced to *suppose* his former statement incorrect. It may be taken for granted, that on a subject which has excited such difference of opinion, nothing decisive can be advanced, but the reasons that have induced the author to form the latter conclusion, are, that in no instance can the Red Sand-stone be traced below the regularly stratified beds, and in all cases it is broken off and lost, in a very abrupt manner, as it approaches the edges of the Strata, at the bases of Cross-fell and Dun-fell.

It may be remarked, that in the neighbourhoood of Kirkby-thore, in Westmorland, the Red Sand-stone contains a bed of Gypsum,* or Alabaster, about five feet in thickness.

—◆—

Having now given a general description of the Section, it may perhaps be acceptable to give some account of the Strata, in other places abounding with Mines. —We therefore insert the three following Tables, which will be found partially to correspond with the upper part of the series already described.

---

* Gypsum is usually called *Alabaster*, or *Plaster of Paris*. Its uses, for chimney-pieces, monuments, floors, &c. are well known. It has very different modifications in the earth, being found in large nodulous masses, and stratified. The latter is fibrous, and its fibres run nearly at right angles from its upper or lower surface. It is of an opaque white, and uniform in its colour. The former is neither fibrous nor laminated, but composed of granules, as sugar, and breaks alike in all directions. Some of these masses are of a fine opaque white, like statuary marble; others are variegated with different colours, as red, green, and bluish. These colours are sometimes so blended with Gypsum matter, as to produce the appearance of Italian marble clouded with blackish veins. It takes a good polish, and though not so hard as marble, is deservedly esteemed for various internal ornamental purposes in architecture, &c. but will not endure the weather.

Selenite, though a gypseous body, is generally found imbedded in clay which is not calcareous It is laminated, transparent, and assumes a variety of forms of crystallization, well known to naturalists.

It may be observed, that Gypsum occurs imbedded in marl, as flint does in chalk, or chert in lime-stone. The Stratum of marl containing Gypsum is very thick. Pits have been sunk in it from eighty to a hundred yards deep, without cutting through it, or even seeing any other than adventitious matter in it.

Marl is sometimes much indurated, and even concreted to a perfect lime-stone. There are instances of its being burnt to lime, but these are seldom known to occur.

TABLE
OF
THE STRATA,
IN ARKENGARTH-DALE AND SWALE-DALE,
In Yorkshire.

Fh. Ft.

1. Mill-stone Grit, thickness not known.
2. Plate and hard beds . . 6 0 Argillaceous
3. Flinty Chert . . . . 2 0 Siliceous
4. Plate and red beds . . 2 3 Argillaceous
5. Crow Chert . . . . 1 3 Siliceous, Inflam.
6. Crow Lime and Coal seam 2 0 Calcareous
7. Plate . . . . . . 4 0 Argillaceous
8. White Grit . . . . 10 0 Siliceous
9. Plate . . . . . . 7 0 Argillaceous
10. Red beds . . . . . 2 3 Siliceous
11. Plate . . . . . . 1 3 Argillaceous
12. Black beds . . . . 2 3 Siliceous
13. Main Chert . . . . 3 0 Siliceous
14. MAIN LIME . . . . 12 0 Calcareous
15. Underset . . . . . 5 0 Siliceous
16. Plate . . . . . . 4 0 Argillaceous
17. Underset Chert . . . 3 3 Siliceous
18. Ditto Lime-stone . . 4 0 Calcareous
19. Grit and Plate . . . 27 0 Siliceous

100 0

TABLE OF THE STRATA,

AT

BELDON,

Three Miles South-West of Blanchland,

In the county of Northumberland.

	Fh.	Ft.	In.
Low Grit	5	1	0
Pebbles	—	—	—
Plate	2	5	0
Lime	0	3	0
Coal	0	1	0
Plate	1	0	0
Hard Strings	—	—	—
Craig's Sill	4	2	0
Plate	1	5	0
Cockle Shells	—	—	—
Pattinson's Sill	2	4	6
Plate	4	1	6
Hazle	0	3	0
Plate	2	0	0
Hazle	4	3	0
Plate	1	2	0
Carried forward,	31	1	0

	Fa.	Ft.	In.
Brought forward,	31	1	0
Little Lime and Black Bed	1	3	0
Hazle	0	4	0
Plate . . . . :	3	1	0
Coal and hard Coal Sill	1	4	0
Grey Beds	1	2	0
Plate and Coal	1	4	0
Low Coal Sill (Sand-stone)	2	3	0
Plate	1	0	0
Hazle	0	3	0
Plate	1	0	0
GREAT LIME-STONE	9	2	0
Tuft	0	4	0
Grey Beds	0	2	6
Hazle	1	1	3
Plate	1	1	6
Hewitson's Lime	0	4	0
	59	4	3

TABLE OF THE STRATA,

AT

SHIELDON,

ONE MILE WEST OF BLANCHLAND,

In the county of DURHAM.

	Fh.	Ft.	In.
Hipple	7	0	0
Plate	7	0	0
High Grit	8	3	6
Plate and Coal	0	3	3
Plate and white Sill	1	1	9
Plate, Coal, and Plate	3	0	6
Low Grit	11	0	6
Plate	1	4	9
Pebbles	1	0	0
Plate, Lime, Post, and Hazle	1	4	0
Crag Sill	4	2	0
Plate	4	3	6
Pattinson's Sill	6	4	6
White Sill	2	0	0
Hazle	4	5	0
Plate	4	0	0

Carried forward, 69 3 3

R

	Fh.	Ft.	In.
Brought forward,	69	3	3
Hazle	0	3	0
Plate	2	1	0
Hazle	0	4	0
Plate	5	2	0
Little Lime-stone	2	1	0
Plate and Coal	0	5	0
Coal Sill	1	1	3
Plate	2	0	0
Coal, &c.	0	3	0
Low Coal Sill	1	2	0
White Sill	3	4	0
Grey Beds	0	0	8
Plate	1	0	0
GREAT LIME-STONE	—	—	—
	91	0	2

The MAIN LIME of the first, and the GREAT LIME-STONE of the second and third of these tables, are supposed to be identical with the Great Lime-stone, No. 153 in our Engraved Section; and, by comparing the beds above this Stratum with those in the tables, it will be seen, that there is a considerable want of agreement, which might easily be expected from the distance of the different places from each other.

We shall now insert an account of the Metalliferous Strata in Derbyshire, extracted from Farey's Derbyshire Report, published in 1811. Previous to entering upon his description of the Strata, we shall present our readers with the following table, in order to supply, in some measure, the place of Mr. Farey's illustrative coloured engraving:

TABLE

OF

THE METALLIFEROUS STRATA,

IN DERBYSHIRE.

No.	Name of each Stratum.	Thickness.			Nature.
		Yds.	Ft.	In.	
1.	Grit Rock	120	0	0	Siliceous
2.	Lime-stone Shale . . .	160	0	0	Argillaceous
3.	First Lime-stone Rock .	50	0	0	Calcareous
4.	First Toad-stone . . .	20	0	0	Basaltic
5.	Second Lime-stone Rock	50	0	0	Calcareous
6.	Second Toad-stone . .	30	0	0	Basaltic
7.	Third Lime-stone Rock .	60	0	0	Calcareous
8.	Third Toad-stone . . .	30	0	0	Basaltic
9.	Fourth Lime-stone Rock	130	0	0	Calcareous

Total Thickness, 650 0 0

The thickness of each Stratum, in the above table, is deduced from Mr. Farey's engraving, before alluded to.

In extracting the following description of the above Strata, from Mr. Farey's treatise, we have been obliged considerably to abridge his observations, but those who wish for more ample information on this subject, are referred to the Derbyshire Report, vol. 1, page 220.

GRIT ROCK.

" The uppermost of the Strata, in the table, is the *Mill-stone Grit* Rock, which, by its thickness and its hardness, and truly indestructible properties, gives rise to the greater part of the Siliceous Rock Scenery in Derbyshire, and the adjacent parts of Staffordshire, Cheshire, and Yorkshire. In several places this Rock has been proved to be 120 yards thick, composed for the greater part, of a very coarse-grained white, yellowish or reddish Free-stone, which is easily worked, considering the extreme hardness of its particles, and its great durability, which appears to me superior, to that of any Free-stone which I have seen used in England. What are known all over England by the name of *Peak Mill-stones*, are from this Stratum,* and, though formerly these were dug and prepared from various parts of the Stratum, yet now,

---

* See page 96.

few, if any, Mill-stones are made, but at Old-Booth
Edge, and other places near Nether Padley, in Hathersage, in a very inaccessible part of the county:
principally, as it seems to me, because here, by long
working, a superior part of the Stratum has been
reached, to what is generally met with on the surface:
for the fact is, that fine blocks of this Rock, of every
size that can be wanted, are so plentifully met with,
loose and above ground, that any thing like a quarry
in it is almost unknown, except in Hathersage.

" Some of the beds of this Grit Rock, which have
usually spherical stains in them of a light red colour,
are perfectly infusible, and form the best *Fire-stone*
which is known, for lining the hearths of iron furnaces and others, where an intense heat is kept up.—
The upper beds of the Grit Rock are often thin, and
capable of further division, so as to make excellent
paving-stones or flags, and even slate for covering
buildings.

" In a Geological point of view, this lowest regular Grit Rock is very important, on account of the
great length that its basset-edge can be traced, with
scarcely any interruption, in the form almost of a
lengthened horse-shoe, terminating at its two ends

against the great east and west or Derbyshire fault, and including within and beneath it, the Great or Lime-stone Shale, and the Lime-stones and Toad-stones, whose descriptions are to follow, and having Coal measures upon and without it.

—*:*—

GREAT OR LIME-STONE SHALE.

"This Stratum is a Black Argillaceous Shale, which decomposes, or falls into Clay or strong Loam on the surface, and forming, where not too wet, a very productive soil; but in some parts the flakes of Shale are durable, remaining for ages in the soil, of the sizes of half-crowns and penny-pieces, whence it is, as I suppose, that such have obtained the name of *penny-shales*.

"This great Shale, whose thickness has been proved by shafts of the Lead Mines in the first Lime-stone Rock underneath it, seems generally from one hundred and fifty to one hundred and seventy yards thick, sometimes entirely consisting of black or brown Shale, in very thin lamina, but subject to great and curious anomalies, the first and most general of which are, accidental beds of fine-grained Siliceous

Free-stone, very full of Mica in minute plates, and
stained with various concentric rings, of different
shapes and shades of yellow and red. In some places,
there are accidental beds of this Shale-stone, of a
canky hardness, and very fit for road making. But
the most extraordinary anomaly attending this great
Shale, is the great masses and accidental beds of dark
blue or black Lime-stone which it produces, some of
the beds, of which, make a Lime, which sets in water,
and is little inferior, for water works, to the famous
Barrow Lime; perhaps these beds contain Manganese.
Iron-stone is found in considerable beds in the Lime-
stone Shale, and sometimes large balls of it occur, but
this Iron-stone is too far from Coals to have been turned to any account since the Charcoal Furnaces were
laid down. Several *Ochrey* and *Chalybeate* Springs
issue from this Great or Lime-stone Shale, and *Sulphur*, in small quantities, is also contained in its cavities.

— ✳ † ✳ —

MINERAL LIME-STONE & TOAD-STONE STRATA.

" The Strata, to be described under this denomination, are seven in number, viz. four Lime-stone Rocks

and three Basaltic Beds or Strata here, called Toad-
stones, the position and average thickness of which
are explained in the table. It must here be observed,
that the Toad-stone Strata are liable to vary in their
thickness, and the Lime-stones also, perhaps, as the
late Mr. Williams showed of the Mountain Lime-
stones of Scotland:—see his Mineral Kingdom, second edition, vol. 1, p. 55, 56, 124, 404.

" The first Lime-stone, the uppermost of the series,
bassets regularly from under the great Shale, which
was last described, all the way from Ranter Mine,
N. N. E. of Wirksworth town, south, to near Quarters House, N. N. W. of Great Hucklow, north, in
an irregular line. The remainder of the boundary of
these Strata, from Quarters House, near Great Hucklow, northward, to Castleton town, is principally limited by a vast Fault; from Wirksworth town, south-
westward, to Hopton, a part of the same great Fault
separates the 3rd Lime-stone Rock from the great
Shale, &c. south of it.

" The western boundary of the Strata I am describing, is marked by the basset-edge of the 3rd or lowest
Toad-stone, and the appearance of the 4th Lime
s

Rock from under it : such boundary, commencing at
the Great Lime-stone Fault, in Hopton, and proceeding first N. W. then W. and then N. E. so as to include Harboro Rocks, then near to Griffe House, and
to the famous Hopton-wood Quarries, till it joins the
Fault above mentioned, one-third of a mile N. W. of
Middleton, by Wirksworth.   From the S. side of
Slaley, the boundary is again to be traced from this
Fault, near to Ible W. and to Grange-mill, thence
to Pike-hall, Dale-head Mine, three-quarters of a
mile N. E. of Newhaven-house, near half a mile
S. W. of Benty-grange, W. of Cronk-stone, W. of
Hurdlow, E. of Great Low Hill, E. of Chelmerton-
town, and W. of the Low, by Flatt-house, Topley-
head, and one-quarter of a mile N. W. of Blackwell ;
it crosses the Wye River above Millers-dale, thence
by the side of Flag-dale, to Great-rocks, thence to
near Small-dale, to Dale-head, three-eighths of a
mile N. W. of Wheston, to Copt, Knowl, Portaway
Mine, and thence across the Cave Dale to Cawler
Hills, and along the same to the Great Lime-stone
Fault, above-mentioned, in Castleton town.

" Within the limits described above, each of the
three Lime-stone Rocks has its regular, but crooked,
range, and basset-edge, from south to north, viz. the

1st Rock, from Wirksworth to Great Hucklow and to Quarters House, a little north of it, abutting at each end against the great Lime-stone Fault, as above-mentioned;—the 2nd Lime, from the Great Lime-stone Fault in Middleton Wood on the north of Middleton, by Wirksworth, to the same Fault again on the south side of the Windmill-houses, near Great Hucklow; and the 3rd Lime, from the same Fault, between Wirksworth and Hopton, south, to the same Fault, against which it abuts, from a point south of Windmill-houses (and passing Hazlebadge, Bradwell, Edingtree, and Pindale) to Castleton Town.

"In like manner the three Toad-stone Strata, each abut against the same Fault, at the south and north ends of their respective ranges."

In order still further to illustrate the position and nature of the Derbyshire Strata, we subjoin the following extract, from Phillips's Geology of England and Wales:—

Speaking of the Strata, whose computed thickness is stated in the table, page 124, Mr. Phillips proceeds,

s 2

" We have to notice the nature of the Strata of Lime-
stone, Toad-stone, Shale, and Grit-stone; and shall
afterwards say a few words on the veins passing through
them.

" The *lowest Stratum of Lime-stone* being that, on
the out-going or out-crop of which are situated the
Peak forest, Buxton, and many towns on the south of
it, passes across Dove-dale and Wetton-dale: the
Weaver hills consist of it.   In it are many caverns,
as the immense one called Elden hole, north of Peak
Forest town; the Devil's hall, connected, by a tunnel,
with Speedwell mine ; Pool's hole near Buxton, and
several of less note.   Its stratification, and that of all
the superior Strata, is, in many places, greatly affected
by what is termed a great Lime-stone fault, but of
which I have not been able to discover any account, except of its direction ; it is very long and circuitous.—
The thickness of this lower Lime-stone Stratum is not
known; we are consequently ignorant of the rock on
which it rests.   It is regularly stratified, consisting of
very many beds, several of which are of considerable
thickness ; some thin ones are described as being a
Free-stone (Sand-stone) : its colour varies from white
to a yellowish stone colour, it rarely includes dark coloured beds.   Small entrochi, numerous anomia, and

other shells and organic remains, occur throughout the whole of this Stratum : in some mines, a thin bed of clay had been found in it. The Lime yielded by this Stratum is preferred to that of the Strata above it. A bed of Toad-stone lies on it, but I propose to notice together the three beds of this substance, and therefore proceed to the

" *Second Stratum of Lime-stone.*—This is about 210 feet in thickness, and consists also of many beds; the superior ones are often of a dark colour, and contain nodules of black chert, shells of the genus anomia, madrepores, &c.; some of the beds are quite black. It contains layers of clay, and towards the lower part of it, some dark beds of Lime-stone contain white madrepores. Imbedded masses of Toad-stone occur in it. On this lies another bed of Toad-stone, to which succeeds a

" *Third Stratum of Lime-stone.*—This, like the two preceding Strata, consists of many beds whose average thickness is about 150 feet: and it is worthy of note, that several of them are of Magnesian Lime-stone. In some places the upper beds partake so greatly of the nature of chert, as to be unfit for the purposes of the lime-burner; these cherty masses are usually called in Derbyshire, *Dun-stone*, or bastard Lime-stone. Here and there are masses of white chert or China-stone. Some few beds contain entrochi; and towards the lower part, are beds of a very black Lime-stone, which, as it takes a very brilliant polish, is termed black Marble. It contains thin beds of Clay. On this Stratum lies the third bed of Toad-stone, on which reposes the

" *Upper Lime-stone.*—This, like the preceding, is about 150 feet in thickness. In it, as in the three lower Strata, some thin beds of Clay are found, and it contains imbedded masses of Toad-stone, though rarely. The upper beds are of that variety of Lime-stone called Swine-stone, and are often dark coloured or black: near the top are found layers of nodules of black chert, similar in their arrangement to the flint nodules in chalk; in the upper beds also the shells called anomia, and others, are common. The middle beds contain vast assemblages of entrochi, and are occasionally quarried as marbles; and it is remarkable, that in some places, where these middle beds basset out on the surface, masses are ploughed up from beneath the alluvial soil, exhibiting the casts of the inside of entrochi in chert; these are commonly called

Screw-stones. Blocks of these were heretofore used in the forming of Mill-stones, which were employed instead of the French Buhr-stone. This Stratum contains beds of what is termed white chert or China-stone, of which considerable quantities are used in the Staffordshire potteries.*

"We come now to the consideration of the *three beds of Toad-stone interstratified with the four beds of Lime-stone.* These are said to be true and regular, and are so calculated upon by intelligent miners ; yet in several places they have proved of great thickness, and in others very thin ; in no place are they entirely wanting; the average thickness of the two undermost beds is about 75 feet, the upper bed is about 60 feet thick. But it is requisite to say, that each of the Lime-stone Strata encloses masses of Toad-stone, which are not connected with the regular Strata of that substance; to which is attributed the suspicion enter-tained by some that it is not stratified at all.

"All the Strata of Lime-stone and Toad-stone are

---

* It is in a mountain composed of Lime-stone, that the beautiful masses of various coloured fluor spar, termed Blue John, are found.

said to basset out in certain places in the district, before mentioned, but their perfect regularity and continuity in this respect, appears to have been greatly affected by the fault, already mentioned.

" The Toad-stone is described as a compact, hard, ferruginous stone, somewhat of the colour of the back of a toad, whence its familiar name. It frequently effervesces strongly with acids, and contains globules of whitish calcareous spar from the size of a pin's head to that of hazle nuts, or larger, having the appearance of rounded pebbles; these nodules, when exposed at the surface, fall out, leaving the imbedding substance with a cavernous or porous aspect. Occasionally it is schistose; in other places it appears as a clay, both in deep mines and on the surface, and is of a bluish grey colour. In these clays, it is said that masses of basalt, and others of the hardest class of these stones, occur, and occasionally in the same shapes as the pentagonal basaltic columns. It is not uncommon to find, in the upper bed of Toad-stone, Chalcedony, Horn-blende, Jasper, Zeolite, and Green Earth.

" In the *cave* at Castleton, which is a deep ravine at the back of the castle, the Toad-stone is seen in the

form of an irregular column, is as hard as ordinary basalt, compact, and contains horn-blende and some
patches or streaks of red jasper: a similar variety is
also found near Buxton, containing zeolite and chalcedony. The Toad-stone has no internal appearance
of stratification; no impression of vegetables, nor of
marine exuviæ, which occur plentifully in the Lime-
stone in which it is interstratified.*

" The *Great Shale,* or *Lime-stone Shale, resting on
the uppermost of the four beds of Lime-stone,* occu-

---

* The great *Whin Sill* of the lead miners in the north of
England, is described as being a bed of *basalt,* coarse-grained
in texture, and composed of white felspar and black horn-
blende, the latter predominating and giving to the rock a dark
greenish grey colour. It lies between beds of Lime-stone, &c.
and therefore in point of situation agrees remarkably well with
the *Toad-stone* of Derbyshire. (Geol Trans. vol. 4, p. 73.)
I am not aware that the latter rock has ever received the name
of basalt, though it occasionally assumes its character and
hardness. The actual distinction between the Toad-stone of
Derbyshire and the basalt of the north of England, has never
been clearly pointed out; and since their geological position is
the same, is there not reason for concluding that they are of the
same origin, and therefore that they ought to receive the same
designation? By the preceding account of the Toad-stone, it
will be observed that its characters differ essentially in different places, which also is the case with some of the basalts of
the northern parts of England, especially of those found in
what are termed *overlying* masses. Both are considered as *trap
rocks* —If the reader be desirous of inquiring into the probable
origin of basalt, and of other rocks usually associated under
the general name of *flœtz trap,* he is particularly referred to a
very candid and ingenious note on that subject by the Rev. W.
Conybeare, inserted in the 3rd vol. of the Transactions of the
Geological Society, p. 208.

T

pies a large tract on the surface. Its thickness is averaged at about 450 feet. Its general colour is black; it disintegrates on the surface, forming a strong loam or clay; which, when it is not too wet, is a very productive soil; but in some places the shale itself is durable, remaining for ages in the soil, of the size of a half crown or penny piece, from which it is presumed to have taken the name of *Penny Shale.*— From the decomposed Shale of this Stratum, bricks and tiles are made in several places. It contains occasional beds of a fine-grained siliceous Free-stone, full of mica in minute plates, and is stained with concentric rings, of several shades of yellow and red. It is considered to be the most perfect Free-stone of the district, and is quarried in several places, having been used in the construction of some of the finest buildings in Derbyshire. This Stratum also contains great masses, and occasional beds of a dark blue or black Lime-stone, which, at Ashford, is quarried as a black marble. The stratification of this Shale is by no means regular, being, in different places, horizontal, inclined, and even contorted. The *Rotten-stone* of Derbyshire is considered to arise from the occasional decomposition of these Lime-stone beds, near or upon the surface. They sometimes contain *Iron-stone.* This Stratum encloses *vegetable impressions;* and some beds of Coal of small extent, varying from a quarter of an inch to two inches in thickness. *Sulphur*, in small quantity, is found in its cavities, and *geodes* of *Lime-stone*, filled with liquid *bitumen*, in several of the mines. The hot springs of Buxton issue from this Stratum.

" We have now arrived at the consideration of the Stratum of *Grit-stone overlying the Stratum of Shale, the four Lime-stones, and three interposed beds of Toad-stone.*—It is requisite here to remark, that this Grit-stone is the Stratum on which the great Derbyshire and Yorkshire Coal measures lie; so that its situation might render it, in some degree, uncertain, whether it ought not to be considered as a member of that important series, rather than as belonging to the Lime-stone formation: but the question seems decided in favour of the latter, by its containing metallic veins in common with the Lime-stone. It is interposed between the Shale and the Coal, and the places at which it crops out on the surface from beneath the latter, are known with great precision along a great length of country. This Stratum has been proved to be 360 feet thick in several places; and is composed, for the greater part, of a very coarse-grained white, yellowish, or reddish Free-stone, which is easily worked, con-

T 2

sidering the extreme hardness of its particles, and is of great durability. It has long furnished Mill-stones, of pretty good quality, of which, formerly, there were several quarries, but they are now chiefly quarried at Old Booth-edge, in a very inaccessible part of the county : hence this Stratum has been termed the *Mill-stone Grit*. It affords also Fire-stone for the hearths of iron-furnaces, since it endures heat remarkably well. The upper beds are very thin ; these are used for paving stones, and sometimes are so thin as to be employed for the roofing of houses.

" The out-going of the Strata, just described, forms the great *Lead district* of Derbyshire ; very numerous veins have been worked in it, principally for Lead, but the ores of zinc, manganese, copper, and iron, also occur in them ; but they are more plentiful and productive when in the Lime-stone, than when in the other Strata. It has been supposed, that Lead Ore has not been found in the Toad-stone, but nineteen instances of its discovery in that situation, in strings and short branches, are mentioned.

" The east and west veins, in descending, are always *cut off by the Strata of Toad-stone*, which, therefore, pass through and divide them ; and, it is worthy of note, that when the vein is again found in the Stratum of Lime-stone, beneath the Toad-stone, it is not *immediately on a line* with the upper part, nor exactly of the same nature; in this case a vein is said to have *squinted.* The Toad-stone is said sometimes to assume the consistence of clay. It has been before noticed, that the Lime-stone Strata contain thin beds of clay, termed, by the miner, *way-boards;* these sometimes pass through and divide the veins of ore in the same manner as the Toad-stone does: and so complete is the separation of the veins of ore by the clay and the Toad-stone, that not even the water in the upper part of the vein penetrates through them into the part beneath."

It will be seen, by referring to Mr. Phillips's note, on the Great Whin Sill or Basaltic Green-stone, page 137, that there is some reason to conclude it identical with the Basaltic Toad-stone of Derbyshire. The author of these pages is far from considering this opinion as destitute of probability, and, although from the rise or aclivity of the Strata, with which the Great Whin Sill is connected, it ought to be far above the Derbyshire series, yet it may easily be thrown down by a slip or a fault, as the great *Burtree-ford*

Dyke ranges southward through Yorkshire, and tilts down to the east near eighty fathoms.

In this view of the matter, the Newcastle Coal form-ation, will correspond with that of Derbyshire; the Mill-stone Grit, and other Sand-stones at the top of the Lead Measures, with the Grit Rock, in the table, page 124; the different Plate beds, numbered in the section, 108, 118, 124, &c. with the Derbyshire Lime-stone Shale; the Lime-stones, No. 145, 153, 160, &c. with the first Lime-stone Rock in the table; the Whin Sill, No. 192, with the first Toad-stone; and the Lime-stones, No. 204, 208, 214, &c. with the second Lime-stone Rock in the table.

Pursuing the same train of reasoning, it might be inferred, that the Cumberland series of Strata, at the bases of Cross-fell and Dun-fell, are underlaid by two other Basaltic beds, and two Lime-stones, correspond-ing with the remaining Toad-stones and Lime-stone Rocks in Derbyshire. This opinion, so far from be-ing hypothetical or absurd, is confirmed by a number of very conclusive circumstances, and, if correct, will set at rest the Controverted Question respecting the Great Red Sand-stone, see page 115.

It will not be improper to insert here, an account of the two late Theories, which have divided the opinions of some of the Geologists of this country, and indeed have excited a good deal of the warmth, and some degree of the asperity, of controversial discussion. The Theories alluded to, are those of HUTTON and WERNER, as stated in Dr. Miller's Edition of Williams's Mineral Kingdom, Vol. II.

THEORY OF HUTTON.

I.—The first general fact in support of this Theory is, that the greater part of the bodies of which the exterior crust of the globe is composed, exhibits the marks of being formed out of the materials of mineral or organized bodies of a more ancient date, and although the spoils of an older world are not found in every piece of rock, yet they are every where visible in the present system, and are so generally diffused as to leave no doubt that the Strata, which now compose the present continents, are formed out of more ancient Strata.

II.—The second general fact on which this Theory rests is, that the present rocks, excepting such as are unstratified, have been all deposited at the bottom of the sea; and having been collected in the form of loose materials, they have been consolidated by some powerful and general agent. This agent is supposed to be subterranean heat, and it is said that the author of the Theory has removed the objections to this assumption, by introducing the principle of compression, which must have prevailed in that region where the consolidation of mineral bodies was effected ; for it is alleged, that under the weight of a superincumbent ocean, the utmost intensity of the heat is unable to volatilize those substances, which at the surface, and merely under the pressure of the atmosphere, are entirely consumed. It is supposed also, that the same degree of pressure, by forcing those substances to remain united, which at the surface are easily separated, might effect the fusion of some bodies which are only calcined in our fires.

III.—The third general argument adduced in support of this Theory is, that the stratified rocks, instead of being in a horizontal position, as it is supposed they were originally, are now observed to be placed in all degrees of elevation, and some even perpendicular to the horizon; and besides, many of the Strata which were once at the bottom of the sea, are now raised up several thousand feet above its surface.— From this circumstance, and from the bendings, the fractures, and separation of the Strata, it is inferred that they have been elevated by means of some expansive force acting under them ; a force which has burst

U

in pieces the solid pavement on which the ocean rests, and has raised up rocks from the bottom of the sea into mountains 15,000 feet above its surface. Thus, according to this Theory, the rocks were first consolidated by heat, and then elevated by the same agent acting with an expansive power.

IV.—The fourth argument in support of this Theory, is derived from the disturbances which abound in the mineral kingdom, and particularly those great breaches among rocks, which are filled with materials, different from the rock on either side. Such are metallic veins, as well as the veins or dykes of Whinstone, Porphyry, or Granite. These are supposed to be of posterior formation to the Strata which they intersect, and in general carry with them the marks of violence with which they have been introduced, and of the disturbance which they have occasioned in the rocks already formed. According to the view of Dr. Hutton, the materials of all these veins have been in a state of fusion, by means of subterraneous heat, and in this state they have been injected among the fissures and openings of rocks already formed. All the masses of Whin-stone, Porphyry, and Granite, which are interposed among Strata, or raised up in pyramids through the midst of the Strata, are supposed to have been in a state of fusion ; and thus, in the fusion and injection of the unstratified rocks, consists the last of the great operations of subterraneous heat on mineral bodies.

V.—The next part of this Theory relates to the changes to which mineral bodies are subjected after they are raised into the atmosphere; and according to it they are all going to decay; the hardest as well as the softest bodies, are wasting, and undergoing a separation of their parts; and being resolved into their elements, are carried down by the rivers, and deposited at the bottom of the sea.

The following general reflections, on this Theory, I shall give in the words of Dr. Hutton's Biographer:—
" On comparing," says he, " the first and the last of the propositions just enumerated, it is impossible not to perceive that they are two steps of the same progression, and that mineral substances are alternately dissolved and renewed. These vicissitudes may have been often repeated, and there are not wanting remains among mineral bodies that lead us back to continents from which the present are the third in succession.— Here then we have a series of great natural revolutions in the condition of the earth's surface, of which, as the author of this Theory has remarked, we neither see the beginning nor the end; and this circumstance accords well with what is known concerning other parts of the economy of the world. In the continuation of

the different species of animals and vegetables that inhabit the earth, we discern neither beginning nor end; and in the planetary motions, where geometry has carried the eye so far, both into the future and the past, we discover no mark, either of the commencement or termination of the present order. It is unreasonable indeed to suppose, that such marks should any where exist. The author of nature has not given laws to the universe, which, like the constitutions of men, carry in themselves the elements of their own destruction; he has not permitted in his works any symptom of infancy or of old age, or any sign by which we may estimate either their future or their past duration. He may put an end, as he no doubt gave a beginning, to the present system, at some determinate period of time; but, we may rest assured, that great catastrophe will not be brought about by the laws now existing, and that it is not indicated by any thing we perceive."

THEORY OF WERNER.

This Theory may be considered as the reverse of the preceding; for, according to it, all mineral substances have been in a state of solution or suspension in water.

According to this Theory, all rocks are divided into three great classes, primary, transition, and secondary; and it is supposed, that the characters of these different classes of rocks, warrant the conclusion, that they have been formed at different periods.

I.—The primitive class of rocks constitutes, not only the highest parts of the surface of the earth, but also supports all other rocks. This class of rocks is characterised by being in a more perfect state of crystallization than the incumbent rocks, and it exhibits no remains of animals or of vegetables. The inferences deduced from these circumstances are, that the rocks possessed of the above characters were the first formed; that they are to be considered as chemical depositions; and that they were produced before the existence of organized beings.

According to the language employed in this Theory, the different classes of rocks are composed of a number of different layers, which are distinguished by the name of *formations*, and these, layers or formations, are supposed to have succeeded each other in a certain determinate order; for, from the observations made by those who have adopted the Theory, they are found in the same relative position in every quarter of the globe. They are, also, from the same circumstances, denominated *universal formations*. The wa-

ter, which held, in solution, the materials, of which
the primitive rocks consist, it is supposed, surrounded
the whole earth to a greater height, than the highest
mountains of the globe. From this fluid, successive
layers or depositions, of various degrees of thickness,
were produced; and, as these formations took place
by a slow and gradual deposition, they are now characterised by a kind of confused crystallization.

II.—After the formation of the primitive class of
rocks, the waters, holding, in solution, the other materials, of which the following classes of rocks are
composed, diminished in height; the primitive rocks
were then above the surface of the water. Part of
those rocks is supposed to have suffered decay from
the action of the weather, and masses were also
broken off by the agitation of the waters; these being
mixed with the solution, were deposited along with
the next class of rocks, which exhibits the characters
of a deposition partly mechanical and partly crystalline. Hence it is inferred, that this class of rocks, being incumbent on the primitive rocks, being less elevated, and of a more earthly and less crystallized
structure, was formed in the circumstances now mentioned. No remains of vegetables or of land animals,
it is said, have been found in this class of rocks; a few
indications of marine animals, have been observed:

and hence it is inferred, that the consolidation of this class of rocks, must have taken place before the existence of vegetables or land animals. The formation of this class of rocks is, also, in this Theory, denominated *universal*, and they have received the name of transition, because they were formed when the earth was passing from an uninhabited to an inhabited state.

III.—As the rocks, thus formed, were more and more exposed by the diminution and subsidence of the waters, they were subjected to still greater disintegration. The materials, thus separated, were mixed, in a greater abundance, with that part of the solution remaining; and hence mechanical deposition became more prevalent, and chemical deposition more sparing. The characters possessed, by the next class of rocks, the secondary, are supposed to warrant these conclusions. These rocks are disposed in horizontal Strata, and they exhibit more of an earthy, and less of a crystalline, appearance, than the rocks which compose the preceding classes. This class of rocks is particularly distinguished, by a great abundance of the remains of organic beings. The formation of the secondary class of rocks, is also supposed to have been universal.

The Strata, which accompany Coal, are deposited in patches, and are therefore supposed to constitute only a partial formation; and hence this class of rocks is distinguished by the name of the *Independent Coal Formation.* The Strata, of which this class of rocks is composed, are incumbent on the transition rocks.— There is another class of rocks, which, according to the Theory, was produced among the last of the series. This has been denominated the *Floetz Trap Formation.* It consists of Basalt, Wacken, and Green-stone, and is incumbent on all other rocks. The rocks belonging to this formation, now exist in detached masses among the secondary Strata, or covering some of the transition rocks, because it has been subjected to a greater degree of waste and decay than other rocks.

The diversity and inequality of surface which appear on the earth, are accounted for, in this Theory, from the different degrees of durability of different rocks, in resisting the waste and decay, which are continually going on. Primitive rocks possessing, from their peculiarity of structure, a greater degree of hardness and cohesion, appear to be the most durable. The present arrangement and position of the various Strata, on the surface of the earth, are also supposed to depend upon the inequalities of the nucleus, on which they were originally deposited.

In all Theories of the earth, the formation of Mineral Veins always constitutes a prominent feature. Accord-

ing to this Theory, fissures were produced after the
subsidence of the waters, by the drying and shrinking
of the newly-formed Strata; and in these fissures, the
various mineral substances, with which they are now
filled, were deposited from solution in water. And as
those veins afford the finest examples of the perfect
crystallization of mineral bodies, this circumstance is
supposed to arise from the waters holding these substances in solution, being less liable to agitation than
during the deposition of the horizontal Strata.

The Theory of Hutton has gradually sunk into dis-
repute, in proportion as Geological facts and observations have been more multiplied and extensive; and
it is not improbable, but even the beautiful Theory of
Werner may share a similar fate, as some parts of it
have met with considerable, and powerful opposition.
The author has, however, inserted, towards the conclusion of this work, a Tabular Representation of the
Order of Super-position of the Strata, in the British
Islands, by the Rev. W. Buckland, which is drawn up
according to the Wernerian Theory; and, as it exhibits a compendious view of the Geological structure
of our island, and points out the position of the district which he attempts to describe, on Wernerian
principles, he thinks it cannot fail of proving acceptable to his readers.

x

SECTION OF THE STRATA.

◆

Part I.—COAL MEASURES.

Local Names.	No.		Yd. Ft. In.	Nature of each Stratum.
Alluvial cover	1		10 0 0	Argillaceous
Brown Post, or Grind-stone Bed	2		24 0 0	Siliceous
Coal	3		0 0 6	Bituminous
Blue Metal Stone	4		5 2 0	Argillaceous.
White Girdles	5		4 1 0	Siliceous
Coal	6		0 0 8	Bituminous
White and Grey Post . .	7		12 0 0	Siliceous
Soft Blue Metal Stone . .	8		10 0 0	Argillaceous
Coal	9		0 0 6	Bituminous
White Post Girdles . . .	10		6 0 0	Siliceous
Whin	11		4 0 0	Basaltic or Siliceous
Strong White Post . . .	12		5 2 6	Siliceous
Coal	13		0 1 0	Bituminous
Soft Blue Thill	14		3 2 0	Argillaceous
Soft Girdles mixed with Whin	15		7 2 0	Siliceous, &c.
Coal	16		0 0 6	Bituminous
Blue and Black Stone . . .	17		7 1 0	Argillaceous
Coal	18		0 0 8	Bituminous
Strong White Post . . .	19		3 0 0	Siliceous
Grey Metal Stone	20		3 1 0	Argillaceous
Coal	21		0 0 8	Bituminous
Grey Post mixed with Whin .	22		3 1 0	Siliceous or Basaltic
Grey Girdles	23		6 1 0	Siliceous
Blue and Black Stone . . .	24		4 2 0	Argillaceous
Coal	25		0 1 0	Bituminous

Carried forward, 128 0 0

☞ *The Italic Letters refer to the different Strata at the bottom of the page, which correspond with the Strata next below those on which the Letters are placed.*

Local Names.	No.	Yd. Ft. In.			Nature of each Stratum.
		Brot. forward, 128	0	0	
Grey Metal Stone , , , ,	26	4	0	0	Argillaceous
Strong White Post , , , ,	27	12	0	0	Siliceous
Black Metal Stone , , , ,	28	6	0	0	Argillaceous
High Main Coal , , , , ,	29	2	0	0	Bituminous
Grey Metal , , , , , ,	30	9	0	0	Argillaceous—a—b
Coal, called Metal Coal , ,	33	0	1	7	Bituminous—c
Blue Metal Stone , , , ,	35	10	0	0	Argillaceous
Coal, called the Stone Coal, part of the 5-qr. on Wear,	36	0	1	2	Bituminous—d—e
Blue Metal Stone , , , ,	39	6	0	0	Argillaceous
Blue Metal Stone and Whin ,	40	0	1	6	Ditto and Basaltic
Strong White Post , , , ,	41	7	0	0	Siliceous
Brown Post with Water , ,	42	0	0	7	Ditto
Blue Metal with Grey Girdles	43	4	2	0	Argillaceous & Siliceous
Yard Coal on Tyne Coal , ,	44	1	0	0	Bituminous

Carried forward, · 194 1 6

Local Names				No.	Yd. Ft. In.			Nat. of each Strat.
a—Post Girdles	,	,	,	31	0	2	0	Siliceous
b—Blue Metal	,	,	,	32	1	1	0	Argillaceous
c—Girdles	,	,	, ,	34	0	1	2	Siliceous
d—Slate Clay	,	,	, ,	37	0	1	6	Argillaceous
e—Post	,	,	, , ,	38	0	1	0	Siliceous

Local Names.	No.		Yd. Ft. In.	Nature of each Stratum.
		Brot. forward,	194 1 6	
Blue Metal , , , , , ,	45		6 0 3	Argillaceous—a
Coal , , , , , , , ,	47		0 0 6	Bituminous
Grey Metal with Post Girdles	48		4 0 6	Argil. & Siliceous—b—c
Blue Metal Stone , , , ,	51		2 2 0	Argillaceous
Grey Met. Stone with Post Gird.	52		5 1 5	Argil. & Siliceous—d
Maudlin seam Wear Coal, and Bensham Tyne Coal , , ,	54		1 0 3	Bituminous—e
White Post , , , , , ,	56		4 0 7	Siliceous
White Post mixed with Whin	57		4 0 0	Ditto and Basaltic
White Post , , , , , ,	58		2 2 0	Siliceous—f
Grey Metal Stone and Girdles	60		4 2 0	Argillaceous & Siliceous
White Post mixed with Whin	61		6 0 0	Siliceous & Basaltic
Whin , , , , , , , ,	62		0 0 7	Basaltic—g
Coal, part of Low Main Wear	64		1 0 6	Bituminous—h
Grey Metal and Whin Girdles	66		3 1 10	Argil. & Basaltic—i—k
Five-quarter Coal, part of Low Main Wear , , , , ,	69		1 0 2	Bituminous—l
		Carried forward,	261 0 3	

Local Names.	No.	Yd. Ft. In.	Nat. of each Strat.
a—White Post , , , , ,	46	1 1 0	Siliceous
b—Strong White Post , , ,	49	2 2 0	Ditto
c—Whin , , , , , , ,	50	0 0 7	Basaltic
d—Blue Metal Stone with Whin Girdles	53	3 1 3	Argil. and Basaltic
e—Blue Grey Metal , , ,	55	1 0 8	Argillaceous
f—Dark Blue Metal , , ,	59	0 2 2	Ditto
g—White Post mixed with Whin	63	2 1 6	Basal. & Siliceous
h—Dark grey Metal Stone ,	65	2 0. 0	Argillaceous
i—Grey Metal and Girdles	67	3 0 0	Argillaceous
k—White Post , , , , ,	68	1 0 0	Siliceous
l—Blue and Grey Metal , ,	70	1 1 0	Argillaceous

Local Names.	No.		Yd.	Ft.	In	Nature of each Stratum.
		Brot. forward,	261	0	3	
Coal , , , , , , , , ,	71		0	0	9	Bituminous
Blue and grey Metal , , ,	72		4	0	0	Argillaceous
White Post mixed with Whin	73		1	1	6	Siliceous and Basaltic
Grey Metal Stone , , , ,	74		2	0	6	Argillaceous
Ditto and Girdles , , , ,	75		2	0	9	Ditto and Siliceous
Low Main Coal on Tyne, Hutton seam on Wear , , ,	76		2	0	6	Bituminous
Grey Post with Blue Stone ,	77		27	0	0	Siliceous & Argillaceous
Coal , , , , , , , , ,	78		0	1	6	Bituminous
Blue Metal Stone , , , ,	79		15	0	0	Argillaceous
Coal , , , , , , , ,	80		0	0	6	Bituminous
Grey Metal with Post , , ,	81		6	0	0	Argillaceous & Siliceous
Coal , , , , , , , ,	82		0	0	2	Bituminous
Grey Metal and white Post ,	83		10	0	0	Argillaceous & Siliceous
Coal , , , , , , , ,	84		0	0	6	Bituminous
Grey Metal Stone , , , ,	85		4	0	0	Argillaceous
Coal , , , , , , , ,	86		0	0	6	Bituminous
Blue Metal , , , , , ,	87		12	0	0	Argillaceous
Coal; Hervey's seam, Wear 3ft. 0in. Whick. St.Coal, Tyne 6 0	88		2	0	0	Bituminous
Grey Metal and Metal Stone	89		10	0	0	Argillaceous
Coal, called Brockwell , ,	90		1	0	2	Bituminous
		Carried forward,	361	1	7	

Local Names.	No.	Brot. forward,	Yd. Ft. In.			Nature of each Stratum.
		361	1	7		
Slate Sill , , , , , , ,	91		5	0	0	Siliceous & Argillaceous
Slate, Clay, or Plate , , ,	92		8	0	0	Argillaceous
Different Girdle Beds , , ,	93		4	0	0	Ditto and Siliceous
Plate , , , , , , , ,	94		4	0	0	Argillaceous
Free-stone , , , , , , ,	95		14	0	0	Siliceous
Coarse Hazle , , , , , ,	96		3	1	0	Siliceous
Plate , , , , , , , ,	97		2	0	0	Argillaceous—a
Plate and Grey Beds , , ,	99		3	0	0	Argillaceous
Hard Stone Ditto , , , ,	100		1	1	0	Siliceous
Plate and Grey Beds , , ,	101		3	0	0	Argillaceous & Siliceous
Grey Beds , , , , , ,	102		1	0	0	Ditto
Plate and Ditto , , , , ,	103		2	0	0	Argillaceous
Mill-stone Grit or grey Mill-stone , , , , , , ,	104		9	0	0	Siliceous
Plate , , , , , , , ,	105		9	0	0	Argillaceous
Hard Hazle , , , , , ,	106		3	0	0	Siliceous
Grey Beds , , , , , , ,	107		3	0	0	Ditto and Argillaceous
Free-stone , , , , , ,	108		15	0	0	Siliceous
Plate , , , , , , ,	109		2	0	0	Argillaceous
Hazle or Slate , , , , ,	110		4	0	0	Ditto and Siliceous
Plate or Famp , , , , ,	111		2	1	6	Argillaceous
Hazle and Plate , , , , ,	112		1	0	0	Ditto and Siliceous
Plate , , , , , , , ,	113		4	1	0	Argillaceous.
Hazle or Slate , , , , ,	114		3	1	6	Siliceous
Plate and Grey Beds , , ,	115		6	0	0	Ditto and Argillaceous

Carried forward, 475 0 7

Local Names.	No.	Yd. Ft. In.	Nat. of each Strat.
a—Blue Whin , , , ,	98	0 2 0	Basaltic

PART II.—*LEAD MEASURES.*

Local Names.	No.		Yd.	Ft.	In.	Nature of each Stratum.
		Brot. forward,	475	0	7	
Alternating thin Strata of Grey Beds , , , , , ,	116		29	1	0	Argillaceous & Siliceous
D						
Grind-stone Sill , , , , ,	117		8	0	0	Siliceous
Plate , , , , , , , ,	118		11	0	0	Argillaceous
Hazle , , , , , , ,	119		3	0	0	Siliceous
Plate , , , , , , , ,	120		3	1	0	Argillaceous
First or Fell-top Lime-stone ,	121		1	1	6	Calcareous
Coal , , , , , , , ,	122		0	0	8	Sulphureous
Hazle or upper Coal Sill , ,	123		4	0	0	Siliceous
Plate , , , , , , ,	124		10	0	0	Argillaceous
Hazle or Whet-stone Sill , ,	125		3	0	0	Siliceous & Argillaceous
Plate , , , , , , , ,	126		4	0	0	Argillaceous
Hazle , , , , , , , ,	127		4	0	0	Siliceous
Plate , , , , , , , ,	128		2	1	0	Argillaceous
Upper Slate Sill , , , , ,	129		8	0	0	Siliceous
Plate , , , , , , , ,	130		2	1	6	Argillaceous
Lower Slate Sill , , , ,	131		7	0	0	Siliceous
Plate , , , , , , , ,	132		10	0	0	Argillaceous
Hazle or hard dry Slate , ,	133		3	0	0	Ditto and Siliceous

Carried forward, 589 1 3

Local Names.	No.		Yd. Ft. In.	Nature of each Stratum.
		Brot. forward,	589 1 3	
Plate , , , , , , , ,	134		7 0 0	Argillaceous
Iron-stone and Coal , , , ,	135 136		1 1 6	Sulph. & Siliceous
Fire-stone , , , , , , ,	137		11 0 0	Siliceous
Plate , , , , , , , ,	138		8 0 0	Argillaceous
White Tuft , , , , , ,	139		3 2 0	Siliceous
Plate , , , , , , , ,	140		4 1 0	Argillaceous
Girdle Bed , , , , , , ,	141		2 0 0	Siliceous
Plate , , , , , , , ,	142		4 1 0	Argillaceous
Pattinson's Sill or Hazle , ,	143		4 0 0	Siliceous
Plate , , , , , , , ,	144		6 0 0	Argillaceous
Second or little Lime-stone ,	145		3 0 0	Calcareous
Plate , , , , , , , ,	146		6 0 0	Argillaceous
Coal , , , , , , , ,	147		0 1 6	Sulphureous
High Coal Sill , , , , ,	148		4 0 0	Siliceous
Plate , , , , , , , ,	149		2 1 6	Argillaceous
Coal , , , , , , , ,	150		0 1 0	Sulphureous
Low Coal Sill , , , , ,	151		3 1 0	Siliceous
Plate , , , , , , , ,	152		6 0 0	Argillaceous
Third Tumbler Beds, black Bed, and Great Lime-stone	153		21 0 0	Cal. and Argillaceous
Tuft or Water Sill , , , ,	154		3 0 0	Siliceous
Plate , , , , , , , ,	155		7 0 0	Argillaceous

Carried forward, 697 2 9

Local Names.	No.		Yd. Ft. In.	Nature of each Stratum.
		Brot. forward,	697 2 9	
mall Lime-stone , , , ,	156		0 1 6	Calcareous
uarry Hazle , , , , ,	157		10 0 0	Siliceous
Plate , , , , , , ,	158		11 0 0	Argillaceous
Till Bed , , , , , ,	159		2 1 6	Ditto and Siliceous
Four Fathom Lime-stone , ,	160		8 0 0	Calcareous
Nattriss Gill Hazle , , ,	161		6 0 0	Siliceous
Plate , , , , , , ,	162		11 0 0	Argillaceous
Fourth, or 3 yards Lime-stone	163		3 0 0	Calcareous
Six Fathoms Hazle , , , ,	164		12 0 0	Siliceous
Plate , , , , , , ,	165		3 1 6	Argillaceous
Fifth, or 5 yards Lime-stone ,	166		2 1 6	Calcareous
Slaty Hazle , , , , ,	167		4 0 0	Siliceous
Plate , , , , , , ,	168		6 0 0	Argillaceous
Sixth, or Scar Lime-stone , ,	169		10 0 0	Calcareous *
Plate , , , , , , ,	170		1 0 0	Argillaceous—a
Coal , , , , , , , ,	172		0 0 6	Sulphureous
Plate , , , , , , , ,	173		2 1 6	Argillaceous
Hazle , , , , , , ,	174		4 0 0	Siliceous
Plate , , , , , , , ,	175		1 0 0	Argillaceous—b
Plate , , , , , , , ,	177		3 0 0	Argillaceous
Hazle , , , , , , , ,	178		0 2 0	Siliceous—c—d
7th, or Cockle-shell Lime-stone	181		0 2 0	Calcareous—e
Plate , , , , , , , ,	183		0 1 0	Argillaceous—f
Plate , , , , , , , ,	185		1 2 0	Argillaceous

Carried forward, 809 0 9

* The Satin-stone occurs about two fathoms below this Stratum, on the
east side of the river Tyne, about a mile and a half south of Alston.

Local Names.	No.	Yd. Ft. In.	Nat. of each Strat.
a—Hazle , , , , ,	171	1 0 0	Siliceous
b—Hazle , , , , ,	176	0 2 0	Siliceous
c—Plate , , , , ,	179	0 2 0	Argillaceous
d—Hazle , , , , ,	180	0 1 0	Siliceous
e—Hazle , , , , ,	182	0 2 6	Siliceous
f—Hazle , , , , ,	184	3 0 0	Siliceous

Local Names.	No.	Brot. forward,	Yd. 809	Ft. 0	In. 9	Nature of each Stratum.
8th, or Single Post Lime-st.	186		2	0	0	Calcareous
Plate ,, ,, ,, ,, ,, ,,	187		1	0	0	Argillaceous
Grey-stone ,, ,, ,, ,, ,,	188		1	0	0	Siliceous
Alternating Plate & Grey Beds	189		18	0	0	Argil. and Siliceous
Tyne-bottom Lime-stone ,, ,,	190		8	0	0	Calcareou
Whet-stone Bed , ,, ,, ,,	191		1	0	0	Argillaceous
Whin Sill ,, ,, ,, ,, ,, ,, ,,	192		40	0	0	Basaltic Green-stone
Plate ,, ,, ,, ,, ,, ,, ,, ,,	193		3	0	0	Argillaceous
Hazle ,, ,, ,, ,, ,, ,, ,, ,,	194		3	1	0	Siliceous
Plate ,, ,, ,, ,, ,, ,, ,, ,,	195		3	2	0	Argillaceous
Hazle ,, ,, ,, ,, ,, ,, ,, ,,	196		3	2	6	Siliceous
Plate ,, ,, ,, ,, ,, ,, ,, ,,	197		1	0	0	Argillaceous
Hazle ,, ,, ,, ,, ,, ,, ,, ,,	198		6	0	0	Siliceous
Plate ,, ,, ,, ,, ,, ,, ,, ,,	199		3	0	0	Argillaceous
Ninth, or Jew Lime-stone ,,	200		8	0	0	Calcareous
Plate ,, ,, ,, ,, ,, ,, ,, ,,	201		2	1	0	Argillaceous
Slate, ,, ,, ,, ,, ,, ,, ,, ,,	202		5	0	0	Siliceous
Plate ,, ,, ,, ,, ,, ,, ,, ,,	203		1	1	6	Argillaceous
Tenth, or Little Lime-stone ,,	204		6	0	0	Calcareous

Carried forward, 926 2 9

Z 2

Local Names.	No.	Yd. Ft. In.	Nature of each Stratum.
		Brot. forward, 926 2 9	
Plate and Grey Beds , , ,	205	5 0 0	Argil. and Siliceous
Hazle Sill , , , , , , ,	206	17 0 0	Siliceous
Plate , , , , , , ,	207	8 0 0	Argillaceous
Smiddy Lime , , , , ,	208	10 1 6	Calcareous
Hazle Sill , , , , , ,	209	4 0 0	Siliceous
Lime-stone , , , , , ,	210	8 1 6	Calcareous
Plate , , , , , , ,	211	1 1 6	Argillaceous
Hazle , , , , , , ,	212	4 0 0	Siliceous
Plate , , , , , , ,	213	1 2 0	Argillaceous
Robinson's Lime , , , ,	214	7 0 0	Calcareous
Hazle , , , , , , ,	215	3 0 0	Siliceous
Plate , , , , , , ,	216	1 0 0	Argillaceous
Great Lime-stone, Rundle, or Melmerby Scar Lime-stone	217	44 0 0	Calcareous
Plate , , , , , , ,	218	4 0 0	Argillaceous
Free-stone , , , , , , ,	219	2 0 0	Siliceous
Plate and Small Coal , , ,	220	2 0 0	Argil. & Sulphureous
Lime-stone , , , , , ,	221	4 0 0	Calcareous

Carried forward,   1054   0   3

Local Names.	No.	Yd. Ft. In.	Nature of each Stratum.
		Brot.forward, 1654 0 3	
Free-stone , , , , , , ,	222	35 0 0	Siliceous
Plate , , , , , , , ,	223	3 0 0	Argillaceous
Free-stone , , , , , , ,	224	2 1 6	Siliceous
Plate , , , , , , ,	225	3 0 0	Argillaceous
Free-stone , , , , , , ,	226	2 1 6	Siliceous
Plate , , , , , , , ,	227	3 0 0	Argillaceous
Free-stone , , , , , , ,	228	3 0 0	Siliceous
Plate , , , , , , , ,	229	3 0 0	Argillaceous
Lime-stone , , , , , ,	230	2 1 6	Calcareous
Hard Free-stone , , , ,	231	4 0 0	Siliceous
Plate , , , , , , , ,	232	14 0 0	Argillaceous
Coal , , , , , , , ,	233	0 0 7	Sulph.& Inflammable
Plate , , , , , , , ,	234	43 0 0	Argillaceous

Carried forward, 1172 2 4

Local Names.	No.		Yd. Ft. In.			Nature of each Stratum.
		Brot. forward,	697	2	9	
Small Lime-stone , , , ,	156		0	1	6	Calcareous
Quarry Hazle , , , , , ,	157		10	0	0	Siliceous
Plate , , , , , , , ,	158		11	0	0	Argillaceous
Till Bed , , , , , ,	159		2	1	6	Ditto and Siliceous
Four Fathom Lime-stone , ,	160		8	0	0	Calcareous
Nattriss Gill Hazle , , , ,	161		6	0	0	Siliceous
Plate , , , , , , , ,	162		11	0	0	Argillaceous
Fourth, or 3 yards Lime-stone	163		3	0	0	Calcareous
Six Fathoms Hazle , , , ,	164		12	0	0	Siliceous
Plate , , , , , , , ,	165		3	1	6	Argillaceous
Fifth, or 5 yards Lime-stone ,	166		2	1	6	Calcareous
Slaty Hazle , , , , , ,	167		4	0	0	Siliceous
Plate , , , , , , , ,	168		6	0	0	Argillaceous
Sixth, or Scar Lime-stone , ,	169		10	0	0	Calcareous *
Plate , , , , , , , ,	170		1	0	0	Argillaceous—a
Coal , , , , , , , , ,	172		0	0	6	Sulphureous
Plate , , , , , , , , ,	173		2	1	6	Argillaceous
Hazle , , , , , , , ,	174		4	0	0	Siliceous
Plate , , , , , , , , ,	175		1	0	0	Argillaceous—b
Plate , , , , , , , ,	177		3	0	0	Argillaceous
Hazle , , , , , , , ,	178		0	2	0	Siliceous—c—d
7th, or Cockle-shell Lime-stone	181		0	2	0	Calcareous—e
Plate , , , , , , , ,	183		0	1	0	Argillaceous—f
Plate , , , , , , , ,	185		1	2	0	Argillaceous

Carried forward, 809 0 9

* The Satin-stone occurs about two fathoms below this Stratum, on the east side of the river Tyne, about a mile and a half south of Alston.

Local Names.	No.	Yd. Ft. In.			Nat. of each Strat.
a—Hazle , , , , ,	171	1	0	0	Siliceous
b—Hazle , , , , ,	176	0	2	0	Siliceous
c—Plate , , , , ,	179	0	2	0	Argillaceous
d—Hazle , , , , ,	180	0	1	0	Siliceous
e—Hazle , , , , ,	182	0	2	6	Siliceous
f—Hazle , , , , ,	184	3	0	0	Siliceous

z

Local Names.	No.	*Yd. Ft. In.*			Nature of each Stratum.
		Brot. forward, 809	0	9	
sth, or Single Post Lime-st.	186	2	0	0	Calcareous
Plate , , , , , , ,	187	1	0	0	Argillaceous
Grey-stone , , , , ,	188	1	0	0	Siliceous
Alternating Plate & Grey Beds	189	18	0	0	Argil. and Siliceous
Tyne-bottom Lime-stone , ,	190	8	0	0	Calcareou
Whet-stone Bed , , , , ,	191	1	0	0	Argillaceous
Whin Sill , , , , , , ,	192	40	0	0	Basaltic Green-stone
Plate , , , , , , , ,	193	3	0	0	Argillaceous
Hazle , , , , , , , ,	194	3	1	0	Siliceous
Plate , , , , , , , ,	195	3	2	0	Argillaceous
Hazle , , , , , , , ,	196	3	2	6	Siliceous
Plate , , , , , , , ,	197	1	0	0	Argillaceous
Hazle , , , , , , , ,	198	6	0	0	Siliceous
Plate , , , , , , , ,	199	3	0	0	Argillaceous
Ninth, or Jew Lime-stone ,	200	8	0	0	Calcareous
Plate , , , , , , , ,	201	2	1	0	Argillaceous
Slate , , , , , , , ,	202	5	0	0	Siliceous
Plate , , , , , , , ,	203	1	1	6	Argillaceous
Tenth, or Little Lime-stone ,	204	6	0	0	Calcareous

Carried forward, 926 2 9

Z 2

Local Names.	No.		Yd.	Ft.	In.	Nature of each Stratum.
		Brot. forward,	926	2	9	
Plate and Grey Beds , , ,	205		5	0	0	Argil. and Siliceous
Hazle Sill , , , , , , ,	206		17	0	0	Siliceous
Plate , , , , , , , ,	207		8	0	0	Argillaceous
Smiddy Lime , , , , ,	208		10	1	6	Calcareous
Hazle Sill , , , , , ,	209		4	0	0	Siliceous
Lime-stone , , , , , ,	210		8	1	6	Calcareous
Plate , , , , , , , ,	211		1	1	6	Argillaceous
Hazle , , , , , , , ,	212		4	0	0	Siliceous
Plate , , , , , , , ,	213		1	2	0	Argillaceous
Robinson's Lime , , , ,	214		7	0	0	Calcareous
Hazle , , , , , , , ,	215		3	0	0	Siliceous
Plate , , , , , , , ,	216		1	0	0	Argillaceous
Great Lime-stone, Rundle, or Melmerby Scar Lime-stone	217		44	0	0	Calcareous
Plate , , , , , , , ,	218		4	0	0	Argillaceous
Free-stone , , , , , ,	219		2	0	0	Siliceous
Plate and Small Coal , , ,	220		2	0	0	Argil. & Sulphureous
Lime-stone , , , , , ,	221		4	0	0	Calcareous

Carried forward, 1054 0 3

Local Names.	No	Yd. Ft. In.			Nature of each Stratum.
		Brot. forward, 1054	0	3	
Free-stone , , , , , ,	222	35	0	0	Siliceous
Plate , , , , , , ,	223	3	0	0	Argillaceous
Free-stone , , , , , ,	224	2	1	6	Siliceous
Plate , , , , , , ,	225	3	0	0	Argillaceous
Free-stone , , , , , ,	226	2	1	6	Siliceous
Plate , , , , , , ,	227	3	0	0	Argillaceous
Free-stone , , , , ,	228	3	0	0	Siliceous
Plate , , , , , , ,	229	3	0	0	Argillaceous
Lime-stone , , , , ,	230	2	1	6	Calcareous
Hard Free-stone , , , ,	231	4	0	0	Siliceous
Plate , , , , , , ,	232	14	0	0	Argillaceous
Coal , , , , , , ,	233	0	0	7	Sulph. & Inflammable
Plate , , , , , , ,	234	43	0	0	Argillaceous

Carried forward, 1172 2 4

Local Names.	No.		Yd.	Ft.	In.	Nature of each Stratum.
		Brot forward,	1172	2	4	
Free-stone	235		10	0	0	Siliceous
Girdle Bed	236		2	1	6	Ditto
Lime-stone	237		6	0	0	Calcareous
Free-stone	238		58	0	0	Siliceous

Carried forward, 1249 0 10

A 2

Local Names.	No.		*Yd. Ft. In.*			Nature of each Stratum.
		Brot. forward,	1249	0	10	
Plate, upper part black, the lower reddish , ...	239		20	0	0	**Argillaceous**
Great Red Sand-stone . . .	240		76	0	0	**Siliceous**
			1345	0	10	

A a 2

A TREATISE,

&c.

PART II.

ON

MINERAL VEINS IN GENERAL.

◆

THIS part treats of the most promising appearances and indications of valuable Mines, and of the three distinct species of Mineral Veins, *viz.* the *Rake* Vein, the *Pipe* Vein, and the *Flat* or dilated Vein.

The *rake* vein (sometimes called, by Naturalists, the *Perpendicular Mineral Fissure)* is the most common, and best known among practical miners, by whom it is generally considered of the same species as that described by the name of *dyke, slip,* or

*fault** in the coal metals. They are both longitudinal gashes, rents, or openings in the rock and
Strata, commonly running in straight lines.

The gash or fissure, called a *rake* vein, in many
instances, cuts all the Strata and rock quite through
from the surface, as far down towards the centre as
that vein descends, which is generally out of our
reach, and as far forward in the line of bearing as that
vein reaches. †

---

* Mr. Farey, in his Derbyshire Report, asserts, that Dykes
and Veins differ very considerably from Slips and Faults; and
in note, page 245, he expresses his surprise, that in the last
edition of this work, I should have confounded the terms together. I must here be allowed to say, that I have carefully,
and repeatedly, perused Mr. Farey's observations on Faults,
both in his Derbyshire Report and in one or two manuscript
communications on the subject, with which he has been so
obliging as to favour me; and I am convinced, that Faults,
either do not occur in this neighbourhood, or that they are
exactly similar to Mineral Veins and Dykes, which heave up
the Strata upon one of their sides. Nearly all the Dykes,
which cross the Newcastle Coal district, are of this description; and in the Lead measures, we have only one instance of
a Vein (viz. at Tyne-head) occurring without perceptible
throw.
  I am, therefore, induced to suppose, that what Mr. Farey
denominates Faults, and illustrates in so elaborate a manner,
in the work, to which I have before alluded, are a species of
Geological phenomena, with which I am totally unacquainted;
and, it must be particularly observed, that, in the whole course
of this work, where I employ the terms, Dyke, Fault, or
Slip, I merely wish to designate the sort of Crack or Fissure,
where the Strata, on one side, seem to be elevated, and on the
other, depressed.

  † Some metallic Veins, in the mining districts of Alston-
moor, Allendale, and Weardale, may be traced for eight or ten
miles on the line of bearing, as, for instance, *High Coalcleugh Vein*,
which is a continuation of *Rampgill Vein*, proceeding to the
westward, and from thence to Breagill Burn, near Nenthead,
it then takes the name of Browngill, from thence, crossing

Sometimes the *rake* vein stands nearly perpendicular, but it commonly over-hangs with less or more slope, which slope is called by miners, *hading*, or the *hade* of the vein. The rock, on both sides of the gash, is called the *sides* or *cheeks* of the vein; and these sides are called the *hanging* side, and the *ledger* or laying side, or the *up* cheek and the *down* cheek. Some miners call them, the *hanging* side and the *hading* side; and the longitudinal line, which the vein follows horizontally, is called the *bearing* of the vein.

Of these *perpendicular fissures*, or *rake* veins, there are two species. The origin of one of these seems to be, a crack or rent, and a slip of the Strata; and the other is a gash or chasm in the rock, without a slip.— The sides of the gash are separated and opened asunder; but the edges of the Strata, on both sides of the fracture, continue opposite to one another, so that there is no slip. An instance of one of these may be

the South-Tyne river, near Garrigill, in Alston-moor, it may be traced crossing Dry-burn, on Rotherhope-fell, about three miles and a half S W. of Alston.

Mr. Bakewell, in his introduction to Geology, second edition, page 283, states, that "Molina, in his interesting history of Chili, mentions a Vein of Silver, at Uspalata, in the Andes, which is nine feet in thickness throughout its whole extent, and has been traced ninety miles. Smaller Veins branch off from each side of it, and penetrate the neighbouring mountains to the distance of thirty miles."

observed about a quarter of a mile above the Smelting-house, near South-Tyne-head, in the county of Cumberland. This vein, or chasm, is about six fathoms wide, the cavity of which is entirely filled with Whin, or Green-stone, with Tyne-bottom Lime-stone opposite, or upon a level on both sides of it, forming, what, among colliers, is called, a *Whin Dyke*. * (See figure 1st.)

It will be necessary to point out some distinguishing marks or characters of each of these two species of veins, to enable the miner to know the one from the other, when he is working them:—the slip veins are seldom wider above than below, but are sometimes narrower; that is, the sides or cheeks of the veins are closer together above, at the superfices of the Strata, than farther down. The slip veins are generally considered more subject, than chasm veins, to *checks* or *twitches*, so called by miners; that is, when the two sides or cheeks, or hanger and ledger, come close together, and no cavity or open space is left between

---

* This Dyke may be traced westward, over Tyne-head Fell, to Kesh-burn; and will probably make a junction, with the Great Sulphur Vein, to the eastward upon Yaud Moss, which is described further on.

them, so that there is no room for any material quantity of ore in a twitch.

There are many of these twitches or checks in all this species of rake veins, which continue for several feet, or for several fathoms ; and the cavities or openings between the several twitches, are wider or narrower, longer or shorter, at all possible uncertainty. The sides of many of the veins, of this description, are very close together, above, at the superficies of the Strata, which nevertheless open to considerable, but very different, degrees of width below ; and these openings are called the *bellies*, or cavities, of the vein. And again, many of them are found regular and uniform, and carry a good rib of ore, for a considerable length, upon the bearing of the vein ; while others may carry some ore, and good enough mineral soil in small quantities, yet never open at all, to any advantage, so far as they have hitherto been tried.

The gash or chasm veins, on the contrary, are always wide above, (as at A, in figure below) and grow narrower as the sides or cheeks come closer together, as they are worked down at uncertain depths; and they often close or check out, below altogether, (as at B.)

B b

A

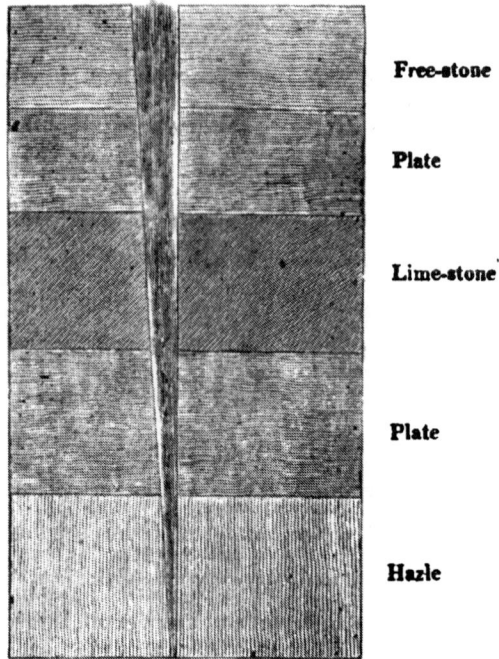

Free-stone

Plate

Lime-stone

Plate

Hazle

B

The gash vein is not so subject to twitches in the line of bearing, as the slips; but it is frequently crossed or intersected by other dykes or veins, or bars of hard stone, which generally move it, a little, to one side of the line of bearing.

According to Williams, a famous vein, of this species was worked at Llangunog, in Wales, in the Duke of Powis's time, whose property it was. Llangunog was, perhaps, the richest vein of lead ore, for the time it lasted, of any yet discovered in this island. They had there a solid rib, for a considerable time, five yards wide, of clean ore, in the middle of the vein, which was poured out of the kebbles at the shaft head into the waggons, and carried directly to the Smelt-ing-house, without being touched by the washers and dressers of ore, besides several feet upon the sides of the vein, which was mixed with spar and other stony matter, and went through the hands of the washers.

This rich and noble vein was at once cut out below, by a bed of black Schistus, or Shiver, or Plate, and that so entirely, that there was not the least fissure or vestige of the vein remaining, nor could any ever be found afterwards, though diligent search was made by the most skilful miners, for several years, and at seve-ral times.*

From what has been said of the gash vein, it ap-

---

* Mr. Farey supposes, that the Llangunog, not being found to penetrate the Strata beneath it, happened, as with the veins in Derbyshire, when they reach the Shale above, or the Toad-stone below. He conjectures, that, at the formation of the vein, the Toad-stone and Shale were not disposed to contract in the same manner as the Lime-stone rock, which they enclose; and that the fissures, at that time, produced in the Lime-stone, have been subsequently filled up, by means which, at present, we cannot explain.

pears, that this species of mineral vein is easily
described, it being an open fissure in the rock, generally running in a straight line, often nearly perpendicular, and always wider above than below, at a considerable depth, if we go deep enough to know it,
(as in figure 1st.)

The other species of rake vein, which we call the
slip, or the *throw,* is not so easily described; there being a great variety of veins of that species, and all of
them subject to a great diversity of accidents.

The kind of vein, generally esteemed the most regular, runs in a straight line, to a considerable distance upon the bearing; it sets downwards, near the
perpendicular, at least it sets down to a considerable
depth, with an equal *hade* or *slope,* has room enough
between the sides, which, we will suppose, should be
at least between three and four feet, or good drift
room; and a good regular vein continues so open, betwixt the cheeks, or hanger and ledger sides, for a
great way forward as we advance upon the line of bearing in it, and for a great depth as we sink down in it,
excepting in the Strata of Shiver or Plate.

Whatever the inclination or hade be, in the Stratum
of Stone, it is generally more in the Strata of Shiver,

or Plate, that is more from the perpendicular,[*] (as in figure below.)

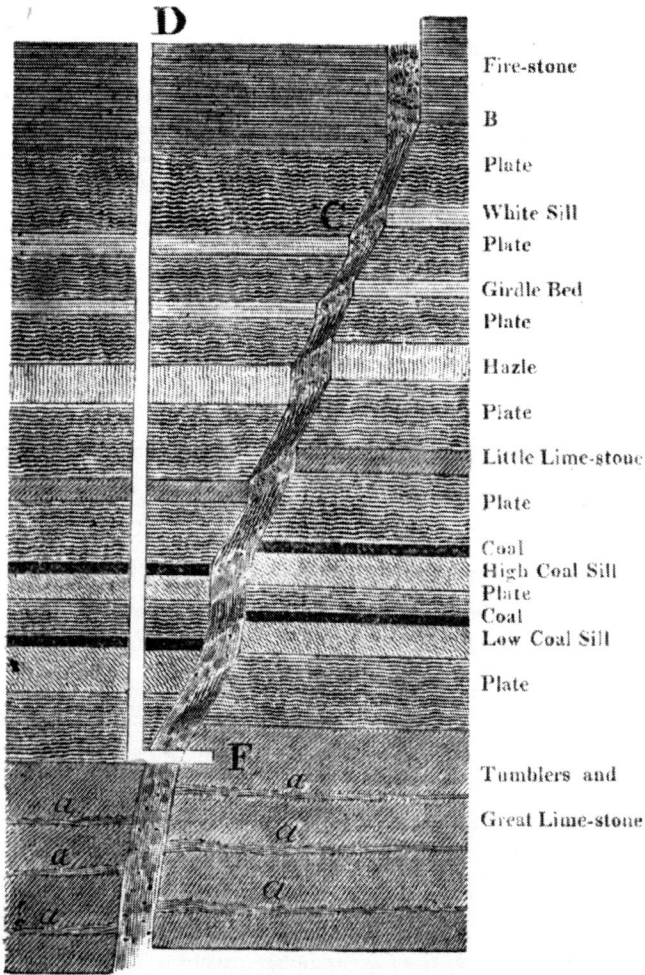

	Fire-stone
	B
	Plate
	White Sill
	Plate
	Girdle Bed
	Plate
	Hazle
	Plate
	Little Lime-stone
	Plate
	Coal
	High Coal Sill
	Plate
	Coal
	Low Coal Sill
	Plate
	Tumblers and
	Great Lime-stone

---

[*] Mr. Farey explains this fact by asserting, that the fissures in the stone are opened to a certain extent, by its

Supposing a vein taking the superficies of the Stratum or Fire-stone, as at **A**, it will set downwards tolerably near the perpendicular, until it comes to the bottom of the cheek **B**; from thence it will hade away in the Plate bed, towards **C**, where it will again stand pretty fair in the Stratum of Hard-stone or White Sill, and again incline or hade in the Plate bed or indurated argillaceous earth, as before, and so on in the same manner.

It must be observed, as a general remark, that the rake veins seldom carry any of the metallic ores in the Plate beds, or indurated argillaceous earths, but frequently a soft clayey substance, commonly called, by miners, *douk* or *donk* of the vein. †

---

shrinking before any fissure existed in the adjacent Shale, but that the further opening of fissures in the stony Strata, when they happened not to be perpendicularly under each other, tore the Shale asunder, and then opened a continuous vein downwards through the Argillaceous Stratum. This he asserts to have happened with some of the more powerful veins, traversing the Lime-stone and the intervening Toad-stone, in the mining field of Derbyshire.

† Although the author of this work has, in some instances, seen the Wernerian Theory, of the formation of veins, remarkably confirmed, yet, he cannot help observing that, the fact here stated seems, in some measure, to militate against it. It was, it seems, the opinion of Werner, that all veins were originally open fissures, which have been gradually filled up by depositions from the surface. Had this been the case we would naturally infer, that the contents of the vein ought to have been pretty uniform from top to bottom, and that the substances it contains in the Siliceous and Calcareous beds, could not so invariably and so widely have differed from its contents in the Argillaceous parts of the Strata. An observation, something similar to this, the author recollects to have seen, made by Mr. Bakewell, in the Philosophical Magazine, and it would be well if the subject was considered by some able supporter of the Theory in question.

Some of these veins are called *quick*, and others *dead.* A quick vein, or a bearing vein, is one that carries ore; and a dead vein is one that only carries some sort of mineral soil, but no ore.

Some of these regular veins, bear a solid rib of ore, of one, two, or three feet wide, for a considerable stretch, forwards and downwards; and some of them bear two, three, or more, thin ribs of ore, of various dimensions, from half an inch, to five or six inches thick, with spar or other mineral matter interposed between them.

Before we proceed any further, it will be proper to point out some general rules belonging to the inclination, or hade, of regular rake veins, or slips. If a vein bears or runs nearly east and west, and throws up the south cheek, or, as the Alston-moor miners term it, *the sun cheek,* that vein, in most instances, will hade downwards to the north; and, on the contrary, if the north cheek be up, the inclination, or hade, will be mostly downwards to the south; and so of any other, *viz.* whatever cheek be up, the hade will generally be the contrary.—See figure, page 189.

There are some veins which are quite irregular in

their inclination, or hade, being of a zig-zag form—
as in the annexed figure,

A

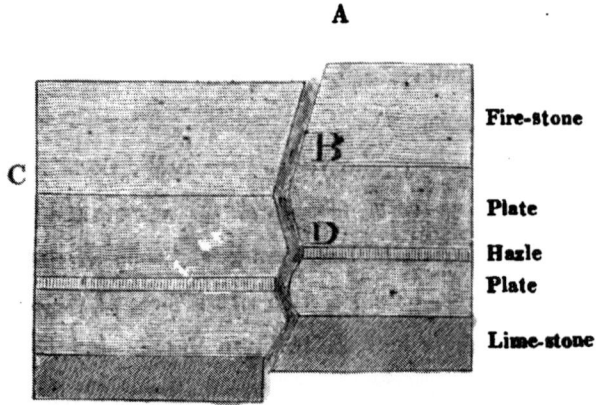

C

Fire-stone

Plate

Hazle

Plate

Lime-stone

Supposing a vein taking the superficies of the Strata
at A, it will hade down through the Stratum of Fire-
stone, or Siliceous earth pretty regularly, until it
comes to the bottom of the upper cheek, B; then,
having the low cheek, C, of Fire-stone or Siliceous
earth, on one side, and Plate or Argillaceous earth
on the other, it will hade back towards D; and so on,
where it has nothing but Plate or Shiver on one side,
and a harder Stratum on the other, until it comes to a
thicker Stratum, where its inclination or hade will be
more regular, having both the sides or cheeks of the
same substance.

There are other veins, of a weaker kind, which have
not so much throw, and are irregular in their hade,

sometimes lying quite flat in a Stratum of Coal, Plate, or Shiver. (See figure below.)

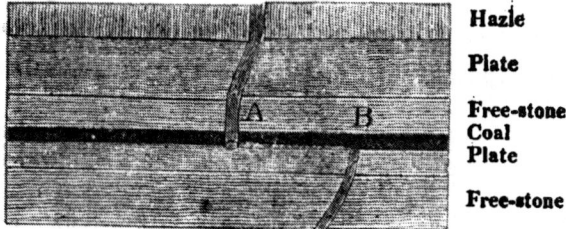

	Hazle
	Plate
	Free-stone
	Coal
	Plate
	Free-stone

When this is the case, the vein or fissure will hade pretty regular, until it comes to some softer Stratum; for instance, Coal, as at A; from thence to B, perhaps three or four fathoms, and then take its regular hade again. But, when this is the case, we must look on the contrary side; that is, on the opposite side of the down cheek.

There are other species of rake veins, which keep pretty regular in their hade or inclination; whatever be the angle the vein makes with the horizon, at the surface it is generally nearly the same, as far down into the Strata as we can reach. These veins being strong, having forty, or even near an hundred, fathoms of throw, for instance, *Old Carrs*, at *Nenthead*, in the county of Cumberland; and the *Burtreeford Dyke*, at *Allenheads*, in the county of Northumberland.

Veins, which occur in the *Blue Rock,* or Grey Wacke Slate, of Geologists, have, in general, a regular hade or inclination, which continues perfectly uniform to the greatest depth, as in the figure below, where the letters A and B show the mineral vein or fissure.

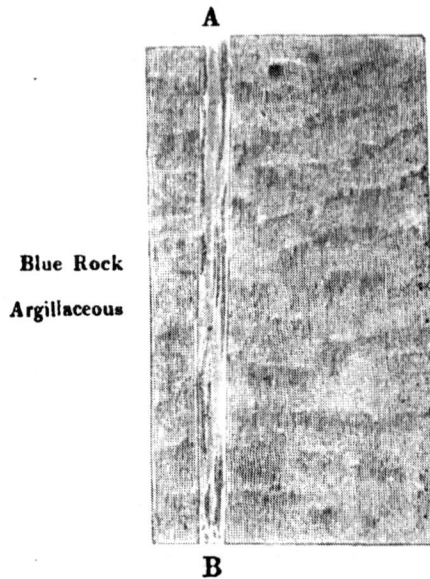

A

Blue Rock
Argillaceous

B

There are, in many parts of Britain, &c. a great many regular veins, which carry no ore at all, where they are tried; and others of them carry a small rib or ribs; but so insignificant, as not to be worth working, though the ore gave five times the usual price; and again, others produce small detached fragments, here and there, as we advance in them, too insignificant to make them worth working.

It is a very common thing, to see *dead* veins, that is, such as bear no ore at all, continue very promising and regular, for a great way, both in driving and sinking. More than fifty fathoms have been driven, in some of these regular veins, under great cover, perhaps twenty or more fathoms down from the surface, where the mineral veins were promising, and what might be supposed likely to produce ore; yet no ore was found, or only so much, as to show the miners what sort of ore they were to expect, and tempt them to proceed, when, nevertheless, they would continue perfectly regular, and the sides about four or five feet asunder all the way.

There are, again, many regular veins, which are not so wide and roomy, between the sides, as those described. But in these have been found several rich mining fields, which have carried ore for two or three miles in length, on the line of bearing, and to the depth of a hundred fathoms or upwards; and, in some places, in every different Stratum, excepting the Plate beds, or indurated Argillaceous earths; for instance, *Rampgill,* at *Nenthead,* in the county of Cumberland, belonging to the Commissioners and Governors of Greenwich Hospital; and *Coal-cleugh,* in the county of Northumberland, belonging to Col. Beaumont. *Rampgill* vein being sometimes twelve

feet wide, nearly of solid ore, in the Great Lime-
stone; and, it has been known, that a single *length*,
(that is, fifteen fathoms in the Great Lime-stone only)
at *Coal-cleugh*, in the course of twelve years, has
raised *Ten Thousand Bings** of Lead Ore.

The writer has, in the course of his perambulations,
seen great numbers of perfectly regular veins, not
two feet wide, which, nevertheless, would frequently
continue fair, and uniform for a considerable length,
especially when washed along the vein by a rivulet,
and where the rocks were made otherwise bare.

Some of these regular, thin, or close veins, contain
ore at the superficies of the Strata, and others contain
none at the surface. What they may carry farther
down, cannot be known, without proper trials; and
it is but seldom that these trials are made.

When two metallic veins, in the neighbourhood of
each other, run in an oblique direction, and of consequence meet together, they commonly produce a body

---

* A *Bing* of Lead Ore is eight hundred weight.

of ore, at the place where they intersect; and if both
are rich, the quantity will be considerable; but if one
be poor and the other rich, then both are either enriched or impoverished by the meeting. After some
time they separate again, and each will continue its
former direction, near to the other; but sometimes,
though rarely, they continue united.

It is a sign of a poor vein, when, in the course of
working it, it separates or diverges into strings; but,
on the contrary, when several of them, as the work
proceeds, are found running into one, it is accounted
a promising appearance.

If two veins have the same bearing, and are consequently parallel to each other, they generally have
the same hade or inclination, if they are within a small
distance of each other; for instance, if they throw the
contrary cheeks up, that is, if one throw a fathom up
to the south, and the other a yard up to the north,
they will both incline, or hade downwards to the
north.

Sometimes there are branches, or strings, without
the cheeks or sides of the vein, in the adjacent Strata,

which often come either obliquely or transversely into
it. If these branches are found impregnated with ore,
or if they appear to underlie or bade faster (as represented in the figure opposite, marked *a, a, a)* than the
true vein ; that is, if they dip deeper into the ground,
they are then said to *overtake* or *come into* the vein,
and to enrich it; or, if they do not, then they are
said to *go off* from it, and to impoverish it. But neither these nor any other marks, either of the richness
or poverty of a mine, are to be entirely depended
upon ; for many mines, which have a very bad appearance at first, nevertheless turn out extremely well afterwards; while others, which, in the beginning
seemed very rich, turn gradually worse and worse.
But in general, where a vein has a bad appearance at
first, it will be imprudent to be at much expence
with it.

Veins of metal, as has been already observed, are
frequently, as it were, so compressed betwixt *hard*
Strata, that they are not an inch wide ; nevertheless,
if they have a string of good ore, it will generally be
worth while to pursue them ; and they frequently turn
out well at last, after they have come into *softer*
ground. In like manner, it is an encouragement to
go on, if the branches or leaders of ore, enlarge,

Plate . . .

Hazle . . .

Plate . . .

Fire-stone .

Plate . . .

White Sill .

Plate . . .

Girdle Bed .

Plate . . .

Hazle . . .

Plate . . .

Lime-stone .

Plate . . .

Coal . . .

High Coal Sill

Plate . . .

Coal . . .

Low Coal Sill

Plate . . .

Great Lime-st.

Tuft . . .

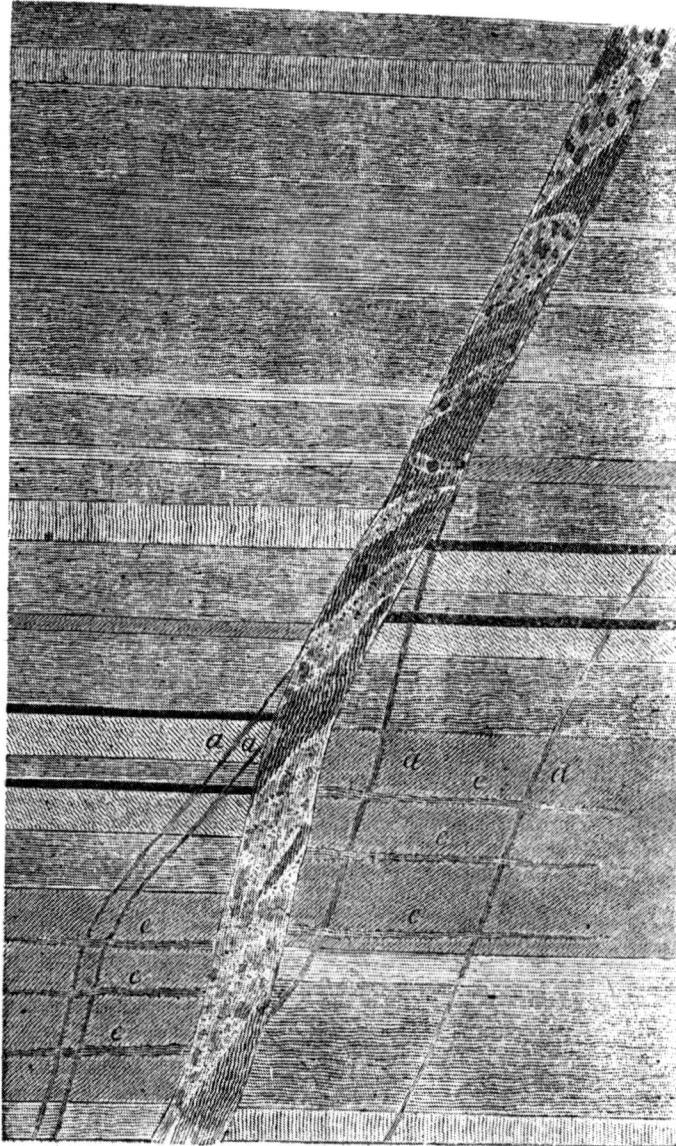

either in width or depth, as they are worked; but it is a bad sign, if they continue horizontal without inclining downwards, though it is not proper always to discontinue the working of a vein, which has an unfavourable aspect at first.

Some of the great mining fields have very large veins, with a number of other small ones very near to each other. There are, also, veins crossing one another; and again, sometimes two veins run down into the ground in such a manner, that they meet in the direction of their depth; in which case the same observations apply to them, which are applicable to those that meet in an horizontal direction; as to the probability of an increase of ore, at their meeting, see plate 4th, figure 3rd.

The fissures or veins of the mines, in *Weardale*, *Allendale*, and *Alston-moor*, mostly extend from east to west; or, more properly, one end of the vein points west and by south, while the other tends east and by north; although, there are other veins, running nearly north and south, commonly called *cross veins;* and it must be remarked, that those cross veins have very rarely been found so productive of metallic ores, as the others, excepting, when the right running veins

p d

and the cross veins intersect, in which case the cross veins generally carry ore, for some distance from the place of intersection, but very seldom in any other Stratum than Lime-stone, and especially the Great Lime-stone, in Alston-moor.

It is again necessary to be observed, that what is usually called the *Great Lime-stone*, (see No. 153, in the engraved Section) is the predominant Stratum for producing Lead Ore, through all the extensive mines in *Alston-moor*, in Cumberland, the two *Allendales*, in Northumberland, and *Weardale* and *Teesdale*, in the county of Durham.

It is not, perhaps, too much to assert, that if a correct estimate of the produce of all the above-mentioned mines was presented to public view, it would be found, that the Great Lime-stone, alone, has produced as much Lead Ore as all the other Strata throughout the whole Section, annexed hereto, and described in Part I.

The writer of these pages has frequently observed, that most of the east and west running veins, in Weardale, throw the north cheek up; consequently their inclination, or hade downwards, is to the south, according to the remark in page 191. He has observed, also, that most of the veins, in *Allendale* and *Alston-moor*, throw the south cheek up, and that their hade or inclination downwards, is to the north.

This correspondence, in the hades of veins over an extensive district, is acounted for, in a very probable manner, by Werner, in his new Theory of Veins.— He observes, that, "When the mass of materials, of which the rocks were formed, by a precipitation in the humid way, and which was, at first, soft and moveable, began to sink and dry; fissures must, of necessity, have been formed, chiefly in those places, where mountain chains and high land existed.

"As, in the first place, these accumulated materials were not equally dense, nor arranged every where of the same degree of thickness and height, it follows, of course, that this sinking did not take place in an uniform manner. From this difference in the sinking and shrinking of the solid materials of our globe, different separations, rents, and fissures, have been produced.

"These fissures and rents must, of course, occur more abundantly where the greatest quantity of matter has been heaped up, or where the accumulation of it has formed those elevations, which are called moun-

tains; because, these being more at liberty and having
less support at their sides, must yield to the consoli-
dating effects of pressure arising from their own
weight, which must have produced interruptions of
the continuity of the mass; in consequence of which,
veins were formed in the lowest parts, for *the mass of
the mountain would naturally incline over to that side
where it found the least resistance.*"

In general, the most regular bearing veins in all the
mining districts, above-mentioned, are veins that have
about a fathom or two of throw, which makes them
have both cheeks of the same Stratum; otherwise,
when they have a larger throw, that Stratum is thrown
past, and perhaps there is a Plate bed opposite, on
the other side of the vein; and, we observed before,
that the Plate beds, or indurated Argillaceous earths,
are seldom productive of metallic ores.

But, although the Plate beds are not, in general,
productive of metallic ores, yet, sometimes, strong
veins carry a *rider* in the Plate beds; when this is the
case, they are frequently productive, or are said to be
mineralized, so far above the bearing Strata, or
below.

When those *right running* veins, as they are called,

are intersected by strong cross veins at right angles,
the right running vein is sometimes moved a very little
way, either to the north or south, perhaps not more
than one fathom; as in figure below.

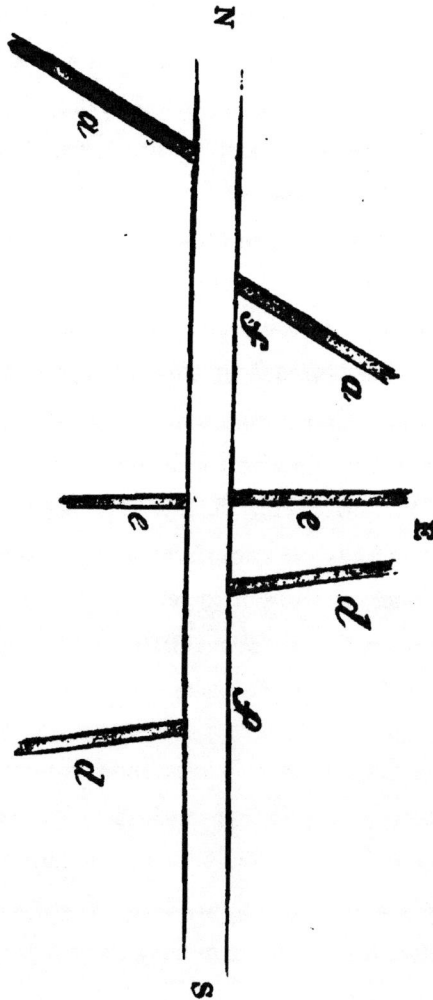

Supposing *f, f,* is a strong cross vein, and *e, e,* a right running vein, intersected at right angles; in such cases, the right running vein will either run directly through the cross vein, or it may be a little to the south or north; but, on the contrary, if it be intersected in an oblique manner, as *d, d,* supposing the right running vein be coming up to the cross vein *f, f,* on the east side, as at *d,* it will be thrown to the south, perhaps ten or twenty fathoms; but, if a vein be coming in the direction of *a, a,* on the east side of the cross vein, it will be thrown as much to the north; and so on, according to the angle that the veins make with each other. A very good instance of the above assertion may be observed at *Nentwater,* in *Alston-moor,* where *Old Carr's* cross vein intersects the other veins. We shall begin with *Goodam-gill* vein, on the east side of the cross vein, which, on the west side, is *Green-gill* vein; next we have *Brownly-hill* vein on the east side, which is *Grass-field* vein on the west side; these veins being thrown about fifteen or twenty fathoms, to a side, by the above-mentioned cross vein.

Plate 4th, figures 1st and 2nd, show two remarkable instances of the influence which veins seem to have upon each other at the points of intersection.— Figure 1st is a ground plan of *Rampgill* vein, which we have before mentioned, as proving remarkably pro-

ductive in several of the beds.　　It is here intersected
by the vein called *Patterdale* vein, and is removed 150
feet from its former direction, occurring ramified into
three parts, on the western side of the intersection.

Figure 2nd shows several veins, which are crossed by
Small-cleugh vein, in *Handsome-mea* lead mine, near
Nenthead.　　The position of these veins, with respect
to each other, is very different on the two sides of the
intersecting vein, but the most singular change occurs
in the *Second Sun Vein*, which, on the south-east side,
tilts nine feet down to the north, and on the north-west
side tilts the same distance down to the south.　　The
arrows, in the plate, are intended to show the dip of
the Strata in the influence of the veins.　　The figures,
1—3, denoting, that the beds, at that place, dip, one
yard in three, in the direction of the arrow's point,
and so on of the rest.　　The arrows, with the figures
1—9, show the true dip of the Strata, at a distance
from the vein.

Veins, however, which have been carried off the direction they were pursuing by the intervention of other
veins, return, in a short distance, to their former
bearing.　　Plate 3rd represents a phenomenon of this
kind, which occurs at *Scale Burn Moss* lead mine,
near *Nenthead.*　　Here, it seems, that *Scale Burn* vein

intersects *Scale Burn* cross vein, which last is found at a considerable distance to the east, and by an abrupt bend, (at X) rapidly regains its line of bearing.

According to Werner, "By the crossing and intersecting of veins, the antiquity, or relative age, of each can be easily assigned. The *distinguishing characteristics*, for the *relative age of veins* and their substances, are the following :

" Every vein, which *intersects* another, is newer than the one traversed, and is of *later formation* than all those which *it traverses*; of course, the *oldest vein is traversed* by all those that are of a *posterior formation*, and the *newer* veins always cross those that are older.

"When two veins cross, one of them, without suffering any derangement or interruption, traverses the other; this last is interrupted and cut across, through its whole thickness, by the former. The first of these is said to traverse the other, and the latter to be traversed by the former. The vein which crosses another is of newer, whilst this last is of older, formation. This crossing of veins is of great importance, and deserves to be kept in remembrance by all who wish to become acquainted with the study of veins; yet, till very lately, it has always escaped the observation of mineralogists."

It is a curious fact, that, in *Alston-moor*, the veins, bearing north and south, called *cross veins*, generally traverse those that are termed *right running veins*, which pursue a point nearly east and west. If the Wernerian doctrines are correct, we may, therefore, infer, that *cross veins* are of a more recent formation. Plate 4th, fig. 3d, shows the crossing of two veins having different hades, but pursuing, longitudinally, the same direction; the letters g, g, show the traversing vein, x, x, the vein traversed, and a, b, c, d, e, represent the Strata, with the throw and influence of the veins.

The curious phenomena that veins present, at the places where they intersect each other, are, in the present state of our knowledge, perfectly inexplicable.

Allowing the traversing veins a posterior formation, we cannot conceive, in what manner, they could influence the *points* of the veins previously in existence. In the instances of *Scale Burn* and *Rampgill* veins, represented in plate 3rd and plate 4th, figure 1st, we might suppose a longitudinal force acting, in both cases, in the direction of the shifts, and removing the veins from their former positions: the bend in *Scale Burn* cross vein, plate 3rd, would almost seem to warrant such a conclusion, but, it will be remembered, that, when these veins were formed, the Strata must have been, in some measure, consolidated, and the veins could not have been removed without the whole mass of Strata accompanying them in the same direction; nor can we conceive, how any longitudinal force could either separate *Rampgill* vein or join it together. If we allow a longitudinal force in these instances, we are compelled to deny it in the cases plate 4th, figure 2nd, where the veins, traversed, seem to be moved in different directions. The same reasoning will apply to almost every instance of the intersection of veins, and would lead us to imagine, that some other course, than either a longitudinal force or the different periods of formation, must have produced these appearances. The author does not presume himself to offer a theory, but he cannot help stating the observations that occurred to him upon the subject.

The greater part of the veins, in the mining district

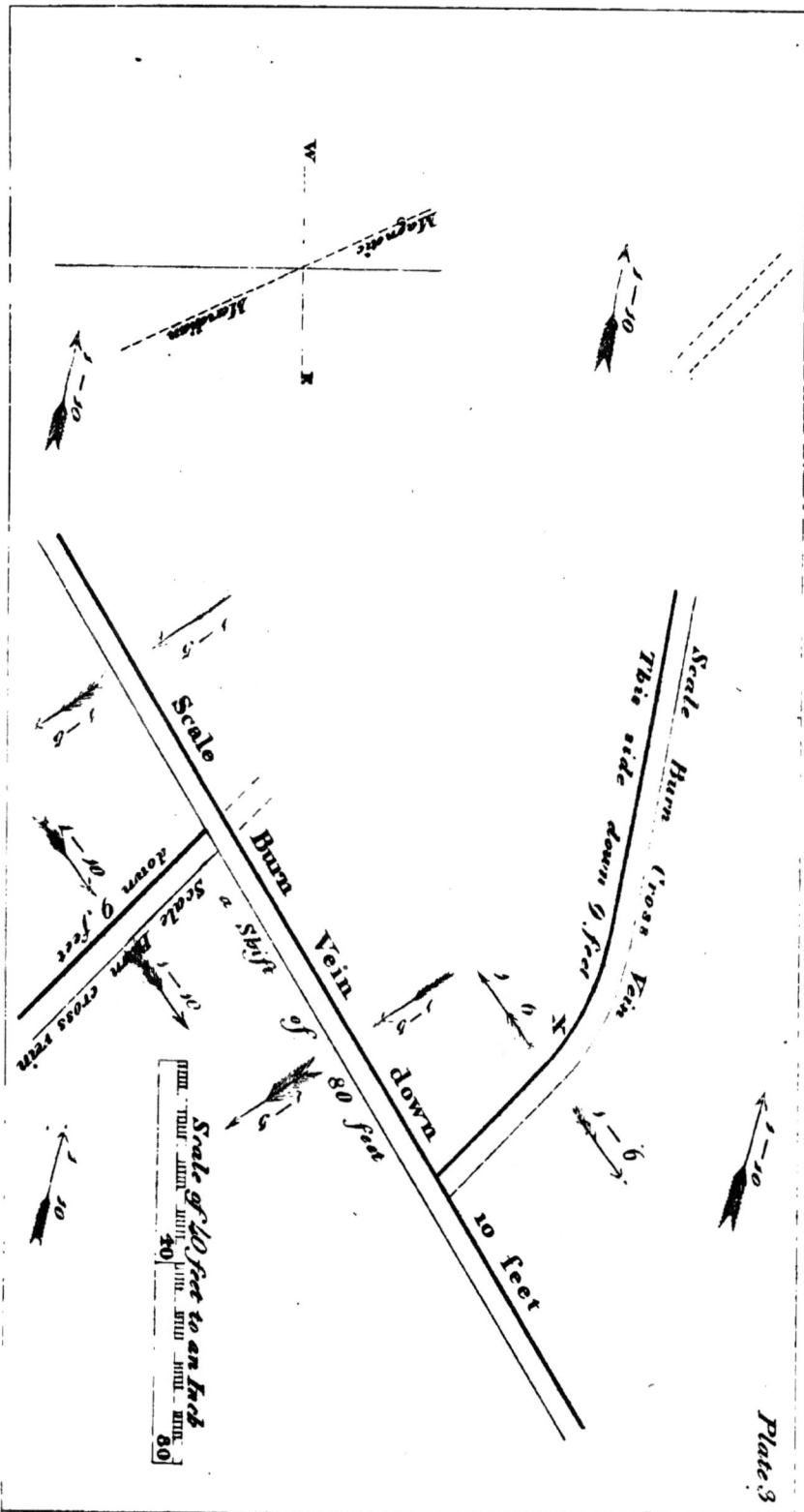

Plate 9.

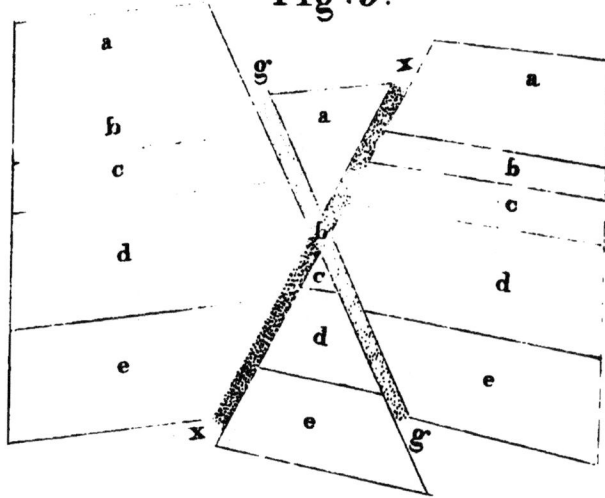

Plate 4

Fig. 3.

a
b
c
d
e

g x
a
b
c
d
e

a
b
c
d
e

x
g

Small Cleugh

Middle Cleugh North Vein 7 fe

Middle Cleugh first

dale Vein 24 feet down

ft of 150 feet

Fig. 1.

Ramgill Vein 13 feet down

of *Alston-moor*, *Allendale*, and *Weardale*, are generally more compressed or squeezed; that is, their sides
or cheeks are nearer together, in the Hazles or Siliceous earths, than in the Lime-stone Strata; and it is
not uncommon to see a vein, or string, in a hard Hazle,
so squeezed, that, perhaps, it is not above six inches
wide, which, nevertheless, will be three or four feet
wide, in the Lime-stone Strata.

It has been before observed, that the two sides of a
mineral vein, are called, by miners, the *hanger* and
ledger, or the *up* cheek and *down* cheek. These sides
or cheeks, are always of the rock or Strata, which
compose the mountain or mining field, the vein being
a crack, breach, or fissure in those Strata, the sides
of which fissure are opened asunder to a vast variety
of degrees.

Thus, the inner part of the fissure, in which the
ore lies, is all the way bounded by two sides of stone,
which are generally parallel to one another, and include the breadth of the vein or lode. Some are very
uncertain in their breadth, as, for instance, they may
be small at their upper part, and wide underneath, and
vice versa. Their regular breadth, as well as their
depth, is subject to great variation; for, though a fis-

sure, or vein, may be many fathoms wide, in one particular place, yet, a little further, east or west, it may not, perhaps, be one inch wide. This excessive variation, happens, generally, in very compact Strata; when the vein, or fissure, is squeezed, as it were, through hard rocks, which seem to compress and straiten it. A true vein, or fissure, however, is never entirely obliterated, but always shows a string of ore, or of a veiny substance; which serves as a leader for the miners to follow, until it sometimes leads them to a large and richly impregnated part. Their length is, in a great measure, unlimited, though not the space best fitted for yielding metal.

In general, the Strata, most productive of the metallic ores, in *Alston-moor, Allendale,* and *Weardale,* are between the Grind-stone Sill and the Four Fathom Lime-stone. See, from No. 117 to No. 160, in the Section.

The richest parts of the Cornwall Strata, for Copper, (according to Mr. Price) is from forty to eighty fathoms deep, for tin from twenty to sixty; and though a great quantity, of either may be raised at eighty or a hundred fathoms, yet the quality is often too much decayed and dry for metal.

What are called *dead* veins, that is, those that have
not been found to bear ore at the surface, nor produce
any upon such trials as may have been made in them,
frequently contain between their sides, in different
places and in different veins, a vast variety of vein
stuff, or mineral stones, and of softer mineral soils.
The most common, and the most promising of the
mineral stones, as concomitants of ore, are the spars
and vein-stones of different species.

A similar compounded stony concretion, found in
many veins, is called, by miners, *a rider;* perhaps,
from its riding, or being suspended in the vein, or separating it longitudinally, into two or more divisions.
This mineral stone is usually hard and heavy, sometimes compact and solid, but frequently cracked and
cavernous, rising in irregular and misshapen masses.
A rider, frequently contains a variety of different substances, or species, as well as different colours, in the
same mass; such as calcareous spar, quartz, apparent
fragments of the rocks near the vein; sometimes pyrites, or sulphur, is found in grains and flowers; and
sometimes different ores, as Lead, Copper, &c. in the
same mass, and all these strongly coagulated or concreted together, by a whitish or a brownish-white substance, somewhat resembling quartz and agate, which

seems to have enveloped the several articles in the composition, when the whole was in a fluid state. This may properly be called *Vein-stone*, or Vein Stuff, a term the most intelligible both to naturalists and miners, it being always found in veins, or on the sides or cheeks of veins,* upon the superficies of them, and in fragments and masses, lying about upon the face of the ground, which have slidden or been forced off the superficies of veins. But the vein-stone, or rider, does not always contain so great a variety in its composition. It is often pretty white, and appears like a quartzy concretion, of a porous, or rather a cavernous, texture; and the inside of the caverns, though small, frequently contain a brownish ferruginous soft soil, of a snuffy appearance; and, sometimes, the insides of these small caverns, are finely lined with great numbers of pointed or prismatical crystals, generally exceedingly beautiful, and sparkling like diamonds. But all the vein-stones, or riders, are not white nor whitish. In many places they are of a brown, a reddish-brown, and several other colours.—

---

* This change of the Strata, which constitutes the sides or cheeks of the vein, ' into *rider*, appears to have been effected by the action of acids, that existed in the solution which filled the vein, at the time of its formation. These acids insinuated themselves into the neighbouring rocks, which they have changed in a greater or less degree.—*See Werner on Veins.*

Strong wide veins, often contain a large rib of this vein-stone, betwixt the sides, several feet thick, but in all degrees of thickness, from a few inches up to several feet. There are strong veins, that carry such a rib, or body, of rider, as to show the same in a ridge above the surface of the ground, a great way; for instance, the Great Vein, commonly called the *Back-bone*, upon *Newn-stones*, in *Alston-moor*, Cumberland, the superficies of the native rock, or Strata, being withered and wasted away from both sides of it.

The next most common stone found in mineral veins, is spar, of which there are several species; and these are frequently tinged with various colours, especially in veins which contain less or more of Copper or Iron.

The mineral spars may be divided into the calcareous and vitrescible; or, to speak as a miner, there are four distinct species of mineral spar, viz. the *calcareous spar, fluor spar, cauk spar* or *barytes*, and *quartzy spar*.

The *calcareous* spar, found in lead mines, is commonly, though not always, of a white and whitish colour, both the homogeneous, and that which is mixed with ore and other mineral matter, unless it happens to be tinged or tarnished with soft soils, in which it is often found, and frequently with mineral water, especially chalybeate, or iron-water, which most of the Plate beds, or Shiver, contain.

Fluor spar occurs in veins in a great many different colours, viz. white, green, violet, yellow, red, and brown. Its most general form, when crystallized, is a cube, but it is frequently met with in the form of an octohedron and cubo octohedron, it also occurs in amorphous shapeless masses.

Calcareous and *fluor* spars, are generally the best, most of them containing indications of lead ore. All the extensive mines in *Weardale*, in the county of Durham, and *Allenheads* and *Coal-cleugh*, in the county of Northumberland, have *calcareous* and *fluor* spars for the matrix; and it is from a mine in *Weardale*, that the beautiful green *fluor* has been procured lately in such quantities.

Cauk, or *barytic*, spar, is not generally of so pure a white as the calcareous spars. The writer of this has seen *cauk* spar of a dead white, but commonly it is of a yellowish, a brownish, or a reddish white, or of a flesh colour, sometimes crystallized and transparent, as at *Dufton-fell*, in the county of Westmorland. It seems to affect the peculiarity of having its crystals laminated, as radiating from a centre, but this radiation seldom amounts to a whole circle. It is commonly a dull ill-looking spar, frequently rising in globes and irregular masses, and so exceedingly heavy, that miners have always imagined it contained metal, only they think, that the proper flux for it is not discovered. No doubt this mineral body is replete with the vitriolic acid, which the art of the chemist may extract. At the same time, there is reason to believe it highly probable, that it is not the ore of any useful metal. This spar is so very ponderous, that it is often extremely difficult to separate it from the metallic ores in dressing them.*

Quartz spar is generally of as pure a white colour as the calcareous, frequently more beautiful, and, sometimes, not unlike it in appearance; but it is of quite a different quality, as it will not effervesce with

---

* There is a vein, in *Welhope*, in the county of Northumberland, belonging to Colonel Beaumont, containing the common cauk spar, or sulphate of barytes, in the upper beds, which changed its matrix in the Great Lime-stone, and contained the aerated or carbonated barytes. It lies mostly in the cavities, or shakes, of the vein, in round balls; and, when broke, it is striated, as diverging from the centre.

aquafortis, nor burn into lime, which are properties of the calcareous spar; on the contrary, instead of calcining, it vitrifies to a glass, or slag, in the fire.

Some of this species of spar, is found of a cubical and of a tabulated texture, resembling the structure of the common blue potter's ore of lead. Much of it has also been found, fine, smooth, uniform throughout, without any visible grain or texture; and it is apt to shoot into prismatical crystals, which are commonly found so pure and pellucid, as almost to vie with the diamond in lustre, and they are frequently so hard as to cut glass.

Most of the mineral spars are frequently found shot into prismatic, cubic, hexagonal, or other figures. These figured crystals are generally transparent, and very beautiful. It is a great curiosity to behold the inside of some of the large cavities in which they are formed. These caverns, lined with crystals, are frequently met with in hard mineral veins; and they are generally called, by miners, *shakes, lochs,* or *loch-holes.*

The miners know nothing of these cavernous vacuities, until they strike into them, as they advance in working; and they are of various dimensions, from the bigness of a nut, up to room enough for three or four men or more to turn themselves in them.

The magnitude of those caverns, is generally in some proportion to the capacity of the veins, in which they are found; and the insides of them frequently exhibit all the variety, beauty, and splendour, of the most curious grotto work.

There is, commonly, a hard concreted stony crust, called *druse*, or *rider*, by the *Alston-moor* and *Allendale* miners, adhering to the inside of the cavity, out of which, as out of a root, an innumerable multitude of short prismatical crystals are shot, which sparkle like a thousand diamonds, with the candle, or when brought up to the sun. Between these clusters of mock diamonds, and sticking to them promiscuously, there are often lead ore, black jack, pyrites, or sulphur, and spar, shot also into prismatic, cubic, or other figures ; and, besides these clusters of grotesque figures, which grow out of one another, and are, as it were, piled upon one another, the whole inside of the cavern is, sometimes, most magnificently adorned with the most wildly grotesque figures which grow upon, and branch out of, one another, in a manner not to be described, and with all the gay and splendid colours of polished gold, of the rainbow, and of the peacock's tail; and all these blended together, and the masses reflecting all the beauty of such an assemblage of gaudy colours.

But, it may be remarked, that these caverns are never so magnificent and glorious, as when there is less or more of yellow copper ore, or of the pyrites, or black jack, in them; as these ores, are found to produce, in hard veins, the most beautiful colours in the world. Many eminent instances, in proof of this assertion, are to be seen in the lead mines at *Allen-heads* and *Coal-cleugh*, in Northumberland, and *Nenthead*, in Cumberland.

These mineral loughs, shakes, or caverns, are the great source of materials for grotto work; and the specimens, collected from the miners, are, generally, the most showy and dazzling articles in the whole arrangement of the splendid grotto.

Neither the calcareous, fluor, nor cauk spars will strike fire with steel, unless there is a mixture of pyrites in them; but the quartzy spar, on the contrary, gives fire plentifully. Pure quartz, of a fine, smooth, uniform texture, breaking like glass, is often found in those mines, where the quartzy spar prevails, and it is frequently mixed with ore.

What is properly called pure quartz, is a white, semi-transparent, hard, and heavy stone, of a fine and uniform texture, of considerable brightness, and not exhibiting any visible grain. It is frequently of an hexagonal form, terminating in a point.

Quartz does not rise in blocks, or large regular masses, neither in the mines nor any where else; it being full of cracks and flaws, so as to break into small irregular masses, with various sharp angles; and it is so hard, as to waste the tools more than any other stone. Where quartz and quartzy spar prevail, the veins are commonly very hard and difficult to work, and it is no easy matter to separate the ore from the quartz in dressing, being so hard, that it requires much labour to break the quartz mixed with ore, small enough, (unless there are crushing or bruising machines for that purpose) and it is also so heavy, that it does not easily separate.

The following is a list and description of such mineral stones as are most generally known, though there are many others, found in different mines, of various colours and textures, too numerous to be described :—

The soft mineral soils are as various, in quality and appearance, as the hard.

The first is a white or whitish mineral soil or clay, sometimes fine, tenacious, and smooth, but often more friable to the touch, not unlike slaked lime mixed with small sand, which frequently bounds in veins near the surface. This species of mineral soil is generally a promising symptom of lead ore.

Red fatty clay in veins, which indelibly stains the hands and clothes, is an indication of iron, and is not uncommon in veins of lead; and the better sorts of iron ores, are generally accompanied with a red staining softness, by which they are easily distinguished; at the same time, it is proper to observe, that some lead and copper veins, contain a considerable quantity of iron, and, consequently, a red or a brownish-red soft soil, especially near the surface.

Bluish and greenish mineral soils, light and friable, and also heavy and tenacious; but these, and

several others, will be treated of, when we come to
examine the symptoms and appearances of mines.

Yellowish, ash-coloured, and marbled soft soils, or
mineral clay; which are frequently not to be distinguished from surface clays of the same colours, but
by the skilful miner.

Black, and blackish-brown soft soils, commonly
light and friable, though there are some of them more
tough and weighty, commonly called *douk* or *donk*, by
the *Alston-moor* miners.

But the most remarkable and distinguished of all
the soft mineral soils, and frequently the most promising, is of a brown colour, and of a lax and friable
texture, often resembling rappee and other snuff, in
colour and appearance, being sometimes blackish, but
generally brown, in all the degrees and shades of that
colour. It is frequently met with in large shakes, or
cavities, lying loose at the bottom, in flat or dilated
veins.

—::::o::::—

Having given this brief specimen of the hard and
soft soils, which are most commonly found in mineral

veins, we will now return to the history of the veins, and of the appearances these soils make in them.

It is very common to find a large body of *rider* in such a strong or hard vein, (as the last-mentioned, page 215) in a rib, or standing in the middle of the vein, like a wall, with a space between it and the sides of the vein ; sometimes, though rarely, there are two or three ribs of rider. This rib of rider, or vein-stone, so situated, divides the vein in two, as there is a space like a vein betwixt this rib, and each of the real sides or cheeks of the vein.

This rib, or body of vein-stone, or rider, (see page 213) is frequently found of various dimensions, from five or six inches, up to five or six feet, thick.— In strong veins, it is not uncommon to find a body of rider, or vein-stone, several feet thick. Sometimes this rider, or vein-stone, is richly flowered, spotted, and veined with ore, and sometimes there is little or no ore found in it; and it frequently happens, that when it is mixed with some ore, it is found in such small specks and threads, and the stone so hard, that it is not worth separating. This rib of rider, in a strong vein, is not always found in the middle of the vein, but is frequently nearer to one side than the

other ; and it is not uncommon to find a similar vein-
stone, adhering strongly to the side, and mixed with
ore, commonly called a *flowery rider,* or a *good rider.*
When a rib, or wall, of rider, is situated in the middle of a wide vein, there is, sometimes, good ore
found upon each side of it, and, at other times, upon
one side only; and this ore is found, either in a continued rib, or in discontinuous masses.

When the ore is found in ribs, betwixt the rider, or
vein-stone, and the real cheeks or sides, these ribs of
ore, as well as that of the rider, are of various dimensions, from two or three inches, up to two or three
feet, or more, in thickness. In strong wide veins,
which have a rib of rider in the middle, it is not uncommon to have a rib of good ore upon each side of
the rider, of one, two, or three feet thick; though it
is not commonly found so thick, upon each side, but
to have a rib, of two or three feet thick, or more, upon
one side of the rider, or vein-stone, and a thin rib
upon the other. *

These continued regular ribs of ore, which are

---

* Mr. Farey says, "the two sides of a large rider, or near
and parallel veins, are seldom, if ever, rich together."—*See
Derbyshire Report, page* 246.

G g

found in wide veins, running parallel to the rib of rider, and betwixt it and the sides, or cheeks, of the vein, are partly solid and partly mixed.

Again, the ore found betwixt a rider and the sides or cheeks of a vein, is not always in regular continued ribs. It is sometimes found in a discontinuous rib or ribs, that is, in large flat slabs or masses, which appear like a rib for two or three feet, perhaps for five or six every way; and then you come to the end of it, if you are working forward horizontally, or to the bottom of the mass, if you are sinking down in the vein; but then, it is not long before you touch the edge of another cake of this discontinued rib. These cakes, or flat masses of ore, in the discontinued rib, are of various sizes; some being very large, and others very small, and the distance between them is as various as the dimensions of the masses. In different veins, and in different parts of the same vein, the masses are often so near to one another, as sometimes almost to touch; and, at other times, there will be a distance of from a foot, to five or six feet, between the masses, and frequently more; but this distance is exceedingly variable, even in the same vein, and often at no great distance in it.

It is proper to be observed here, that these discontinuous ribs of ore are generally in soft mineral soils, that is to say, all the masses or slabs of ore, are encompassed with soft soil, and the same softness continues betwixt mass and mass; and, it is further to be observed, that, although the rib is really discontinued, and there is less or more space betwixt the different masses of ore, yet the several masses are thinner and thinner, towards the edge of the mass, and do not break off at once when at their full thickness. The discontinuous, as well as the continued and regular ribs of ore, are of various dimensions or thickness, from one inch, or less, up to two or three feet, or more, in rare instances.

But there are, again, a great many veins which do not carry any rib of rider, or vein-stone, in the middle of them, but frequently, the sides or cheeks of the veins are *ridered*, for two, three, or six feet, from the sides or cheeks of the vein; and some veins do not carry any rider at all in one part of the Strata, and yet, the same vein will be ridered in another part.— When a rider is specked with spar or ore, it is called a *promising* rider; but when it has a dead appearance, and light, it is accounted a *bad* rider. A great many of the riders are impregnated with arsenic, and other semi-metals.

Rider, in a vein, is seldom found in a continued rib, but more frequently found in a discontinuous rib, sometimes in a vein that is rather hard and close, but generally among softness, in a vein that is loose and open; and, moreover, rider is not only in ribs of several dimensions, and in several degrees of continuity, but it is also found in larger and smaller globes and irregular masses. These globes, and irregular masses of rider, or vein-stone, in wide, soft, loose veins, are found of all dimensions, from the size of the fist, up to the size of a hogshead, and much bigger.

In some very wide loose veins, irregular masses of rider will be found, in one side of the vein, and irregular masses of ore in the other; and both the masses of rider, and those of the ore, will be found lying without any order among soft loose mineral soil, and without the least appearance of continuity; sometimes the masses being pretty near and contiguous to one another, and, sometimes, the miners have to work downward several feet through the soft soil, before they touch one of them.

These large masses of rider, are frequently so very hard, even among the excessive softness of the loose

soil which surrounds them, that they cannot be broken
to pieces with any tools, or strength of man, without
gunpowder.

These masses of rider, or vein-stone, found loose,
and detached among softness, are of all colours; as
white, yellow, red, brown, black, green, and ash-coloured, in all their shades and varieties; and frequently, several of these colours are found blended together, in the same mass. These masses of rider, in
softness, in wide loose veins, are sometimes poor,
sometimes rich, in ore; and they are frequently found
to contain none at all. When they are poor in metal,
they are then to be called *riders mixed with ore;* but
when they are very rich in metal, they may be called
masses of ore mixed with rider. It is not uncommon
to find these riders mixed with several species of ore
in the same mass; for instance, lead, copper, iron,
hemitite, pyrites, &c. which mixture, generally renders them all very useless; the riders being often so
hard, that it is not easy to break them small enough
for separation; and the different ores found so mixed
and combined together, that clean ore can hardly be
made out of any one of them.

Again, wide, soft, loose veins, sometimes, only

produce larger and smaller masses of ore, without any rider at all, in the inside of the vein, yet it very seldom happens, but the sides or cheeks of the veins are more or less ridered.

The dimensions of these globes and masses of ore, in soft wide veins, cannot be accurately stated. It is common to find detached bits amongst the soft soils, as small as pease, and even smaller; but, generally, so coated over, as to be imperceptible, until they happen to be crushed or bruised between two hard bodies, when their bright metallic quality appears.

Bits and masses of ore, are commonly found detached, and surrounded with softness, as big as eggs, the fist, the head, and so on, up to the large unwieldy masses, which cannot be stirred from the place where they are found, but must be wrought out piece-meal; and, in some very wide soft veins, they sometimes, although not often, meet with masses so large, as to produce a great many tons of lead out of one lump.

These larger and smaller lumps of ore, in some soft works, are all pure and solid; in others, they are less or more mixed and blended with spar, rider, stone, and other heterogeneous bodies.

In some soft veins, pure and mixed masses of different species of ore are found, such as lead, copper, iron, &c.; and there are often found, in the softness, masses of all sizes, of different kinds of stone, besides spar and sparry rider; and every substance, found in the inside of these soft loose veins, has, generally, the appearance of having been corroded and wasted; the masses, large and small, of ore and other substances, being of no determined or regular shape, but having much the appearance of some degree of corrosion, and a partial wasting as they have hardened; they have generally a lax texture, and an appearance like slaked lime or snuff. It was hinted before, that the lax dusty soils are of various colours, though a snuffy colour, and darker brown, are the most common. The phenomena of the inside of these veins, are so various, that it is almost impossible to go through every point of description, observing only, that all bold, wide veins, are not soft. Many of them are, on the contrary, very hard, and various in their appearances and contents. Some of these bold veins, have produced large bodies of lead ore, in several great mining fields, both in the rock and change of beds; as at *Wanlockhead* and *Lead-hills*, in Scotland, where, it is said, they have frequently had veins, from six to fourteen feet wide, of solid lead ore, in the rock. In *Allendale* and *Alston-moor*, veins have been found from six to twelve feet wide, of solid lead ore.

About six years ago, a very rich mining field was opened, in *Alston-moor*, by John Wilson, Esq. and Company, known by the name of *Hudgill Burn*, which is now raising considerable quantities of lead ore: the mine consists of two principal veins, denominated the sun vein and north vein, with other collateral strings or veins, between them; the east forehead of the north vein, is now above three feet wide, of pure *Galena*, in the Tuft, or Water Sill. (No. 154 in the Section) Besides, it is seventeen feet wide, consisting of four ribs of Galena, from two to four feet each, in the Great Lime-stone. (No. 153 in the Section) The sun vein is also about twelve feet wide, blended with Galena. Including altogether, the mine has produced upwards of 9000 *bings* of ore in one year. This is one of the richest lead mines that have been discovered in *Alston-moor*, or perhaps in the world, during the time that the mining operations have been carried on, as the number of miners employed has not exceeded eighty. *

---

* A most singular and curious phenomenon occurred in this mine. About fifty fathoms below the surface, in the vein,

But the cavities, or rather the spaces, betwixt the sides of bold hard veins, are not always filled up with pure and solid ore; it may rather be asserted, that such a thing seldom happens. They generally contain, besides the ore, a great quantity of rider, spar, and other hard matter. Hard bold veins, containing no metal to begin with, are very discouraging for mineral trials; the ground being so difficult to cut, that efforts in them soon become expensive; though sometimes this difficulty is, in part, removed, by a thin strake, or seam of clay, betwixt the rider and the side or sides of the vein, which miners call a *steeking*, and which helps them forward greatly, because they can cut this out first, the length of a pick helve, which frees the *hards*, and makes them more easily wrought with gunpowder, or otherwise.

It is almost as difficult to describe, fully, the inside of a hard vein as that of a soft one, the riders, spars, and ores, usually appearing in such a variety of conditions and mixtures in different veins.

---

surrounded with Galena, was found a PIECE of WOOD, about six inches in length and about four in breadth, not in a fossil state, but by appearance like a chip, or piece broken from a tree, rather convex on one side. Mr. Thomas Wilson, who related this to me, had the specimen then in his possession, which he produced. This fact cannot be accounted for by any Theory yet advanced !

It has been observed before, (in page 224) that some hard veins carry a rib or body of rider, with a rib of ore upon one or both sides of the rider. These ribs of ore, are of various dimensions or thickness, from less than one inch up to three, four, or five feet.

Sometimes these ribs of ore, running parallel to a rider, in hard wide veins, are more frequently found mixed and debased with spar, and other heterogeneous matter. It is uncommon to find any ore in one of these hard veins, but what is mixed and blended with a prodigious body of strong rider, of great width, which, at any rate, is very difficult to work, and therefore the ore must be in considerable quantity, when so mixed, to defray the expense of raising and dressing it.

And again, there are some bold, regular, good-like veins, containing a considerable quantity of ore, which is all spoiled and rendered useless by its being blended with cauk, spar, or black jack, from which it cannot be separated at a moderate expense; and some good veins of ore are spoiled and rendered useless, by being mixed with a great quantity of pyrites, mundic, or sulphur-stone. Sometimes a rib of three or four feet, or more, of the pyrites, is found in a wide vein, with a considerable quantity of fine lead ore intermixed with it.

If the lead ore happens, luckily, to lie in a rib, or otherwise, in one side of the vein, it may be wrought with profit; but if they are blended together, it is ten to one that the lead is worth working; the pyrites, or sulphur, being so ponderous, that, sometimes, they cannot be separated to advantage.

Wide sparry veins, sometimes carry two or three, or more, narrow ribs of ore, separated from one another by so many ribs of spar, as not to be always worth working; for it too often happens, that, when ore is, in this or any other way, divided, it is rendered unprofitable; this, however, depends upon the quality and goodness of the ore. If the ribs are, each of them, some inches thick of pure solid ore, they may be worked very well; but, sometimes, such divided ribs are not above a quarter of an inch a-piece, and even less.

We will now proceed to give some account of such rake veins as may be called irregular; and these are, First, such as open suddenly into very wide bellies, and close or check again, as suddenly. Second, waving veins, or such as open and close alternately, at very short distances, as you work forward horizontally in them.

Some hard veins come under the description of those above-mentioned; and it is not uncommon to see a pretty wide and rich belly of good solid ore, which does not continue, for any considerable length, upon the bearing of the vein, but soon checks or twitches out, by the sides coming together as you advance horizontally; that is, the ore fails at the end of a few fathoms, where the sides of the vein unite, either suddenly, or more gradually; and the *twitch*, when the sides of the vein come together, is either total, or in part. Some of these *twitches* carry a small rib of solid ore quite through, until the vein opens again, and produces another belly; and in other twitches, we have a rib of rider going quite through the twitch, and this rider is sometimes mixed with ore, and at other times it is quite barren; and again, in many of these twitches we have neither ore nor rider, but in some of them the sides of the vein are squeezed as close together as a joint between two hewn stones, and especially in the Blue Rock, or Grey Wacke Slate.

Sometimes there will be found a thin strake or

seam of clay, perhaps not an inch thick, or not above one or two inches at most. Miners call this thin seam of clay a *sticking*, when there is either a thread or small rib of ore, either pure or mixed with spar or rider, or else a rib of barren rider, leading through the twitch; or again, where there is a sticking of clay, there is no difficulty in the case, except in point of labour and expense, because an inexperienced miner may find his way through the twitch well enough. But where the sides come perfectly close, and are run or cemented together, which is often the case, it then requires the care and attention of an observing experienced miner, to keep or follow the vein with certainty as he drives through the twitch, and especially if it proves a long one.

In general, the veins do not close at once when one of these twitches is coming in or commencing; but the belly of ore begins, from the widest part, to wear gradually less and less, until at last the sides of the vein are come pretty close together, and the ore wears out to a point or thin edge. It is, in some twitches, squeezed out altogether, and in others, is reduced to a small thread or rib, which goes through with them.

These twitches are of various lengths. No miner,

when his vein is checked or twitched out, can possibly
tell, how long it is to continue; or, in other words,
how many fathoms he has to drive through it before
the vein opens again, unless he has cut through the
same twitch, either higher up or lower down; and this
uncertainty, in the length or extent of twitches,
is one of the most puzzling dilemmas, or, perhaps, greatest difficulty, met with in the practice of
mining.

Some of these bars, grips, or twitches, betwixt
bellies or wide places in a vein, will continue for ten,
twenty, thirty, or forty fathoms, and even up to sixty,
eighty, and a hundred, or more; so that we are frequently left in extreme doubt, after we have driven
ten or fifteen fathoms in an unknown twitch, and, in
such cases, it is no easy matter to determine, whether we should push forward or stop short.

When the miners have cut a drift through a twitch,
they find the vein begins to open, and the sides or
cheeks to part asunder again upon the other side. If
they had a thin rib of ore, serving to lead them
through the twitch, it begins to grow thicker; but if
they had none, they now meet it at an inch thick, or
even less; but as they advance forward, the ore

usually increases gradually, and grows better and better, until they come to the best and widest part of the belly, something like a fish's tail, increases gradually from the point, forward, to the thickest part of the body.

These bellies of ore, are of indeterminate dimensions, both as to length and breadth, or thickness; some of them are but a few fathoms long, in all; others continue for a great many fathoms. Some continue at full wideness, where the ore is best, for several fathoms; and others begin to dwindle or wear thinner, almost as soon as you arrive at the best and thickest part of the belly; and again, they vary as much in width or thickness as in length, as they are found in different veins, and sometimes in different places in the same vein, from a few inches, up to several yards wide. It sometimes happens, that the miners meet with a false appearance while driving through a twitch, that is, with a small quantity of ore, which does not continue, neither as they advance, nor up or down; but, in such case, they soon lose it again, which proves a great disappointment, as they naturally expect that they have got hold of, or reached, one edge of a belly of ore, and it proves a false belly, or only a small nest.

When one belly of ore proves pure and solid, it generally happens, that all the bellies prove so, in the same vein, and especially so in the contiguous parts of the same mining field. The contents, or produce of a vein, frequently change greatly at any considerable distance.

There have been remarkably rich bellies of lead ore, in the mining field, at *Allenheads*, where the flat or dilated veins, and the rake veins, come together.

Instances have been known of eight hundred bings of ore being raised by six miners, in one of those shakes, or bellies, in the space of nine weeks.

In this species of vein, mention has only been made of solid bellies of ore; but it must be observed, that, where ore is found, in this description of vein, it is not always solid; on the contrary, it is oftener found mixed with spar and rider, than solid, and too often, also, the bellies, in this sort of hard vein, contain only spar or rider, without any ore, or so little that it is not worth working. It is in these veins that the open cavities, or drusses, lined with perfectly formed crystals, are most frequently met with, many of which are exceedingly curious.

When this species of hard vein proves barren of
ore, the spars and riders are found in bellies in them,
in like manner as the ore is found in the bearing veins;
and these barren hard soils begin and end in a narrow
or thin edge at the extremities, and swell out gradually in the middle of the belly, exactly as the ore
does; and the cheeks or twitches are the same in the
barren as in the bearing veins. Sometimes a thin rib
of the spar or rider, which they contain, leads through
the twitch; and sometimes a thin sticking of clay, or
else the sides of the vein are found squeezed together,
as described before, in page 236.

This species, of big-bellied veins, are as often found
soft as hard; but the soft bellies are much more difficult to describe than the hard, and likewise more difficult to work.

The soft soils, found in the bellies of this sort of vein,
are much the same, as those already described in the
soft and wide regular veins; and the ore is found in
them much in the same manner, excepting, that there
are no regular ribs found in these bellies. The ore,
in the wide and spacious cavities of these soft veins, is
generally found in globes or irregular masses, frequently of a globous, roundish, or oval figure, and

of as various dimensions as can well be imagined, surrounded with, and buried in, soft soils.

It is no uncommon thing to find the soft openings,
in this sort of vein, swell out to an enormous width,
so as sometimes to make it difficult to find the real
sides of the vein; and sometimes the real sides are
shaken and loose, occasioned by the softness of the
soil within the real sides, yielding to the pressure of
the sides. Working these soft wide veins, is the most
difficult part of mining.

There is no proceeding a foot in these, without ad-
vancing square timbers as far as the drifts go, in form
of a trance or passage into a house, each pair of
which timbers are composed of two door cheeks, or
side posts, and of a lintel and sole tree. The miners
stand within this square timber, where they work,
and still set more timber before them, as they can
make room for it. This is expensive, troublesome,
and dangerous, if they have not good skill in setting
the timber, for the soil is generally quite soft and
loose, and being commonly mixed with lesser and
greater globes and masses of ore and stone, the
whole will frequently rush down with violence before, or in front of, their timber, to a greater height

than they incline. A skilful miner does all he can to prevent the soil from running or washing down before his timbers, by driving in polins, or sharp-pointed stakes. He enters these above the lintel or head tree, and without the side posts of his foremost pair, and with his mallet drives them forward, past the square timbers, into the softness; and if a mass of ore, or any hard substance, retards the point of one of his polins, he draws it out of the way with his pick; and when the end of his polin is freed, he drives again, until it is far enough up. When they are all driven as far up, or forward, as it is wished, he works out room to set another pair within those polins, and enters another course of polins, and so on; and, whether they advance horizontally, sink down, or rise upwards, in these soft places, they must do all with square timbers, which is very troublesome and expensive; but it frequently happens, that the ore is so plentiful and good, in these veins, as abundantly to compensate for all this trouble and expense.

The second sort of irregular rake vein, is called the *waving vein*. This is a rake vein, or perpendicular fissure, which opens and closes at very short distances. This vein is very near a-kin to the last described, as it consists of bellies and twitches; but the twitches are

so numerous, and so near to one another, that there is
neither room nor distance enough between them, for
any of the bellies, in this vein, to open out to any
considerable wideness, and, of course, this vein is
never so rich and valuable as the last-mentioned;
there not being room enough in these small cavities or
openings, for any considerable quantities of ore.

As the concavities or bellies, in this vein, are small
, and of short continuance, so it generally happens, that
the twitches, grips, or bars between them are also
short, and of no great continuance; and, as the
small openings and twitches are so frequent and near
to one another, it may be properly called the *waving
vein*, as the small bellies in this vein resemble the hol-
lows between the waves on a pool of water. The writer
has dwelt the longer upon the history of the rake vein,
or perpendicular mineral fissure, because it is the
most common and frequent of all veins. He will now
proceed to the history of the *pipe vein*; but will first
give a brief account of some of the *strings*, and other
partial veins, which branch out from the principal ones,
as these strings most properly belong to, and accompany, the rake veins.

A *string*, in mining, is a weak vein, or mineral fissure, which flies out in a right line, but with an acute angle, from the principal continued vein; and when it has stretched in that line to an indeterminate, though no great distance, it ends in a point, and is squeezed out to nothing by the two sides or cheeks coming close together, coalescing, and leaving no marks or vestige of a vein. Or, if there be another vein, at no great distance, running parallel to the principal continued vein, then the string will continue its bearing, until it joins or comes into the other vein. The opposite end joins the principal vein, somewhere, and comes into one side or other of it in an acute angle, but does not cross it; for if it should cross the vein, and is found quite through upon the other side, it is not a string, but an oblique or diagonal vein.

When a string has really joined, and is come into a vein, they are both afterwards considered in that line, as no more two, but one, the line of the string, and the string itself, being lost in the vein, and the vein only continues the line of bearing. These strings fly out from the veins in all directions, though always diagonally; and they are sometimes as rich, and for a short time even richer, than the vein itself.

A *skew* is an irregular discontinuous mineral fissure, striking out from the principal vein in an uncertain direction, and lies in a very slanting irregular position. These imperfect mineral fissures seldom stretch out to any considerable distance from the principal veins.

A *back*, or *sweep*, is a mineral fissure, which often resembles a segment of a circle. It breaks off from the hanging or upper cheek of the vein, strikes out to a less or greater distance, fetches a sweep, and comes back into the same vein again, at a distance from where it first set out.

All these inferior branches produce good ore in some mines.

A *pipe* vein resembles, in many respects, a huge irregular cavern, pushing forward into the body of the earth, in a slanting or sloping direction, but many of them with very different degrees of slope; some of them, having but a few degrees of slope from the horizontal flatness, and others declining precipitately, so as to be nearer the perpendicular position than the angle forty-five. In short, they stand in all positions, between the perpendicular and the horizontal.

The pipe, in general, does not cut the Strata like the rake vein, but is an opening between them, so that, if the lay or position of the Strata is nearly horizontal, so is the bearing of the pipe; but if the declivity of the Strata is precipitous, the pipe shoots down headlong, almost like a shaft. Some pipes are very wide and high, others are very low and narrow, and they are sometimes not so large as a common mine or drift, and others, again, are of all the intermediate mean dimensions.

Some pipe veins are hard, and others are soft. The hard ones contain all the variety of mineral matter, which is commonly found in hard rake veins. Some of them are found quite full of solid ore, others are full of ore mixed with spar, rider, &c.; and some, again, are full of spar or rider, without any ore at all. Large pipe veins, where they are full of solid ore, are exceedingly rich.

Soft pipe veins are as frequently met with as the hard; that is, such as contain soft mineral soils within the tubulous concavity of the pipe. The soft pipes are found in various positions, as well as the hard: some put down with a quick, and others with an easy, slope.

It should be observed, that pipe veins do not always approach the tubular form. Several of them are much wider than they are high; and these more flat pipes frequently come to be very low between the roof and sole, or upper and lower Stratum, towards the skirts or extremities of the pipe upon the right and left hand.

All pipe veins do not continue betwixt two distinct beds of stone. Sometimes they burst their way up through the Strata, and then they have a much greater slope than the ordinary declivity of the Strata, where they are found.

The bearing of such pipes, as continue between the Strata, is exactly the same as the declivity of the Strata; that is to say, the bearing of such, runs parallel to a line drawn across the Strata, from crop to dip; and it should be understood, that pipes have, in general, no longitudinal bearing whatever: their bearing is in a declining or sloping line, and mostly towards the same point of the compass as the declivity or dip of the Strata.

It was observed before, that the slope of one of these pipe veins is the same as the declivity of the

Strata in the mining field, and even in that part of the
field where they are found; and as the declivity of the
Strata is extremely various, and changes so often, the
slope of these pipes must be as various in different
places.

With respect to the other species of *pipe* veins,
which have burst their way up through the Strata, it
is more difficult to point out their bearing, as they generally dip down precipitately, and may be said to
have no bearing at all, as the one end dips down towards the centre, and the other end points up towards the surface; and such of them as do not stand
so near the perpendicular, seldom or never run in a
straight line, but wind downwards in a sloping and oblique direction. The kind of vein, or deposition of
metallic ore, that comes next under our consideration
is the *streek*, or *flat*, or *dilated vein*, which is the third
in the order of those called *principal veins*. Neither
this nor the *pipe* can, perhaps, come under the denomination of mineral fissures, as in fact they are scarcely
fissures at all. The flat, or dilated vein, is a space or
opening between two Strata or beds of stone; one of
which lies above, and the other below, this vein, in
the same manner as the roof and pavement of a Stratum of Coal are above and below that Coal. When

the Strata, between which this kind of vein is found, lie nearly parallel to the horizon, the vein is likewise in the same horizontal position; and when the Strata vary from the horizontal position, the dilated vein varies likewise, with some degree of declivity; and this of necessary consequence, as the vein does not burst the Strata, but always continues between the same two beds of stone.

These flat veins, lie between the Strata in some respects, as seams of Coal are found; at the same time, there is no further resemblance between them, than that they are both found between the Strata, and have exactly the same horizontal or declining position, as the Strata of the place where they are found. In these respects they are to be investigated upon the same principles as the Strata, or seams of Coal; and there is also this further resemblance, that these veins are subject to be interrupted, broken, and thrown up and down by dykes, slips, or faults, and other interruptions of the regular or plane position of the Strata, as in figure below.

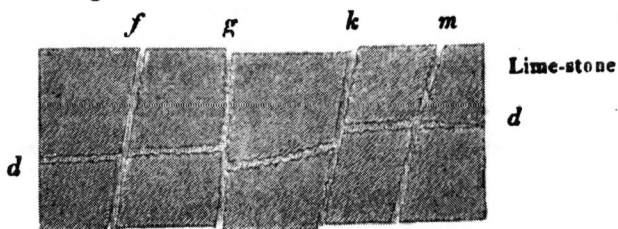

Suppose the flat, or dilated vein the Stratum of Lime-stone, as at *d*, it will continue its regular course until it comes to the mineral fissure, vein, or string, *f*; and from thence to *g*, *k*, and *m*, being thrown up and down by those slips, veins, or fissures, in the same manner as in the seams of Coal; with this difference only, that in working Coal these interruptions are generally real troubles, and the getting over them is so much pure loss of money and time; whereas, on the contrary, when they are met with in working a flat vein, they often prove a great advantage, as they are, in fact, other mineral veins of different denominations and descriptions; so that, as often as these interruptions are met with in a flat vein, it is an adventitious increase of the reality; or, at least, the chance of meeting with more treasure in the same field. In other respects, the theory of the flat vein and the seam of Coal is widely different: the seam of Coal preserves an equal thickness betwixt roof and pavement, and, in fact, is a Stratum fully as regular as any of the Strata above and below it; whereas, on the contrary, the flat, or dilated vein, is, or was, only an opening or space between the Strata, of very unequal depth or height, which space is now filled with mineral matter.

Sometimes these flat or *Strata* veins, as they might be called, open wide betwixt the roof and floor, or lid and sole, which openings contain a variety of mineral matter, soft and hard, and generally with a less or greater mixture of ore; and, not unfrequently, the whole space is filled with good solid ore. In some rich mining fields the flat, or dilated veins, produce nearly as much lead ore as the rake veins; for instance, *Coalcleugh*, in Northumberland, and *Nenthead*, in Cumberland. These two mining fields have produced a prodigious quantity of lead ore, in the flat, or dilated veins, in the Great Lime-stone; and, it is necessary to be observed, that these flat, or dilated veins, in the above mining fields, are generally mineralized by the rake veins; for the flats or streeks seldom carry ore to a great distance from the rake veins, except there be smaller strings or cross veins found in working the flats, by which, if it should be the case, they are generally enriched, and especially by cross strings. The flat, or Strata veins, are frequently discovered by sinking or working downwards in the rake veins; and, when it so happens, it is reckoned a lucky accident, as they can turn off, and work away horizontally, with the same shaft, &c. as in the following figure.

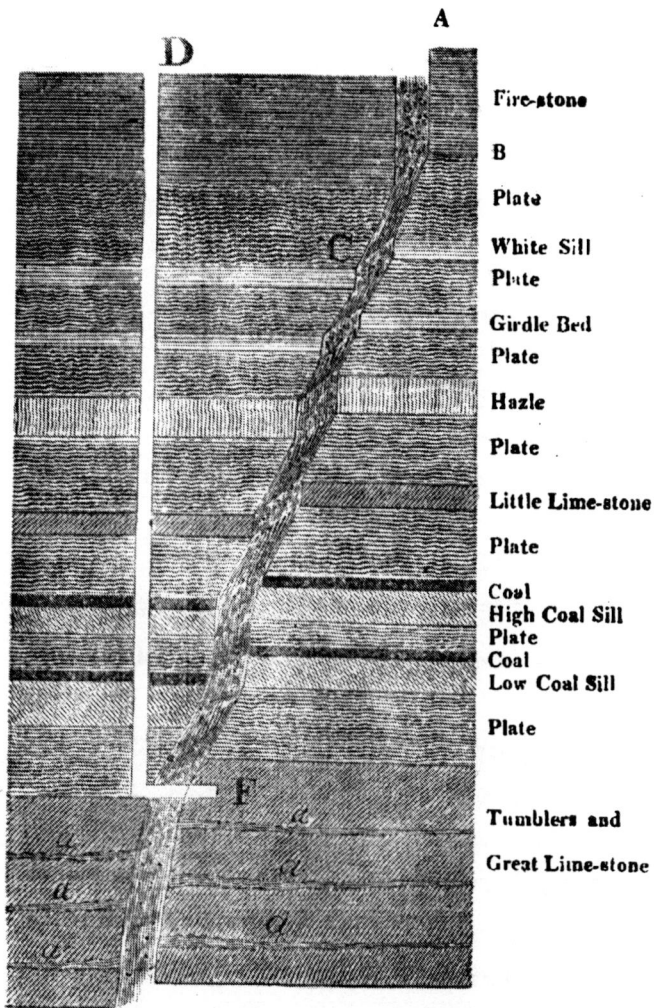

A

Fire-stone

B

Plate

White Sill
Plate

Girdle Bed
Plate

Hazle

Plate

Little Lime-stone

Plate

Coal
High Coal Sill
Plate
Coal
Low Coal Sill

Plate

Tumblers and

Great Lime-stone

Where D is a shaft sunk down upon the Lime-stone,
and cut through the vein at F; and the three flat, or
dilated veins, a, a, a, may be worked by the same

shaft. It must be further observed, that the flats seldom carry ore close up to the sides or cheeks of strong rake veins, but there is generally a rider, for a fathom or so, on the sides or cheeks of the vein, which obstructs the flat, or dilated veins, from coming close up to the rake veins.

These flat veins, found between the Strata, are discovered in some mining fields, in several species of stone; but they are most frequently found in Limestone, lying, either in a horizontal or declining position.

Some of these veins are found (in Argillaceous Strata, or Plate; in which the vein itself is frequently nothing more than a soft Argillaceous Stratum) often containing nodules or masses of pyrites, spar, quartz, and other stones.

The flat, or Strata veins, open and close as well as the rake veins. Sometimes the Stratum, which is the immediate roof or lid of this vein, comes down, and joins close to that below it, and to such a degree, that there is, perhaps, no spar left between them, and little or no vestige of a vein left; and these twitches, or closings of the roof and sole of the vein, will continue to a less or greater distance, and the vein be entirely, or in part, squeezed out from betwixt the two layers of stone, as is found in the rake veins, when they check or bring their sides or cheeks close together.

Sometimes the Strata veins will continue of a moderate and pretty regular height, between the roof and sole, for a considerable extent; and at other times, the roof and sole come together, and open again, at short distances.

Sometimes the space, which we may call the *concavity* of the vein, is but low, betwixt the roof and sole, so that, where the ore is worth working, part of the roof, or rock above it, must be worked away with the ore, to give the workmen room to advance; and, at other times, they open wider or higher, so as to furnish sufficient space for a good body of ore; and again, they sometimes open up to an enormous height, which places may be called the *bellies* of these flat veins.

In some mining fields there are frequently three flat, or dilated veins, worked at the same time, as in fig. p. 199, at *e, e. e*, or in fig. p. 253, at *a, a, a*, commonly called the high, low, and middle flats.

It was observed before, that the species of pipe which approaches in affinity to the streek, or flat vein, lies mostly between the Strata, and consequently it has, in such cases, the same declivity with the Strata as the streek, or flat vein, so that there is an original affinity between them; and when twitches run parallel in one of these streeks, and the roof rises up to a considerable cavity between the twitches, the name *pipe* is then usually imposed by the miners.

The fourth and last capital vein, is the *accumulated pipe vein*. The accumulated, concentrated, or conical vein, is not easily described, so as to convey a distinct idea of it. Some of these veins approach to the form of vast irregular cones, and others of them have some resemblance to inverted cones; but whatever is the form or description of this vein, it frequently contains a great deal of wealth, in a small compass of ground, the accumulated pipe veins being often the richest of all mines.

From some of these large pipes, a great, and from others a less, number of nearly perpendicular fissures or rake veins meet, and join in one common centre, as in the annexed figure.

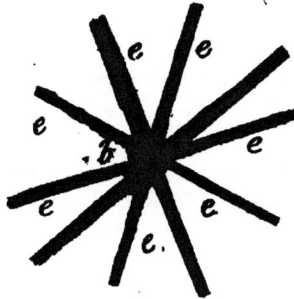

Where *b* is the pipe or accumulated vein, and *e, e, e,* &c. so many different fissures or rake veins, from which they spread out, like radii, to different distances from the main body of the shaft or cone; and these branches frequently contain rich bodies of ore, which, being worked out, there remains a vast perpendicular arched concavity, as it were, hanging upon pillars.

The main pipe or shaft, of the accumulated vein, somewhat resembles the inside of a glass-house, and the vast capacity of this vein is often stored with a rich body of metallic ore, frequently bedded with soft mineral soil; but the veins and branches which join this pipe, or diverge from it, commonly resemble our rake veins or perpendicular mineral fissures. In fact, the accumulated vein is nothing more than a number of rake veins intersecting one another, and is the centre of intersection, as represented in the last figure.

There has been a number of pipe, flat, and accumulated veins, worked at *Pike-Law*, in the county of Durham, where many rake veins meet, and intersect each other.

When the ore is worked out of a large accumulated vein, it exhibits a horrid and frightful gulph, some of which may be fifty or sixty feet wide below, and they are often worked down to a great depth from the surface.

The excavation of the perpendicular irregular pipe, is, of itself, sufficiently frightful; but when the hanging rocky sides, of the main pipe or cone, are slitted up and opened, perhaps from top to bottom in many places, in working collateral diverging veins, the appearance of this horrible gulph is then awful beyond description.

It must be observed, that some of the accumulated pipes are very irregular at all depths, sometimes standing nearly erect, and then turning to a slanting or a spiral position; and, with respect to the capacity of this kind of pipe, it is sometimes of middling wideness, but it often contracts, and dilates again, to various dimensions. It sometimes opens out to an enormous width, far down, as well as at the surface, when it may be truly called an *accumulated pipe vein.*

Many iron mines are found to occur in this description of vein, and lead and copper ores are frequently found, and worked, in both the sorts of accumulated veins.

Having now gone through the description of the different kinds of mineral veins, viz. the rake, the pipe, the flat or streek, and the accumulated pipe veins, which usually carry the greatest quantities of the metallic and other mineral ores, that are found beneath the surface of the earth, it may be proper to remark, that mineral veins are subject to several accidents, which may be expected to be met with in the progress of working them; some of which are the more dangerous, as they may occasion the entire loss of the vein, if not well understood; and therefore, as it is possible, that these troubles or accidents, are not in general sufficiently well known to all miners, they deserve to be investigated with attention.

The flat vein, found between the Strata, is frequently liable to be twitched or squeezed out, by the roof and sole coming together ; however, when there is no more in the case than the roof and sole coming together, the miners may be pretty sure, that the vein will open again, and that they will find it upon the same level, when they have cut through the squeeze or twitch that has troubled them.

But it may be remarked, that flat, or dilated veins, in general, do not carry metallic ores, to any great distance from the rake veins ; and the richest flats are generally, in large mining fields, in a complication of veins, as *Nenthead*, in Alston-moor, and *Allenheads* and *Coalcleugh*, in Northumberland ; and it may be further remarked, that soft sparry veins are seldom so productive of flat, or dilated veins, as the hard ridery veins, and frequently veins, that have more or less of black jack, or sulphuret of zinc, blended in them,* have flats attached to them.

Grips or twitches are generally pretty well understood by most miners, who have been used to flat

* Considerable quantities of blend, or black jack, and calamine, are now raised in Alston-moor. One of the largest spelter or zinc works, in England, has been lately established, by Mr. Thomas Shaw and Company. It is worthy of remark, that, for many years previous to this establishment, the black jack was commonly thrown away as waste, when dressing and washing the lead ore.

works; but there are other troubles or accidents incident to these veins, which are not so generally known, nor so easily investigated; such as dykes, slips, gashes, or chasms, which have been described before.

These breaks, irregularities, and dislocations of the Strata, are too often very troublesome in the coal field, but they do not always prove distressing in the mining field; very often they are quite the contrary; for often, both sides of a Whin-dyke, and of the gashes in the Strata, prove to be very rich and fruitful veins.

The slips, which are the most numerous of all the interruptions of the regularity of the Strata, are also the most frequent, and the most durable mineral veins; so that there is mostly the greater chance of success, the more of these interruptions of regularity there are found in a mining field, and for a very good reason, because they, such are all mineral veins.

A rake vein is sometimes thrown off its course to one side, either by a close joint, or by an open cross vein. When a vein is started, or thrown out of the line of bearing, to one side or other, it is proper to observe, that the vein is, in this case, generally cut

off by a smooth joint, which meets the miners full in
the face, instead of the vein they had been following;
and behind this joint, straight forward in the line of
bearing, there is usually not the least appearance of
the vein, because it is thrown off its former course to
one side.

There is one circumstance relating to this back joint,
which deserves to be particularly remarked : if the
vein is started to the right hand side, the smooth
joint, which cut it usually off, meets the miner first on
the left hand; and, on the contrary, if the vein is
thrown to the left hand, the joint usually meets the
miner first on the right hand, and so passes on, in a
slanting or diagonal direction, across the fore-head of
the mine, or fore-most working in the vein.

Having now given a description of MINERAL VEINS
IN GENERAL, we shall present to the reader a few
more particular local observations on the mines, in the
different mining fields of *Derwent, Weardale, Teesdale, Allendale,* and *Alston-moor.*

At the conclusion of this part will be found an Al-
phabetical List of these Mines, but it may be thought

necessary to give a more detailed account. We shall commence by enumerating the different cross veins, or those which pursue a direction nearly north and south, beginning at the eastern part of the mining district, and concluding with the most western cross vein that occurs, of any magnitude.

The first, worthy of notice, is *White-heaps* vein, in *Derwent,* which is a wide sparry vein, bearing a south-east and north-west direction, but without any great throw or dislocation, visible on its two cheeks. It was worked by the London Lead Company formerly, and raised a considerable quantity of lead ore, but was never rich, being very much blended and intermixed with spar and rider. There is a cross vein, at a little distance to the west, running nearly north and south, but considerably weaker than the above, called *Linn-bank* vein.

The next remarkable cross vein, or dyke, is the *Great Burtree-ford Dyke,* which is the strongest vein yet found in the mining districts before-mentioned.— It crosses at the west end of the mining field of *Allen-heads,* and at *Burtree-ford,* (from which it has taken its name) in *Weardale,* and may be traced for several miles southward, into Yorkshire; first at *Chronckly*

Scar, on the river **Tees**; and again in *Lunedale,* in
the manor of the Earl of Strathmore. (See pages
141 and 142.) Its course may be ascertained to the
north of *Allenheads,* at *Bridge Eals,* where it crosses
the *East Allen* river, about two miles below *Cattan,* in
Northumberland. It throws more than eighty fathoms* up to the west, and its bearing is nearly north
and south.

About two miles to the west of the last cross vein,
is another vein, called *Whetstone Mea* cross vein,
running rather in a south-east and north-west direction; which divides into two branches southward of
West Allendale Burn, in Northumberland, where
they make a junction, at *Barney Crags,* one mile
N. of *Coalcleugh;* the east branch thrown down to the
west about twenty-four fathoms, and the western
branch throws down to the east about eighteen fa-

---

* Whatever be the throw or difference of level occasioned
in the measures by these dykes or veins, it never happens, as
might be expected, that a precipitous face of the rock is left
on the elevated side, or that the lower side is covered by an
alluvial deposit, which connects the inequality of the beds that
are *in situ,* but the surface of the ground, covering the vein,
is rendered level by the absolute removal of the rocky Strata,
on the elevated side. The same phenomena have been observed in other parts of the kingdom, and render evident the
operation of a most powerful agent, employed in tearing up
the surface, and in dispersing the fragments of the ruin.

thoms, they cross and intersect the mining field of *Coalcleugh*, to the eastward; and from thence, passing a little to the west of *Kilhope Law Boundary Currock*, into the county of Durham; intersecting the mining field of *Kilhope*, to the eastward, and will probably make a junction with the *Great Burtree-ford Dyke*, not far from *Wears-head*, in *Weardale*; and will probably intersect with the *Great Stublick Dyke*, or Vein, between *Cupola* Bridge and *Langley* Smelt Mills.

There are three or four weaker veins running parallel with these on the west side, which have been cut through at *Coalcleugh*; some of these throwing up, and others down, towards the east. There is likewise another cross vein, at the west end of the mining field of *Coalcleugh*, called the *Bounder-end* cross vein, which throws about one yard up to the west, running nearly north and south. It has been productive, in some tolerably rich flat or dilated veins connected with it, in the Great Lime-stone, both at *Coalcleugh* and *Rampgill*.

To the westward of the *Bounder-end* cross vein, about two hundred fathoms, there is another vein, called *Moss* cross vein, which throws about six fathoms

M m

up to the east, and down to the west; its bearing is nearly north and south. The next vein is *Handsome Mea* vein, running in a south-east and north-west direction, and throwing the east, or rather the north-east, cheek up about twelve or fourteen fathoms.—This vein has yielded a considerable quantity of lead ore, both in the vein and the flats, in the Great Lime-stone.

From the last-mentioned vein, at a little distance to the west, we have *Old Carr's* cross vein, running nearly north and south, which is the strongest vein that is found in *Alston-moor*, its throw being in some places nearly forty fathoms up to the west. Very good flat, or dilated veins, have been worked along the side of this vein at a little distance, and some remarkable rich cavaties of lead ore, &c. have been wrought, in or near it, at different times.

About four hundred fathoms further west we have another cross vein, called *Black Eshgill* vein, running nearly north and south. It throws about six fathoms up to the east, and has been tolerably rich, in the Great Lime-stone, both at *Black Eshgill-head,* (from which it takes its name) and likewise at *Dowgang* and *Nenthead* fields.

About three miles further west, we have another cross vein, called *Sir John's* vein, running nearly parallel to *Black Eshgill* vein, which also has a throw up to the west.

The next principal cross vein is the *Great Backbone*, or sulphur vein, running south-east and north-west, and throwing the south-west side or cheek up near about twenty fathoms. This great vein contains quantities of pyrites or sulphur-stone, blended with yellow copper ore, in *Cross-gill* Burn, *Alston-moor*; but the produce of copper was so inconsiderable, when it was formerly worked, that it would not defray the expense of procuring it. The workings in this vein were never prosecuted to any great extent, on account of the quantity of water which inundated, and rendered useless, the different shafts; but the Commissioners and Governors of Greenwich Hospital have lately thought proper to re-open the workings at their own expense, and there is the greatest probability of the vein proving productive. Their operations are conducted in a manner likely to produce an effectual trial, as they are now driving a water level under the Scar Lime-stone, which will drain the former workings, and greatly facilitate their future operations.

It is exceedingly probable that this, as well as some other strong veins which traverse the mining district, may contain metallic ores in the lower parts of the Strata, and, if the present trial should confirm this supposition, it will open a new field for mining adventurers.

This vein may be traced, for a considerable distance on its line of bearing, first, to the northward it may be seen, at a waterfall, or cascade, known by the name of *Kesh Burn Force,* which falls over the Great Whin Sill, or Basaltic Green-stone, about five miles S.W. of *Alston,* and again upon the summit of *Hartside.* There is great reason for supposing it to be the same vein that crosses the river *Eden,* at *Armithwaite Bay.* By applying the bearing, taken upon *Newnstone,* viz. N. 72 W. true meridian, (about two miles and a half S. W. of *Garrigill Gate)* to a map of Cumberland, it will be found nearly to correspond with the above-mentioned places; and by reversing and pursuing the course to the southward, it may be seen crossing the *South Tyne* river, (See Part I. page 111) from thence it passes through *Tyne-head* Fell, over *Yuad Moss,* near the mines at *Eshgill-head,* in *Harewood,* in the county of Durham, (the property of the Earl of Darlington) and intersects with the *Great Burtree-*

ford Dyke, or vein, in *Weardale,* and then passing down the *Billing Pasture,* on the west side of the river *Wear,* where some specimens of iron shot copper ore, have been procured ; from thence there is some reason to suppose it identical with the great vein that traverses the *Cock-field* Coal field, about twenty miles S. W. of the city of *Durham.*

Since the Commissioners and Governors of Greenwich Hospital commenced driving the level in *Crossgill,* under the Scar Lime-stone, No. 168 in the Section, the miners (under the direction of Mr. JOHN DICKINSON, of Lowbyer, the Moor Master) have cut through a collateral string, or vein, on the north side of the principal vein, which has produced some very fine specimens of copper pyrites, or yellow copper ore, blended with malachite, which is a strong indication of the mine being productive in the lower or underlying series of the Strata.

An observation will be found frequently to occur in the course of this work, that the mines, on the east side of the *Great Burtree-ford Dyke* or vein, are generally of a softer nature than those on the west side, as at *Allenheads,* and all the extensive mines in *Weardale* and *Derwent,* which are on the east side of the

Burtree-ford Dyke; likewise, that the mines, which are on the west side of the above-mentioned vein, are generally of a harder nature, frequently containing a great deal more of black jack and rider, as at *Coal-cleugh*, all the mines in *Alston-moor* and *Kilhope*, and the mines in *Teesdale.*

It may be further observed, that there are several veins, on the west side of the above great vein, which contain a great deal of cauk, or barytes, and especially in *Teesdale* and *West Allendale;* whereas, on the east side, the veins contain mostly the calcareous or fluor spars.*

———◆———

Having gone through the description of the principal cross veins, it becomes the duty of the writer, to give an account of some of the most valuable mines

---

* A great variety of fluors, compact and *foliated, amorphus,* and *crystallized,* are found at *Allenheads,* and in the different lead mines in *Weardale* and *Alston-moor.* Crystals cubical, with the edges sometimes bevelled, octoedrical, polygonal, irregular. Colours very numerous; red, green, blue, yellow, purple, violet, colourless, and all gradations, from very pale, to almost black. Often of a drusy surface, composed of different minute crystals, and not unfrequently frosted over with marcasites. Very commonly found mixed with lead ore, cloud, spar, &c. Sometimes, though rarely, studded with brilliant quartz, crystals, and with crystallized galena,

that have been worked, and are working, in the mining districts before-mentioned.

The first lead mine which we find, after leaving the
Coal measures, is that of *Healy Field*, which has
been worked for a great number of years, and still
continues to produce lead ore, although in smaller
quantities than formerly.

The next mining field, about 6 *m.* to the west of the
last-mentioned mine, is that of *Shieldon*, in *Derwent*, which was formerly in the possession of the
London Lead Company, and at that time yielded a
considerable quantity of lead ore, in the higher parts
of the Strata. The works were, however, abandoned
for a number of years, until they were re-opened, some
time ago, by Easterby, Hall, and Company, who
drained the mines, by means of powerful steam engines, and sunk into the Great Lime-stone, which, on
account of the declivity of the Strata, lies buried at a
great depth in this part of the mining district. (See
the Section of the mines at *Shieldon*, page 121.) Their
endeavours, unfortunately, did not prove successful.

Jeffrey's Rake, another vein, about two miles
south-west of *Shieldon*, was worked, in the Great

Lime-stone, by the same mining company, and at present produces ore in small quantities.

The mining fields, which lie contiguous to those of *Derwent*, are *Allenheads*, in Northumberland, and *Rookhope*, in Durham; the former having been a valuable lead mine for several years. Although we have no certain information when these mines were first discovered, yet it is probable that they were worked near two hundred years ago, as they have belonged to the Blackett family, for upwards of 120 years. The main water level, called the *Haugh* level, was begun by Sir William Blackett, in the year 1684, as appears by the inscription upon a stone found at *Shield-ridge* level mouth, the main water level at *Coalcleugh;* and it is supposed, that these two levels were begun about the same time.

There is a complication of veins, at *Allenheads*, very productive of lead ore, both in the rake veins, and in the flat or dilated veins; and several large and remarkably rich cavities of lead ore have been found in the Great Lime-stone, some of which have produced upwards of one thousand bings; most of the ore being found in a loose state, upon the soles of the cavities, which has probably fallen from the roof, at some remote period of time.

The Strata, towards the west end of the mining field of *Allenheads*, has a great acclivity or rise, supposed to be occasioned by the *Great Burtree-ford Dyke* or vein, before described, the Strata rising or inclining about a yard in two, before it reaches this great dyke; and it may be necessary to observe, that the veins at *Allenheads* have not yet been proved, through the above great dyke or vein, although most of the veins have every appearance of being the same as those in *Kilhope-head.*

The third mining field, is *Wolf-cleugh*, in *Rookhope*, in the county of Durham, which has raised a considerable quantity of lead ore, at different times, though these mines have of late been very poor.

There are several veins in *Rookhope*, besides those at *Wolf-cleugh*, which have been worked at different times.—(See the List of Mines, subjoined to the end of this part.)

The next mining field, is *Middlehope*, in *Weardale*. The principal bearing veins that have been worked in *Middlehope*, are those running south-east and northwest, although most of the veins in *Rookhope* intersect the principal veins in *Middlehope*, and are thought to

N n

enrich them; among others, the *Lodge-field* veins are supposed to be some of them.*

The greatest part of the mines in *Weardale,* are soft workable mines; the veins commonly carrying much soft fluor spar, the miners working a great deal of ground, and raising immense quantities of Bouse, † before they obtain any considerable quantity of ore; but the mine-masters, in *Weardale,* raise large quantities of lead ore, by employing numbers of workmen, and slitting out much ground in one year.

The best lead mine, which was working in *Weardale,* in 1809, was *Birkonside,* or *Brecon-sike,* lead mine. This famous mine has, it is said, furnished, in some years, near ten thousand bings of lead ore. It is intersected to the westward by the *Burtreeford Dyke.*

The next principal mining field, is *Coalcleugh,* in Northumberland, in which there are three leading

---

* The Governor and Company have lately opened a very valuable mine, in *Middlehope,* which raises considerable quantities of lead ore.

† *Bouse,* undressed ore, in the state that it is drawn out of the mine.

veins worked, viz. *High Coalcleugh* vein, *White-wood* vein, and *Low Coalcleugh* vein. This valuable lead mine has produced a considerable quantity of ore for several years past.

Contiguous to *Coalcleugh*, are the extensive mines in *Alston-moor*, belonging to the Comissioners and Governors of Greenwich Hospital, which are more numerous and productive, in the same space of ground, than almost any others yet discovered in the world; * (see the List of Mines, at the end of this part) these mines are generally worked by private mining adventurers, excepting those at *Nenthead*, which have been for many years in the possession of the London Company. The manor of *Alston-moor* affords an excellent opportunity for working the mines or making discoveries, as the bearing Strata basset out on each side of the vales of the *Nent* and the *Tyne*, and levels can be drove, in the Plate beds, to the different veins, at a comparatively trifling expense.

---

* The value of the lead mines, in *Alston-moor*, was taken from the Moor Master's Book, for the three following years,—

	£	s.
In the year 1766—18,600 bings, worth, on an average, £2. 15s. per bing	61,950	0
1767—24,500	77,162	10
1768—18,730	62,213	10

The next valuable lead mine, is *Cross-fell* mine. *
This noble vein was discovered only a few years ago, and
carried lead ore up close to the moss, in the coal sills,
as may be seen in the Section. It is in the uppermost
part of the Strata, at the place where this vein was
first discovered to be so rich, although other and
higher beds put on or cover them, as we ascend towards the summit of the *Cross-fell* mountain, which
is upon the line of bearing of the vein, and the throw
of the vein is about a fathom up to the north, the matrix, in general, amorphus fluor spar.‡   It is worthy
of remark, that the same veins, which are here generally filled with fluor spar and galena, are on the west
side of the *Cross-fell* range of mountains, filled with
sulphate of barytes and galena.

Having thus given a description of the principal
mining fields upon the line of acclivity of the Strata,
commencing in *Derwent*, and continuing to the westward towards *Cross-fell*, we shall proceed now with
the history of *Float* and *Shoad* ore.

---

* *Cross-fell* mine has raised, in some years lately, nearly
5,000 bings of lead ore, the average price, per bing, £5. 10s.

‡ There are other veins in this neighbourhood, that have
raised considerable quantities of lead ore, which were opened
by John Little, Esq. and Company, of Raise-house, near
Alston.

Float ore differs from the shoad; the former being water-worn, the latter not. The float ore is generally mixed with water-worn bullets and gravel; the shoad never, unless it hapens to be washed off the superficies of the vein, by some rivulet or stream of water.

Shoad, ore is a pretty sure indication of a vein where it is found, or a little above, or higher on the acclivity of the surface; but you must judge of the distance above, by the greater or less acclivity of the slope. If the side of the hill is very steep, it may slide a great way down; but if there is little declivity downwards from the vein, the shoad will be found proportionally at a less distance. The shoad ore is found of all sizes, from very large masses, down to the size of peas, and smaller grains; and it has been produced, by the weathering or decomposing of the sides or cheeks of the vein, so as to leave the ore standing higher than the superficies of the rock, which exposed ore has, in time, slidden off where the ground is sloping.

It is a common thing, in some mining countries, for the miners to go *a Shoading*, that is, to search for shoad, on which occasions, they traverse rivulets, gullies, scars, and other places, where the surface of the ground is broken, and in places where the superficies of the Strata rise up to the grass-roots or surface. From the description of the float and shoad ore, already given, there is no doubt that an intelligent person, though no miner, will be able to distinguish the one from the other; but in case either of them should be found, it may be proper to point out the methods which should be taken to discover the vein.

Shoad ore is found in rough irregular globes or masses, of all sizes, and is frequently coated with white upon the outside. When such ore happens to be discovered upon a level piece of ground, a cross trench should be cut to the rock, in the very place where it is found; but if it is found upon a slope, or immediately at the foot of a slope, then look for the vein at a less or greater distance above, in proportion to the slope or declivity of the ground. When shoad is found upon a slope, or at the foot of it, the first business is to look about on all sides, to see if any other symptoms of a vein can be discovered; and if not, then you must judge, from circumstances, what method is most likely to discover the vein.

If you find, that the cover of alluvia, or rubble,

upon the superficies of the rock is thin, and the distance from the place where the shoad was found, to the highest part of the slope, is but short, you may begin a cut to the rock, upon the spot where you found it, and push your trench right up the slope, keeping the surface of the rock until you discover the vein. But if you should fail to discover the vein, by cutting upwards in a right line, then come down again to the foot of your trench, and there cut a little across, that, in case the vein should run in a right line, up and down, parallel to your cut, or in a diagonal direction, and you have been a little to one side at first setting out, you may by this means intersect it. If the cover upon the superficies of the rock is thick, it will, in that case, be troublesome and expensive to cut a long trench; and therefore, the best method is to sink a small shaft down through the cover, until you come to the solids, or undisturbed rock or Stratum.

Particular notice must be taken of every thing you see in going down with this shaft; and if you find bits of ore, of spar, or of good rider or vein-stone, it is to be supposed, that you are still below the vein; but if you can discover no mineral soil, nor any symptom of a vein, neither as you go down nor on the superficies of the rock, you have, perhaps, overshot the vein, and must come lower down, and sink another shaft about half-way between the first and the place where the shoad was found. On the contrary, if you find small pieces of ore, or lively mineral soil, in going down with the first shaft, in that case you should sink another, still further up in the line of the first, from the place where the shoad was found; and if the symptoms continue stronger in the second shaft, a third, a fourth, &c. must be sunk, still keeping the line.

If the symptoms should appear stronger, and more in quantity, in one side of your shaft than in the other, it is probable that the vein runs up and down the slope, parallel to your line of pitting. In this case, you should go to the shaft which contains the most and best mineral matter, and drive across, upon the face of the firm rock, into the most promising side; and if the symptoms increase as you advance, push forward your drift until you cut the vein.

With respect to the float ore, it is not presumed safe to advise any method of trial for discovering the vein it originally came from, until such vein is otherwise first discovered, it being very difficult to know how far the ore has been carried by the water, before it was lodged in its present bed; and, therefore, diligent search should be made on all hands, especially towards the higher grounds, to see if any other symptoms of a vein can be discovered, before you proceed to expensive trials for it. But, notwithstanding this caution against proceeding to expensive trials for the vein, it is highly proper to make trials upon the float ore itself, in order to discover what quantity there is of it, that you may be able to judge whether or not it is worth pursuing.

In trying the float ore, it is proper to make a trench or cut, quite down to the surface of the rock, and to push your trench forward in the way that most ore appears. It is likewise proper to push forward cross-cuts · from your first trench, every way where any ore leads you, as there may be nests or accumulated parcels of it, lodged on either hand, where not expected, and therefore it is proper to follow every symptom, and to examine every probable spot, especially flat or hollow places.

Whatever way the float ore may be discovered, it is expedient to make trials upon it every way, by trenching to the rock; and if the cover of clay, gravel, earth, or any other loose rubbish which lies above the

o o

float ore, should be in any place too thick for trenching, in that case you should put down pittings upon
it here and there; and if a quantity of ore is discovered
worth working, you are then to judge whether you
can raise it cheapest by throwing off the cover which
lies above, so as to lay the whole ore bare, or by mining it under-ground, and securing it over-head with
timber. Whatever method is chosen, as the ore lies
upon the surface of the rock, it is to be observed, that
there is a chance of discovering a vein, in trying and
raising the float ore.

Where either float or shoad ore is found in a settle,
or small flat spot in the middle of a sloping piece of
ground, or near the bottom of a slope, there is a very
good method of trial, besides trenching and pitting,
called *Hushing,** which is often practised with success;
and where circumstances are favourable, it is undoubtedly the most effectual, and at the same time the most
frugal method of trial for making discoveries; but it
is necessary that several favourable circumstances con-

* Considerable quantities of float ore have been procured
at *Greengill* mine, in *Alston-moor* by Hushing; and the same
mode of working continues to raise a considerable quantity,
under the direction of Mr. Thomas Shaw and Company. It
will be also necessary to remark, that this mine produces a
great quantity of white lead ore, or fine white crystals of carbonate of lead.

cnr to make hushing convenient.   In the *first* place,
a slope of considerable declivity, is absolutely necessary ; and in the *second* place, it is proper that water
can be collected into some convenient place, for making a dam-head, or reservoir, for the water, and the
higher up, such a head can be made, the better; but
the dam must be so situated, that you can make small
collateral diagonal cuts across the slope, on both sides,
to lead or conduct the water from small rivulets or
higher springs, and also rain water, into your reservoir.   If a little dingle, settle, flat, or hollow place,
can be had for the site of this reservoir, so much the
better, as the head can, in that case, be made with
the less expense to hold much water; but where such
a convenient spot cannot be had, they are often made
upon the inclining plane of the declivity in the form
of a crescent.   A large dam is always better than a
small one, if it can be had; and where the sloping
ground, to be hushed, is of any considerable length,
from the hush-dam down to the bottom of the slope,
the reservoir must contain a considerable quantity of
water, otherwise its force will be spent too soon, before
it proves effectual, to carry down the great quantity
of rubbish which the water will raise in a long hush-
gutter; and therefore, if your dam or reservoir has
not a level area, for the water to spread upon a consi-

derable superficies, it is necessary that the head
should be the higher, in order to make up in depth
what is wanting in the length and breadth of the piece
of water. It is necessary to hint, in general, that the
head of this reservoir and the sluice, must be wide, in
proportion to the quantity of water to be let out at
once, and to the strength of water necessary for securing the hush-gutter.

From this hush-dam you draw a line right down the
hill, unless there be some hillock or other obstruction
by the way, in which case you must draw your line in
such a direction as the water will run best in a trench,
or hush-gutter, when made. When you have marked
out the line of the hush-gutter all the way down to
the bottom of the slope, then cut off the sod or upper
surface of the ground out of it, about two or three
feet wide, and about a foot or a foot and a half deep,
all the length, to make room for it to contain a small
run of water; and when the gutter is so prepared, let
out but a small quantity or run of water at first, in
proportion to the capacity of the gutter; and when
the water is let out, the first two or three times, the
men must be divided, at proper distances from each
other, with their tools in their hands, to help to loosen
the earth for the water to carry away, and to take out

obstructions, which may stop the water, and turn it out of the gutter. The steeper the declivity, and the longer the gutter is, the greater force the water will exert.

The writer has seen stones of several tons weight, and as big as little huts, carried several hundred yards down a large hush gutter; and the water and stones, of all sizes, which the torrent carries down, wears, at last, not only the surface cover, which lies above the rock, but it also wears down, by the friction of the stones, a considerable depth of the superficies of the rock itself, and in consequence, it must discover and wash clean all the veins, useful and curious stones, &c. which cross the line of that gutter in any direction, by which means valuable discoveries are often made; and where water can be had, and can be properly used, hushing is, by far, a more effectual method, than either trenching or pitting.

When a hush is worn pretty deep, where there is a weighty cover, above the superficies of the rock, great stones or other obstructions will sometimes turn the water, to wear one side of the gutter more than the other; and sometimes both sides wear, undermine, and fall in, alternately, until the water is spread so wide, in that part of the gutter, that its force is lost.

In these cases, it is necessary to turn the big stones out of the way, on both sides, so as to give the water room to run, as near as possible, in a straight line, which is the only way to make it scour the bottom effectually.

This method of discovering veins by the help of water, in the manner pointed out, is very effectual, where the figure of the ground and other circumstances are convenient for this mode of trial; and it surely deserves the preference, because it may be said to bare the bone, and show us every thing that is to be seen in that section of the hill.

Mineral veins may be, and frequently are, discovered, in all places where the superficies of the Strata and rocks are to be seen, such as upon the rocky shores of the ocean and of lakes, in rocky precipices, in the rocky banks and beds of rivers and rivulets, in dingles or ravines, scars cr cliffs, and on all other places, where the solid superficies of the Strata are either to be seen, or have so thin a cover, that some of the mineral shoads are found mixed with the upper soil; but where there is a thick cover of clay, sand, and other loose matter, upon the surface of the rock, all mineral symptoms may then be perfectly concealed from our view, until such cover is cut through by some ditch or trench, or washed away by some rivulet or current of water, &c.

Wherever the regularity of the Strata is broken and interrupted, or any breach or fracture appears in the rock, there is some reason to suppose, that it is occasioned by a mineral vein; and therefore, when a considerable gash or crack is observed in the face of a rock, cutting across the Strata, it should be taken notice of and examined. The fissure of a vein may be distinguished from such a recent crack as is occasioned by undermining, by water, or the gradual yielding of a precipice.

The sides of an accidental recent fissure are generally rough, unequal, and jagged, and the chasm or space between the sides is generally empty, at least of mineral matter; whereas, the sides of the mineral veins are more regular, and may be traced in pretty straight lines, whether the vein stands nearly perpendicular, or in a heading or slanting position; and the space between the cheeks or sides, whether the vein is narrow or wide, is always filled, either in whole or in part, either with ore, or with such other mineral fossils, hard or soft, as usually accompany ore in the veins.

The Strata, which are generally the most productive of the metallic ores, are Lime-stones; most of the indurated argillaceous mountain rocks, of which there are many varieties, appearing in thick, thin, and middling Strata, some of these rocks are very hard, and others of moderate hardness. These mountain rocks are of various colours, though mostly of some of the shades of grey. Many rich and valuable mines are found, and worked, in granite, or moor-stone rocks; such, for instance, are the lead mines of *Strontian*, in the Highlands of Scotland, and several mines in *Cornwall*, &c. These three orders or classes of rocks, and Strata, are most commonly cut and intersected by mineral fissures, containing, in many instances, great quantities of the metallic and other mineral ores.

We shall now endeavour to give a List of the Mines, in *Alston-moor*, in the county of Cumberland; the two *Allendales* and *Derwent*, in Northumberland; *Weardale* and *Teesdale*, in the county Palatine of Durham; and also certain mines in Westmorland. It is necessary to observe, that some of the mines mentioned in the following List, are continuations of the same vein, on account of granting leases, or possessions of mines, on each vein, when of considerable length, each of which has its own name.

A LIST OF LEAD MINES,

Which are, or have been, worked

IN THE MANOR OF ALSTON,

In the county of Cumberland,

Belonging to the Commissioners and Governors of Greenwich Hospital; including the Mines at Cross-fell and Tyne-head; together with an Account of the other Mineral Substances they produce.

1 *Blagill,* one mile and a half E. of *Alston;* Lead, some Blend or Black Jack, with a little Fluor Spar and Quartz in the Coal Sills, Great Lime-stone, and Tuft or Water Sill.—Two Horse Levels.

2 *Brownley Hill,* four miles S. E. of *Alston;* Lead, much Blend or Black Jack, with some Fluor and Quartz, principally in the Great Lime-stone.—One Horse Level.

3 *Browngill,* one mile E. by N. of *Garrigill Gate;* some Lead, with Amorphous Fluor and Calc Spar, in the Strata, from the Fire-stone, to the Tuft or Water Sill (see Section, page 165).—Two Horse Levels. Occupied by the London Lead Company.

P p

4 *Blagill Foot* Cross Vein, one mile and a half E. by S. of *Alston;* some Lead, in Three Yards Lime-stone and Six Fathom Hazle below; cut in *Neat Force* Boat Level.

5 *Benty Field,* three-quarters of a mile N. E. of *Garrigill Gate;* some Lead, with Quartz, in the Coal Sills and Great Lime-stone.

6 *Backbone,* or Sulphur Vein, one mile and three-quarters S. W. of *Garrigill Gate;* a very broad Vein, composed of Amorphous White Quartz, with Pyrites, and Pyritical or Yellow Copper Ore, in Strata, from the Four Fathom Lime-stone to the bottom of the Scar Lime-stone (see Section, page 169).—One Draining Level.

7 *Baxton Burn,* four miles W. by S. of *Alston;* a Trial, in the Coal Sills and Great Lime-stone.

8 *Birch Bank,* four miles and a half S. W. of *Alston;* some Lead, with a little Fluor and Quartz, under the Four Fathom Lime-stone.

9 *Black Eshgill Head* Cross Vein, three miles and a half S. E. of *Garrigill Gate;* Lead, in Strata, from the High Coal Sill to the bottom of the Great Lime-stone.—One Horse Level, and one Water

Wheel Engine, under-ground. Occupied by the London Lead Company.

10 *Brigal Burn*, one-quarter of a mile W. of *Nent-head*; Lead, with Quartz and Fluor Spar, in Strata, from the High Slate Sill to the Tuft or Water Sill (see Section, page 167).—One Horse Level, and a Crushing Machine.

11 *Brigal Burn* Cross Vein, one-half mile W. of *Nenthead*; Lead, and Calamine, principally in the Great Lime-stone.

12 *Bayle Hill*, one-half mile S. of *Alston*; Galena, with Carbonates of Lead, and some Calc Sinter, principally in the Great Lime-stone.—One Horse Level.

13 *Cable Cleugh*, two miles S. by W. of *Nenthead*; Lead, with Crystallized and Amorphous Fluor Spar, in Strata, from the Fire-stone to the bottom of the Great Lime-stone.—One Whimsey Shaft. Occupied by the London Lead Company.

14 *Copper Slit*, three miles S. E. of *Garrigill Gate*; some Lead, with Iron Pyrites, principally in the Great Lime-stone.

15 *Clargill*, in *Tyne-head* Fell, four miles and a half

S. by E. of *Garrigill Gate;* Lead, rich in Silver, principally in the Scar Lime-stone.

16 *Clargill,* three miles N. E. of *Alston;* a Trial, in the Great Lime-stone.

17 *Cross Fell,* seven miles S. S. W. of *Alston;* much Lead, and Amorphous Fluor Spar, in Strata, from the Fire-stone to the Four Fathom Lime-stone.— One Whimsey, and two Horse Levels.

18 *Calvert,* in *Tyne-head* Fell, four miles and a half S. of *Garrigill Gate;* Lead, with Amorphous Fluor Spar, in Strata, from the Quarry Hazle to the bottom of the Scar Lime-stone (see Section, page 169).—One Horse Level.

19 *Cow Hill,* one-half mile S. W. of *Nenthead;* much Lead, principally in the Great Lime-stone.

20 *Cow Hill* Cross Vein, one-half mile S. W. of *Nenthead;* Lead, principally in the Great Lime-stone.

21 *Craig Green* Sun Vein, two miles and three-quarters S. by W. of *Alston;* Lead, principally in the Great Lime-stone, and Tuft or Water Sill.—One Horse Level, and one small Crushing Machine.

22 *Cowper Dyke-heads,* one mile N, N. E. of *Garri-*

gill Gate; Lead, with a little Fluor Spar, in Strata, from the High Coal Sill to the Four Fathom Lime-stone.—Two Horse Levels.

23 *Cornriggs,* two miles and three-quarters W. by S. of *Garrigill Gate;* Lead, with Quartz, and Iron Shot Copper Ore, in Strata, from the Four Fathom Lime-stone to the bottom of the Scar Lime-stone.—One Horse Level.

24 *Cash Burn,* three miles and a half W. by S. of *Garrigill Gate;* Lead, with some Pyritical Copper Ore, in Strata, from the Scar Lime-stone to the Single Post Lime-stone (see Section, pages 169 and 171).—One Water Wheel Engine here formerly.

25 *Craig Green* Middle Vein, one mile and three-quarters N. of *Garrigill Gate;* much Lead, principally in the Great Lime-stone.—One Horse Level.

26 *Craig Green* North Vein, one mile and a half S. of *Alston;* Lead, in the Great Lime-stone.—One Horse Level.

27 *Dowgang,* one-quarter of a mile W. of *Nenthead;* much Lead, principally in the Great Lime-stone. —One Horse Level,

28 *Dowpit Sike*, two miles S. by E. of *Alston;* Lead, in the Fire-stone, Coal Sills, and Great Lime-stone.—Two Water Levels.

29 *Doukes Burn*, four miles and a half S. W. of *Garrigill Gate;* Lead, in Strata, from the Four Fathom Lime-stone to the bottom of Nattriss Gill Hazle.—One Water Level.

30 *Eshgill Field*, one-half mile S. S. E. of *Garrigill Gate;* Lead, with Crystallized Quartz and Calc Spar, in the Scar Lime-stone.—One Water Wheel Engine here formerly.

31 *Flow Edge*, one mile and three-quarters S. S. E. of *Alston;* much Galena, with Carbonates and Oxides of Lead, and some Amorphous Fluor Spar, in Strata, from the High Slate Sill to the Tuft or Water Sill (see Section, page 167).—One Horse Level. One Crushing Machine here formerly.

32 *Fairnberry*, one mile and a quarter S. by E. of *Alston;* some Lead, principally in the Great Lime-stone.—One Draining Level.

33 *Fletchers*, one mile and a quarter N. E. of *Garrigill Gate;* Lead, with Fluor and Quartz Spar, in Strata, from the High Slate Sill to the Tuft or

Water Sill, but very poor in the Great Lime-stone.
—One Horse Level.

34 *Foreshield Grains*, one mile and a quarter, S. by
E. of *Alston*; a Trial, under the Four Fathom
Lime-stone.—One Horse Level.

35 *Greengill*, one mile and a quarter N. by W. of
Nenthead; much Lead, considerable quantities of
Shoad and Float Ore, with Carbonates and Oxides
of Lead, principally in the Slate Sills.—One
Horse Level.

36 *Grass Field*, one mile and a half N. of *Nenthead*;
much Lead, principally in the Great Lime-stone.
One Horse Level, and a large Crushing Machine.

37 *Gallygill Sike*, two miles N. N. W. of *Nenthead*;
Lead, principally in the Great Lime-stone.—One
Horse Level.

38 *Gallygill Sike* North Vein, two miles and a quarter N. N. W. of *Nenthead*; Lead, in the Four Fathom Lime-stone.

39 *Goodam-gill Moss*, three-quarters of a mile N.N.E.
of *Nenthead*; some Lead, with much Blend or
Black Jack, in the Great Lime-stone. Occupied
by the London Lead Company.

40 *Green-castle*, four miles S. W. of *Alston*; Lead, and Amorphous Fluor Spar, in Strata, from the top of the Great Lime-stone to Nuttriss Gill Hazle.—One Horse Level.

41 *Hudgill Burn*, two miles and a half S. by E. of *Alston*; very rich in Galena, with Carbonates and Oxides of Lead, in Strata, from the Fire-stone to the Quarry Hazle.—One Horse Level, and a Crushing Machine.

42 *Holey Field*, one mile and a half S. S. E. of *Alston*; much Lead, and Crystallized Arragonite, principally in the Great Lime-stone.—One Horse Level.

43 *High Tyne* Green Vein, in *Tyne-head* Fell, six miles S. of *Garrigill Gate*; Lead, with Amorphous Fluor Spar, in Strata, from the top of the Scar Lime-stone to the bottom of Tyne-bottom Lime-stone.—One Horse Level.

44 *Handsome Mea*, or Small Cleugh Vein, one mile S. by W. of *Nenthead*; much Lead, principally in the Great Lime-stone.—One Horse Level, and a Crushing Machine. Occupied by the London Lead Company.

45 *Lee House Well*, two miles and a half S. by W. of

Garrigill Gate; Lead, principally in the Six Fathom Hazle.—One Horse Level.

46 *Long Cleugh,* one mile and three-quarters S. of
Nenthead; much Lead, and Amorphous Fluor
Spar, with some Quartz, in Strata, from the Fire-
stone to the Tuft or Water Sill. Occupied by the
London Lead Company.

47 *Longhole Head,* two miles E. of *Garrigill Gate;*
much Lead, with Amorphous Fluor Spar, in Strata, from the High Slate Sill to the Four Fathom
Lime-stone.—One Whimsey. Occupied by the
London Lead Company.

48 *Little Gill,* two miles and a half S. E. of *Garrigill Gate;* Lead, with some Sulphate of Barytes,
and Calc Spar, in Strata, from the Fire-stone to
the bottom of the Great Lime-stone.

49 *Lough Vein,* two miles and a half E. of *Alston;*
Lead, Strata, Coal Sills, and Great Lime-stone.

50 *Middle Cleugh* Mines, two miles S. of *Nenthead;*
much Lead, with Crystallized Fluor and Quartz,
some Blend or Black Jack, in Strata, from the
top of the Fire-stone to the Tuft or Water Sill
(see plate 4th, figure 2nd). Occupied by the
London Lead Company.

51 *Nattriss* North Vein, two miles S. by E. of *Alston;* Lead, in Strata, from the Slate Sill to the bottom of the Great Lime-stone.

52 *Nattriss Red Groves,* two miles and a quarter S. by E. of *Alston;* Lead, in Strata, from the Fire-stone to the bottom of the Great Lime-stone.—One Horse Level.

53 *Nenthead Fields* Cross Vein, one-quarter of a mile E. by N. of *Nenthead;* much Lead, with Calamine, and some Blend or Black Jack, principally in the Great Lime-stone.—One Horse Level.

54 *Nentsberry Hags,* three miles and a half S. by E. of *Alston;* Lead, principally in the Great Lime-stone.—One Horse Level.

55 *North Grains* Cross Vein, alias *Cocklake;* Lead, principally in the Great Lime-stone.

56 *Nenthead Field,* alias *Pity Mea,* one-quarter of a mile E. by S. of *Nenthead;* Lead, principally in the Great Lime-stone.

57 *Old Carrs,* three-quarters of a mile S. by E. of *Nenthead;* much Lead, with Calc and Quartz, some Crystallized Arbestus, principally in the Great Lime-stone.—One Whimsey.

58 *Peat Stack Hill,* one-quarter of a mile W. of *Nenthead;* Lead, in the Tuft or Water Sill (See also *Dowgang).*

59 *Rampgill,* one-quarter of a mile S. of *Nenthead;* formerly exceedingly rich in Lead Ore, with Quartz and Blend or Black Jack, and Crystallized and Amorphous Fluor Spar, in Strata, from the Grind-stone Sill to the Four Fathom Lime-stone. —Five Whimseys, one Horse Level, one Water Wheel Engine under-ground; one Crushing Machine. Occupied by the London Lead Company.

60 *Roderhope Cleugh,* three miles and a half S. W. of *Alston;* Lead, with some Fluor Spar, principally in the Six Fathom Hazle.

61 *Scale-burn,* one-quarter of a mile S. of *Nenthead;* Lead, with Blend or Black Jack, some Fluor Spar, and Quartz, in Strata, from the High Slate Sill to the bottom of the Great Lime-stone (see Section, page 167).—One Horse Level and two Whimseys. Occupied by the London Lead Company.

62 *Smittergill Hills,* four miles and a half S. W. of *Alston;* Lead, with Amorphous Fluor Spar, in Strata, from Nattriss Gill Hazle to the Scar Lime-stone.

63 *Sir John's* Vein, two miles and three-quarters S. by
E. of *Garrigill Gate;* Lead, with double refracting
Calc Spar, in Strata, from the top of the Scar
Lime-stone to Tyne-bottom Plate.—One Horse
Level.

64 *Slote,* alias *Bunker's Hill,* one mile and a quarter
E. of *Alston;* some Lead, with Witherite or Car-
bonate of Barytes, and Calc Sinter, in the Coal
Sills (see Section, page 167).

65 *Thorngill,* East and West, one mile and a half E.
of *Alston;* Lead, with some Fluor and Calc Spar,
in Strata, from the Fire-stone to the Four Fathom
Lime-stone.

66 *Thoughtergill,* one mile and a half E. by N. of
Garrigill Gate; Lead, with some Fluor Spar, in
Strata, from the High Coal Sills to the bottom of
the Great Lime-stone. Occupied by the London
Lead Company.

67 *Tyne-bottom,* one-quarter of a mile N. of *Garrigill
Gate;* Lead, with Crystallized and Amorphous
Calc Spar, Slickensides or Specula Lead Glance,
principally in Tyne-bottom Lime-stone.—One
Water Wheel Engine; one Horse Level. Occu-
pied by the London Lead Company.

68 *Windy Brow*, three miles and a quarter S. E. of *Garrigill Gate*; Lead, with Fluor Spar, in Great Lime-stone and Scar Lime-stone.—Two Horse Levels.

69 *Welhope Knot*, one mile S. by E. of *Garrigill Gate*; Lead, with Amorphous Fluor Spar, from the top of the Great Lime-stone to the bottom of the Scar Lime-stone.

LIST OF LEAD MINES,

IN THE

TWO ALLENDALES,

In the Manor of Hexham, and County of Northumberland,
Belonging to Colonel and Mrs. Beaumont.

◆

1 *Allenheads*, seven miles S. of *Allendale Town*, and four miles E. of *Coalcleugh*, consisting of several Veins, viz. *Poverty Vein, Sun Vein, Diana Vein, Blackett Vein, Style Vein, Christopher Mills' Vein, Grind-stone Vein*, &c.; much Lead, with Crystallized Cubical Spar, blue, purple, amber, &c., and also Carbonates of Lead, some Blend or Black Jack, with Quartz, in Strata, from the Grind-stone Sill to the Four Fathom Lime-stone (see Section, page 165).—One Horse Level, upon the Fire-stone,

called *Fawside* Level, begun in the year 1776, under the direction of the Author's Father; one Water Level, known by the name of the Haugh Level, begun in Sir William Blackett's time; four Water Wheel Engines, under-ground; seven Whimseys, one of them under-ground; and a large Crushing Machine.

2 *Coalcleugh*, two miles E. of *Nenthead*, and seven miles and three-quarters S.S.W. of *Allendale Town;* consisting of several veins (see page 275); much Lead, and Blend or Black Jack, with coloured Cubical and Amorphous Fluor Spar and Quartz, in Strata, from the Grind-stone Sill to the Four Fathom Lime-stone.—One Water Wheel, and one Pressure Engine, under-ground; five Whimseys, two of them under-ground; two Horse Levels, viz. *Coalcleugh* Level and *Barney Crag* Level; and one Water Level, begun in Sir Wm. Blackett's time; one Large Crushing Machine.

3 *Hearty Cleugh*, in *Welhope*, three miles and a half N. W. of *Coalcleugh;* Lead, with some Calc Spar, principally in the Great Lime-stone.

4 *Kearsley Well*, four miles and a half N. by W. of *Coalcleugh;* Lead, principally in the Great Lime-stone.—One Horse Level.

5 *Swinhope Head*, one mile and a half E. of *Coal-cleugh*; Lead, with some Blend or Black Jack, principally in the Great Lime-stone.—One Horse Level, begun under the direction of Mr. William Crawhall, the Agent; and one Crushing Machine.

6 *Sipton*, four miles N. of *Allenheads*; a Trial, in Slate Sills and Fire-stone.

7 *Welhope Head*, one mile and a half N. W. of *Coal-cleugh*; Lead, with Sulphate and Witherite or Carbonate of Barytes, in Strata, from the High Slate Sill to the bottom of the Great Lime-stone.—Two Horse Levels, begun under the direction of the late Mr. Joseph Dickinson.

LIST

OF SOME MINES IN DERWENT,

In the counties of Northumberland and Durham.

1 *Jeffries' Rake*, two miles and a half S. W. of *Blanchland*; Lead, with Fluor and Quartz Spar, Strata, Slate Sills, &c. down to the Great Lime-stone.—One Steam, one Water Wheel Engine, and one Crushing Machine.

2 Old and New *Shieldon*, one mile N..of *Blanchland;* Lead, with Fluor and Quartz Spar, Strata, from the Fell-top Lime-stone to the Great Lime-stone.— One Steam Engine, and one Crushing Machine.

3 *White Heaps*, three miles and a half W. of *Blanch-land;* Lead, with Fluor and Quartz Spar, Strata, Slate Sills, and Fire-stone.—One Pressure Engine.

LIST OF THE LEAD MINES,
IN WEARDALE,

Belonging to the Right Rev. the Bishop of Durham;

And principally occupied by Col. & Mrs. Beaumont.

1 *Black Dean*, one mile N. E. of *St. John's Chapel;* Lead, with Fluor Spar, Strata, from the top of the Great Lime-stone to the bottom of the Four Fathom Lime-stone.

2 *Birkon-side*, or *Brecon-sike*, three miles and a quarter N. E. of *St. John's Chapel;* much Lead, and Fluor Spar, Strata, Coal Sills, and Great Lime-stone.—One Horse Level, one Water Wheel Engine, and one large Crushing Machine.

3 *Bolts Burn*, in *Rookhope*, four miles and a half
N. E. of *Stanhope;* Lead and Fluor Spar, principally in the Coal Sills and Great Lime-stone.

4 *Brandon Walls*, in *Rookhope*, four miles N. by E.
of *Stanhope;* Lead, with Calc and Fluor Spar, in
Strata, from the top of the Great Lime-stone into
the Five Yards Lime-stone.—One Water Wheel
Engine.

5 *Cowhoes*, in *Kilhope*, five miles N. by W. of *St.*
John's Chapel; Lead, raised by Hushing, in the
Coal Sills, Great Lime-stone, Tuft or Water Sill,
and Quarry Hazle.

6 *Corbit Mea*, and *Grove Rake*, in *Rookhope*, eight
miles and a half N. by E. of *Stanhope;* Lead,
raised by Hushing, principally in the Slate Sills
and Fire-stone.

7 *Chapel Pasture*, one mile W. of *St. John's Chapel;*
Lead, with Fluor Spar, Strata unknown.

8 *Crawlaw*, one mile S. of *Stanhope;* Lead, with
Fluor Spar, Strata, Coal Sills and Great Lime-
stone.

9 *Foul Wood*, in *Rookhope*, five miles and a half N.
by E. of *Stanhope;* Lead and Fluor Spar, in

R r

Strata, from the Fire-stone to the Great Lime-stone.

10 *Guinea Grove*, four miles N. by E. of *St. John's Chapel*; Lead, in Strata, from the top of the Coal Sills to the bottom of the Great Lime-stone.

11 *Green Field*, in *Weardale*, three miles and a half N. by E. of *St. John's Chapel*; Lead, with Fluor Spar, in Strata, from the top of the Coal Sills to the bottom of the Great Lime-stone.

12 *Hazly-hill* Vein, in *Kilhope*, five miles and a half N. of *St. John's Chapel*; Lead, principally in the Great Lime-stone.

13 *Harehope Gill*, two miles and a half W. N. W. of *Wolsingham*; Lead and Fluor Spar, in Strata, from the High Coal Sill to the bottom of the Great Lime-stone.

14 *Ireshope*, two miles N. by E. of *St. John's Chapel*; a Trial, making by the London Lead Company, in the Scar Lime-stone.—One Water Wheel Engine.

15 *Kilhope Burn*, or *Burn Grove* Vein, three miles and a half N. of *Nenthead*; Lead, principally in the Great Lime-stone.

16 *Kilhope Head*, North and South Veins; Lead,

with Blend or Black Jack, and Fluor Spar, in Strata, from the Fire-stone to the bottom of the Great Lime-stone.

17 *Level Grove*, in *Kilhope*, six miles N. by E. of *St. John's Chapel*; Lead, some fourteen-sided Galena, principally in the Great Lime-stone.

18 Three, *Lodge-field*, or *New-house* Veins, two miles N. by E. of *St. John's Chapel*; Lead, with Amorphous and Crystallized Fluor Spar, in Strata, from the Fire-stone to the Four Fathom Lime-stone.

19 *Level Gate*, one mile N. E. of *St. John's Chapel*; Lead, with Fluor Spar, principally in the Coal Sills and Great Lime-stone.—One Horse Level.

20 *Midge Pits*, three miles N. E. of *St. John's Chapel*; Lead, with Fluor Spar, in Strata, from the High Coal Sill to the bottom of the Great Lime-stone.

21 *Middlehope* Old Vein, two miles and a half N. E. of *St. John's Chapel*; much Lead, with Amorphous and Crystallized Fluor Spar, in Strata, from the Slate Sills to the bottom of the Great Lime-stone.—Two or three Whimseys, and one Horse Level.

22 *Middlehope* New Vein, two miles and a half N. E. of *St. John's Chapel;* much Lead, with Amorphous and Crystallized Fluor Spar, in Strata, from the Slate Sills to the bottom of the Great Lime-stone.— One Horse Level, one Pressure Engine, and one Crushing Machine. Occupied by the London Lead Company.

23 *Middle Grove* Vein, in *Kilhope*, five miles and a half N. by E. of *St. John's Chapel;* Lead, principally in the Great Lime-stone.

24 *Old Faw*, two miles and a half N. by E. of *St. John's Chapel;* Lead and Fluor Spar, in Strata, from the Fire-stone to the bottom of the Great Lime-stone.

25 *Pudding Thorn*, five miles N. by E. of *St. John's Chapel;* Lead, in Strata, from the High Coal Sill to the bottom of the Great Lime-stone.—One Horse Level.

26 *Pasture Grove*, three miles and a half N. E. of *St. John's Chapel;* much Lead, with Crystallized and Amorphous Coloured Cubical Fluor Spar, Strata, from the Fire-stone to the bottom of the Four Fathom Lime-stone.—One Horse Level; one Water Wheel Engine.

27 *Quarry Hill,* one mile and a half W. of *Stanhope;* Lead, principally in the Great Lime-stone.

28 *Rispey,* in *Rookhope,* six miles N. by E. of *Stanhope;* Lead and Fluor Spar, in Strata, from the Coal Sills to the bottom of the Great Lime-stone.

29 *Stanhope Burn,* one mile and a half N. E. of *Stanhope;* Lead, principally in the Great Lime-stone.

30 *Scraith Head,* four miles and a half N. W. of *St. John's Chapel;* Lead, with Fluor Spar, principally in the Great Lime-stone——One Horse Level.

31 *Sedlin,* three miles and a half N. by E. of *St. John's Chapel;* Lead, with Fluor Spar, in Strata, from the Slate Sills to the bottom of the Great Lime-stone.—Four Whimseys; one Horse Level.

32 *Scar Sike,* in *Rookhope,* six miles and a half N. by E. of *Stanhope;* Lead, with Fluor and Quartz Spar, Strata, Coal Sills, and Great Lime-stone.

33 *Softly Side,* one mile and a half W. of *Stanhope;* Lead and some Fluor Spar, Strata, from the top of the Great Lime-stone to Tyne-bottom Lime-stone.

34 *Wears Head,* two miles and a half N. by E. of

St. John's Chapel; Lead, with Fluor Spar, Strata, from the top of the Great Lime-stone to the Scar Lime-stone.

35 *Wolfcleugh,* Old and New Veins, seven miles and a half N. by E. of *Stanhope;* much Lead, with Coloured, Cubical, and Amorphous Fluor Spars, Strata, from the top of the Fire-stone to the bottom of the Great Lime-stone.—One Water Wheel Engine, and two Whimseys.

36 *White's Level,* one mile E. by N. of *St. John's Chapel;* Lead, with Coloured, Cubical, and Amorphous Fluor Spar, Strata, Coal Sills and Great Lime-stone.

LIST OF LEAD MINES,

IN TEESDALE,

In the County of Durham,

The Property of the Earl of Darlington.

◆

1 *Armstrong* Vein, at *Pike Law,* six miles and a half N. E. of *Middleton;* much Lead, with some Fluor Spar and Honey Comb, or Vesicular Iron Spar, principally in the Great Lime-stone.

2 *Ashgill Head,* thirteen miles N. W. of *Middleton;* much Lead, with some Fluor Spar, Strata, from the Low Slate Sill to the bottom of the Four Fathom Lime-stone. — One Horse Level, three Whimseys, and one Crushing Machine.

3 *Blakeley Green,* four miles and a half N. W. of *Middleton;* a Trial.

4 *Beadley Hill,* six miles and a half N. E. of *Middleton;* Lead, principally in the Great Lime-stone.

5 *Beck Head,* six miles W. of *Middleton;* a Trial.— One Horse Level, in the Tuft or Water Sill.

6 *Caldberry,* one mile and a half N. of *Middleton;* much Lead, with some Fluor Spar, Strata, above the Low Coal Sill.—One Horse Level; one Crushing Machine.

7 *Comes,* eight miles N. W. of *Middleton;* a Trial.

8 *Dubby Sike,* twelve miles W. of *Middleton;* Lead, with Sulphate of Barytes, and some Calc Spar, Strata, Scar Lime-stone down to the Whin-stone.

9 *Elphytorey,* one mile and a half N. E. of *Middleton;* a Trial.

10 *East Reveling,* one mile and a half N. by W. of *Middleton;* Lead, Strata, Coal Sills.

11 *East Cowgreen*, ten miles W. of *Middleton;* Lead, with Sulphate of Barytes, Strata, Scar Lime-stone and Tyne-bottom Lime-stone.

27 East and West *Rake*, two miles E. of *Middleton;* Lead, worked in the Great Lime-stone.

12 *Flakebridge*, three miles E. of *Middleton;* Lead, with some Fluor Spar, Strata, Coal Sills.

13 *Flushamea*, five miles and a half N. E. of *Middleton;* Lead, with some Fluor Spar, principally in the Great Lime-stone.

14 *Grass Caldberry*, ten miles N. W. of *Middleton;* Lead, worked in High Brig-stone Hazle, or Quarry Hazle.

15 *Grass Hill*, twelve miles N. W. of *Middleton;* much Lead, some Carbonates and Phosphates of Lead, Strata, from the Coal Sills to the Four Fathom Lime-stone.—One Horse Level.

16 *High Dike* Cross Vein, one-quarter of a mile E. of *Middleton;* Lead, principally in the Great Lime-stone.

17 *Harbury Hill* Vein, one mile and a half N. E. of *Middleton;* a Trial.

18 *Hungary* and *Harrison* Veins, four miles N. W. of *Middleton;* Lead, principally in the Great Lime-stone.

19 *Hope Slit,* two miles N. W. of *Middleton;* Lead, with some Fluor Spar, principally in the Great Lime-stone.

20 *High Hurth,* six miles and a half N. W. of *Mid-dleton;* Lead, worked in the Low Coal Sill.

21 *Harthope,* seven miles and a half N. W. of *Mid-dleton;* a Trial.

22 *Hawksike,* twelve miles N. W. of *Middleton;* Lead, worked in the Brig-stone Hazle.

23 *Hunter Moss,* fifteen miles N. W. of *Middleton;* a Trial.

24 *Langdon Head,* eight miles N. W. of *Middleton;* Lead, worked in the Great Lime-stone.

25 *Mannergill,* two miles E. of *Middleton;* much Lead, worked in the High Coal Sill.

26 *Mannergill* North Vein, three miles N. of *Middle-ton;* Lead, worked in the Great Lime-stone.

27 *New Streak, Tarnstreak,* and *Wester-head* Veins, at *Pike Law,* six miles W. of *Middleton;* much

Lead, with some Fluor Spar, worked in Coal
Sills and Great Lime-stone.

28 *North and South Side,* six miles W. of *Middleton;*
Lead, worked in the Great Lime-stone.

29 *Old Marlbeck,* one mile and a half N. E. of *Middleton;* Lead, worked in the Great Lime-stone.

30 *Old Langdon,* eight miles N. W. of *Middleton;*
Lead, worked in the Great Lime-stone.

31 *Red-groves, Lodge Sike,* and *Wiregill,* one mile
N. of *Middleton;* Lead, worked in the High Coal
Sill.

32 *Racket Gill* and *Parken Grove,* three miles and a
half N. E. of *Middleton;* Lead, worked in the
Great Lime-stone.

33 *Skeers,* one mile and a half N. E. of *Middleton;*
Lead, worked in the Great Lime-stone.

34 South *Long Cleugh Head,* thirteen miles N. W. of
Middleton; Lead, worked in the Four Fathom
Lime-stone.

35 *Trough Head* Vein, ten miles N. W. of *Middleton;*
worked in the Great Lime-stone.

36 *West Cowgreen,* eleven miles W. of *Middleton;*

Lead, with Sulphate of Barytes, Strata, Scar Lime-stone down to the Whin-stone.

37 *Willy Hole*, twelve miles N. W. of *Middleton*; Lead, with Sulphate of Barytes, in the Scar Lime-stone.

38 *West Reveling*, one mile and a half N. by W. of *Middleton*; a Trial. *

A LIST

OF

SOME MINES IN WESTMORLAND,

The Property of the Earl of Thanet.

◆

1 *Dun-fell*, eight miles N. E. of *Appleby*, and four miles N. by E. of *Dufton*; Lead, with Calc Spar, and some Sulphate of Barytes, in Strata, from the Fire-stone to the bottom of the Great Lime-stone.

---

* I beg leave to return my Acknowledgments, to Mr. Barnes, of Eggleston, for his kind assistance with the above List, of the *Teesdale* Mines.

2 *Dufton-fell*, three miles and a half E. by N. of *Dufton;* Lead, with Amorphous and fine Crystallized Sulphate of Barytes, Strata, principally Tyne-bottom Lime-stone.—One Crushing Machine.

3 *Force Burn*, six miles and a half E. by N. of *Dufton;* Lead and Sulphate of Barytes, in the Whinstone, close by the river Tees.

4 *Hard Shins*, seven miles and three-quarters N. E, of *Dufton;* Lead, principally in Tyne-bottom Lime-stone and Whet-stone Bed.

5 *Hilton* and *Merton* Mines, two miles E. of *Hilton;* Lead, with Massive Sulphate of Barytes, Strata, Tyne-bottom Lime-stone and the Jew Lime-stone. —One Crushing Machine. The property of Earl Lonsdale; occupied by John Bland, Esq.

6 *Knockergill Head*, three miles and a half N. E. of *Dufton;* Lead, with Massive and Crystallized Sulphate of Barytes, Strata, principally Tyne-bottom Lime-stone.

7 *Low Hearth*, six miles N. E. of *Dufton;* a Trial, in the Scar Lime-stone.

8 *Nether Hearth*, seven miles and a half N. E. of *Dufton;* Lead, with Calc and Fluor Spar, principally in Tyne-bottom Lime-stone.

9 *Silver Band*, seven miles N. E. of *Appleby*, and three miles N. by E. of *Dufton;* Lead, with Massive and Crystallized Sulphate of Barytes, in Strata, from the Fire-stone to the bottom of the Great Lime-stone (see Section, page 167).

10 *Stake Beck*, five miles E. by N. of *Dufton;* Lead, with Fluor Spar, Strata, from the Four Fathom Lime-stone to the bottom of the Six Fathom Hazle.

11 *Tees Side* Mine, eight miles N. E. of *Dufton*, and six miles S. by E. of *Garrigill Gate*, in Cumberland; Lead, with Massive Fluor Spar, Strata, Tyne-bottom Lime-stone, Whet-stone Bed, and Whin-stone.—One Water Wheel Engine; occupied by Mr. Wm. Todd, of *Alston.*

12 *Thralkeld Side*, three miles E. by N. of *Dufton;* Lead, with Massive and Crystallized Sulphate of Barytes, Strata, Jew Lime-stone and Smiddy Lime-stone.

A TREATISE,

&c.

PART III.

OF

THE DISCOVERY OF MINES.

◆

THE principles of the Investigation and Discovery of Mines, depend upon a particular sagacity or acquired habit of judging, from particular signs, that metallic matters are contained in certain parts of the earth, at no great distance below its surface. The peculiar signs of a latent metallic Vein, seem reducible to general heads : such as, 1st, the finding pieces of ore on the surface of the ground. 2nd, the discovery of certain mineral waters.* 3rd, the finding

---

* The presence of copper, in any water, is easily discovered, by immerging in it a small piece of polished iron, which will thus instantly be turned of a copper colour, by reason of the precipitation of the metal upon it. A candle, or a piece of tallow put into water of this kind, will, in a short time, be tinged of a green colour.

of Vein-stone or Rider. 4th, the finding of metallic sands. 5th, the discolouration of the trees or grass, in particular situations. 6th, the ascension of warm exhalations and the like; all which are so many encouragements for making stricter search, near the places where such symptoms appear.

But when no evident mark of a mine appears externally, the skilful mineralist usually sinks or drives into the earth, in such places, as, from some analogy of knowledge, gained by experience, or by observing the situation, course, or nature of other mines, he judges, may contain metallic ores. When the mineralist has reason to suppose, that certain Veins bear towards any particular spot, the most effectual way of proving their existence, is by driving an adit or level from the lowest ground, across the bearing of the Veins, by which means there is a certainty of cutting all the Veins, within the limits of his level, at twenty, thirty, or forty fathoms deep, if the level admits of it. In driving adits or levels across to *unwater* mines already discovered, there are, sometimes, many fresh Veins found, which frequently prove better than those to which they were driving.

After the mine is discovered, the next thing to be

considered is, whether it may be worked to advantage; and in order to determine this point, we are duly to weigh the nature of the place and its situation, as to wood, water, carriage, healthiness, and the like, and compare the result with the richness of the ore, and the charge of digging, crushing, stamping, washing, and smelting.

Particularly the form and situation of the spot should be well considered. Mountains and hills are wrought with the greatest ease and convenience, chiefly because the drains and burrows, that is, the levels or adits may be, in these situations, readily cut, both to drain the water and to form *gang-ways* for bringing out the ore, &c.

In all cases, we are to look out for the Veins, which rains, or other accidental circumstances, may have laid bare, and if such a Vein be found, it may often be proper to open the mine at that place, especially if the Vein proves tolerably large and rich, otherwise the most commodious place for a situation is to be chosen for the purpose.

_____

ON

THE OPENING OF MINES.

◆

When it is once ascertained, that Ores of a Metal can be worked to advantage, in any particular place, the Mine-master proceeds in his operations, by endeavouring to extract the metallic matter by all the mechanical means which the art possesses. These consist in sinking Shafts, driving Levels or Adits, employing various Machines, to raise the water, renew the air, favour the ascent and descent of the workmen, prevent the earth from giving way, &c.

In general, after having proved that the ground contains Ores, or if their existence is rendered probable, by the various indications before stated, a Level or Adit, is driven, if the nature of the situation will admit it, but if a Level cannot be driven, a square perpendicular Shaft is sunk in the ground, sufficiently wide to contain ladders for the convenience of ascent and descent. In this Shaft may be placed also Pumps, to draw out the water which may collect at the bottom,

T t

and over it Machinery for the purpose of raising and lowering the Buckets or *Kibbles,* and pumping the water.

If the Ore be too deep for a single Shaft to reach it, at the bottom of the first Shaft, a horizontal Gallery is opened, at the end of which a second Shaft, or *Sump,* is sunk, and in this manner the workmen proceed till they arrive at the bottom of the Mine; but, in cases where a quantity of water is to remove from the Mine, by means of Pumps, it is generally necessary to have a single perpendicular Shaft from the surface to the lowest part of the workings.

When the Rock, to be perforated, is hard and solid and capable of supporting itself, the Shaft will not require to be guarded within; but if it be soft and friable, or threatens to fall in during the excavation, it becomes necessary to support the Shaft and Gallery with pieces of wood-work covered with planks all round, or a circular stone wall, where stones can be procured.

It is also of the utmost consequence to obtain a free current of fresh air. Where it is practicable to obtain a Gallery, which shall lead from the bottom of the

Shaft to the day or open air, a current is easily established by this simple artifice; but if this is not possible, a second Shaft is sunk, at the extremity of the
Gallery, opposite to the first, and if it opens at a different Level from the other, a circulation and conse-
quent renewal of air immediately takes place. If the
secondary Shaft be of equal height with the former,
the circulation will not take place spontaneously, and
a lighted furnace must be employed near the bottom
of one of the Shafts, to destroy the equilibrium of the
confined air.

The destructive Elastic Fluids, which are so frequently disengaged in the cavities of Mines, and particularly the Carbonic Acid Gas, and different species
of mixed Hydrogen Gasses, are among the most for-
midable enemies of miners. The former of these
Gasses is more generally known by the term *Choak
Damp*, or *Foul Air*, and the latter by that of *Fire
Damp*. Galleries, fires, ventilators, inflammation,
by means of torches held at a great distance, in those
parts of the Mines which are thus mephitized, and
particularly the various methods of causing fresh air
to enter, are the only remedies which until lately have
been opposed to these subterraneous evils. Within
these few years a Lamp has been invented by that dis-

tinguished Philosopher Sir Humphrey Davy, the flame of which is covered with wire-gauze, and by that means prevented from igniting the inflammableGasses. The occurrence of Choak Damp, or Foul Air, is very common in many of the Mines, which we have before described, but the Fire Damp has not been met with except in the Great Aqueduct Level, called *Next Force* Level, where it has once or twice exploded.

ON

THE WORKING OF MINES.

In treating of this part of the Art of Mining, we shall commence with the most proper method of Working the Mines of an extensive district. In the first place, it becomes necessary to commence by collecting and arranging all the knowledge we can acquire respecting the various Veins which traverse the district in question, as well as the relations they severally bear to one another. We should afterwards construct a Geognostic Plan of the district, and attach to it a Geognostic Description. This Plan and Description should be formed according to the same principles, be equally complete, and have such a relation

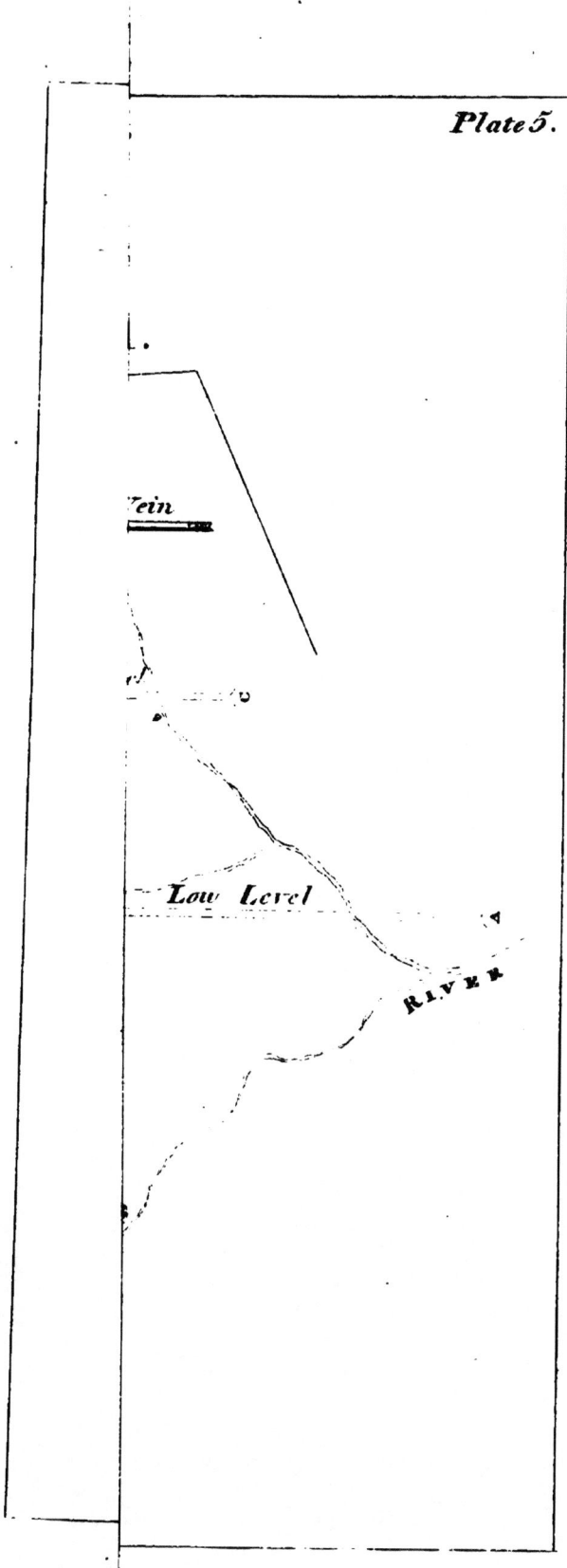

Plate 5.

Vein

Low Level

RIVER

to each other, that the same explanation may apply to both. If these two works are properly completed and made with accuracy they will form a Ground-work, from which may be drawn, in the surest manner, all the Plans and Schemes relative to the future working of the Mines, in the district to which they are adapted.

The Geognostic Plan should consist of two Maps or principal Designs: one the Ground Plan, taken at the surface, which may be called the External Plan of the district; the other should be a Horizontal Plan, accompanied by a Vertical Section, made to represent the interior of the ground, and it is upon this, that all remarkable Geognostic objects are to be traced.

On the External Plan should be marked the situation of each Vein, as, for instance, let us suppose the Vein D (figure 1st, plate 5th) makes its appearance at the out-burst, or basset, of the *High Coal Sill*, the low Level, or principal draining Level, commences at A, upon the *Great Lime-stone*, and the uppermost Level, C, is drove upon the *High Coal Sill*, &c.

The throw of each Vein ought to be represented

upon the Plan thus $\overline{\overline{}}^{a}_{b}$ the upper side or cheek
with a weak line, as at *a*, and the lower side or cheek
with a strong line, as at *b*; this being of great importance respecting the crossing and traversing of veins.

On the Internal Plan, or Horizontal Map, should
be represented, all the windings and turnings of the
different Levels drove upon the Veins, with all the
subterranean Shafts, or *Sumps*, made from those
Levels, and each separate Level should be distinguished by different colours, as in plate 5th, figure 2nd.
Those who wish for further information, relative to the
Surveying of Mines, are referred to Mr. Thomas
Fenwick's Treatise on Subterraneous Surveying.

The Internal Section, plate 6th, figure 3rd, shows
the depth of each subterranean Shaft, or *Sump*, sunk
into the Strata upon the vein, and will correspond
with the Horizontal Map, plate 5th, figure 2nd.
Upon the south Vein, at *e, e, e, e, e,* and *d*, the *Low
Level* is driven through the *East Cross Vein*, at *g*,
and the Horizontal Map shows the intersection and
traversing. At *r*, plate 6th, figure 3rd, is a Shaft sunk
from the surface, in order to make a current of air cir-
culate through the different workings made upon the

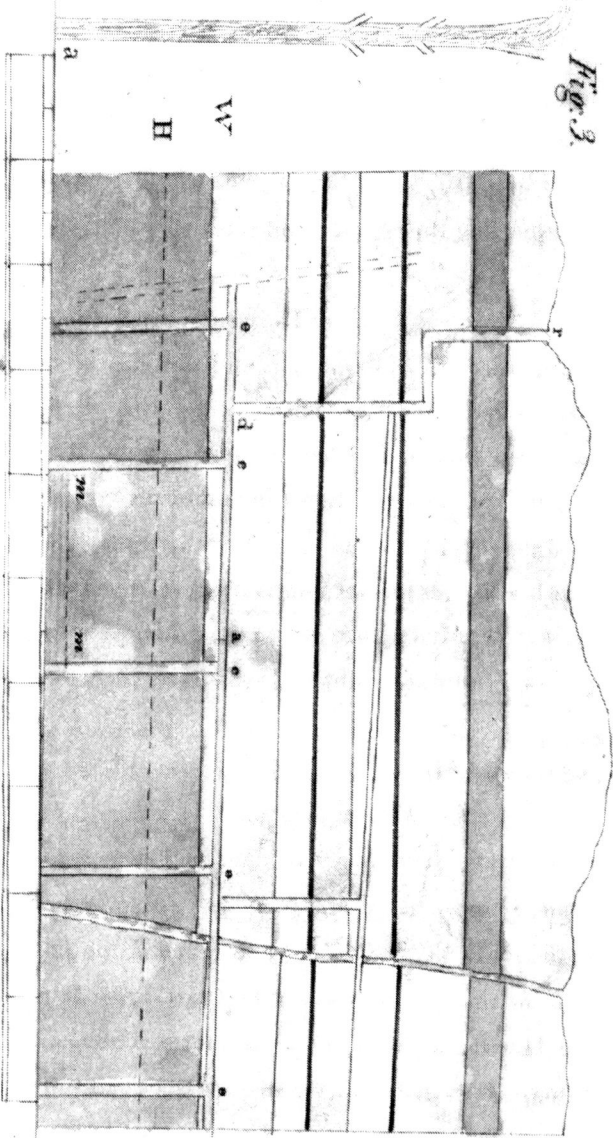

Fig. 3.

Fig. 5.

vein, and the darker shade, *m, m, m, m,* is to show the part excavated in procuring the Metallic Ores.

There ought, likewise, to be a Description of the Mining District, an account of its External Surface, of its Situation, Limits, and the Strata, which it contains; this description ought also to contain an exact account, both general and particular, or rather individual, of the different known and remarkable Mineral Repositories contained in the district.

There should also be kept Books of Record, specifying all the traversings, ramifications, and throws, of the different Veins, as far as can be ascertained; together with the general rise and dip of the Strata, both within the influence of the different Veins and at a distance, when they seem to pursue their natural inclination.

The Section of the Strata, plate 6th, figure 4th, is intended to show the inclination or hade of the south Vein, with its influence upon the Strata on both sides; and this Section will be found to correspond, either with the External Plan, plate 5th, figure 1st, or the the Internal Plan, figure 2nd. The distance, *e, a,* shows, how far the Sump, *e,* ought to be from the

Vein, at *a,* in order to meet with it again near the bottom of the Stratum of *Lime-stone.* S. N. and *x, x,* are two Cross Cuts into the Vein, supposed to have been driven in the course of sinking, the dotted lines are intended to show the occurrence of the *Black Bed, High, Middle,* and *Low* Flats (see page 103.)

There should likewise be kept Books of all the Bearing of the different Veins occurring in the district, and these bearings should be reduced to the true meridian, on account of the variation of the needle.

The expense of working Mines varies greatly at different mining fields and in different countries; it is, therefore, impossible to state any general estimate which will universally apply; I shall, however, endeavour to give an idea of the charges, in the Mines at *Alston-moor* and the places adjacent. But even here the expense of Mining depends a great deal upon the various situations of the places where the Mines occur, with respect to draining of water, drawing out the stone and ores, and likewise the different Strata, to drive or sink in.

As Mines generally occur in hilly or mountainous grounds, and may be drained by means of Levels or

Adits, drove from the bottoms of the hills or mountains, we shall commence with the expense of driving, those Levels, per fathom, in the different beds which have been most productive of Metallic Ores, and in the *Plate Beds*, or indurated Argillaceous Earths, in which Ores have been very seldom found to occur, but these last are better to drive in than other beds of harder Stone ; therefore, when there is a situation for Draining the Mines, by Levels, and a Plate Bed can be found to answer the purpose, it is preferable to any other.

The measures generally used, in *Alston-moor*, for Horse Levels, are, from three feet four inches to four feet wide, and six feet high, or thereabouts, and such Levels may be driven, at first, in a Plate, to the length of twenty or thirty fathoms, for, from One Pound to One Pound Ten Shillings, per fathom, exclusive of the charge for *arching*, *wooding*, and *railing*. But, as the Level proceeds further into the hill, the incumbent weight becomes greater, the Plate, Shale, or Schistus, more indurated, and the distance longer to remove the rubbish, and it may be necessary to increase the price, per fathom, to three or four pounds or upwards.

It sometimes happens, that a *Plate Bed* cannot be found to answer the intended purpose, when it may become necessary to drive in Lime-stone, hard Sand-stone, or Hazle. These rocks can very seldom be worked without Blasting with Gunpowder; * and, when this is the case, such Levels will require from four to five, six or eight pounds, per fathom, exclusive of the *railing*, &c. as before. When those Levels have proceeded to the length of 50 or 60 fathoms, the miners generally require a circulation of fresh air; and for this purpose, either a *bore-hole* may be put down, or a Shaft sunk, so as to communicate with the farthest part of their workings. If there is a small stream or rivulet of water at the surface, it may be allowed to fall into a cistern or tub, at the bottom of the *bore-hole* or Shaft, and it has the effect of carrying down, along with it, a current of air. This contrivance is called, by the miners, a *water blast*, and is represented in plate 6th, figure 5th, where *a* is the

---

* The method of Blasting is performed thus:—The miners bore a long cylindrical hole, like the hollow of a large gun barrel, with an iron instrument, hardened with steel at the end, like a chisel, which is called a *jumper:* after the hole is bored as far as they think necessary, it is then filled with a proportionate quantity of gunpowder; and another instrument introduced into the hole, called a *pricker:* then, they firmly ramming down the charge, with Plate, or hardened Clay, with another instrument, called a *driver* or *drivel*, the pricker is withdrawn; after that they introduce a squib, at which they leave a match to fire it.

pipe or shaft through which the water descends into the cistern; and *b* the box, that conveys the accumulated air to the workmen. The manner in which it operates is evident, from the Plate, and by this simple artifice, a Level may be drove to the length of four or five hundred fathoms. *

The expense of sinking likewise depends much upon the depth that they are from the surface or Level, as the expense of drawing out the stone or earth increases, according to the depth, and the different beds become harder or more indurated.

The measures used for *Whimsey* or Horse Engine Shafts, are generally about four feet six inches long by 3 feet broad, and the price, per fathom, depends a great deal upon the Strata through which there is occasion to sink. Whimsey Shafts may be sunk to the depth of ten or fifteen fathoms, at from about two pounds ten to three or four pounds, per fathom, and after that from five to six or eight pounds, per fathom, exclusive of the charge for timber, walling, &c.

---

* In some machines of this kind, the constructors seem to have been of opinion, that a great height was required in the waterfall, but Doctor Lewis, who hath made a great number of experiments upon the subject, shows, that an excess in height can never make up for a deficiency in the quantity of the water.

In *Alston-moor*, after a Mine is opened and appears
to be productive, the miners take a certain piece of
ground, commonly called a *length*, in which they propose to raise Ore, for a certain time, at so much per
Bing,* according to the richness of the Mine or working.† A length of ground is commonly either twelve,
fifteen, or twenty fathoms, and the price of procuring the Ore, depends much upon the hardness, the
expense of drawing the Stone or Ore out of the
Mine, and the probable quantity of Metal that can be
raised. The miners generally take *bargains*, in *part-
nerships*, consisting of from two to four, six, or eight
men, and the prices are from eight to fifteen, twenty,
thirty, forty, or fifty shillings, per Bing; the miners
always paying for Candles, Gunpowder, the expenses
of drawing the Ore or Stone from the Mine, working,
dressing, and preparing it, fit for the process of
Smelting.

But it frequently happens, that the quantity of
Ore in a Vein is so inconsiderable, that it becomes necessary to give the workmen both so much per bing

---

* A Bing is equal to eight hundred weight.

† After a *length* of ground is properly opened, it is excavated by blasting, or working down the roof, commonly called
roof work, and sometimes by working the sole of the Mine,
called *stope work*.

and per fathom ; and, occasionally, when a Vein is *twitched*, and hard Riders are to be driven through, it will require the price, per fathom, to be advanced to eight, ten, or twelve pounds, or upwards. *

The expense of drawing the Ore or Stone, out of the Mine, when Horses are employed, is pretty considerable, and depends much upon the length of the Level or Adit, and depth of the Mine. In *Alston-moor*, it is usually drawn out at so much per *Shift*, and at some mines, a Shift contains eight Waggons, at others only six. A miner's Waggon, calculated for an *Eight Waggon Shift*, will contain Thirty *Kibbles*, and the capacity of each *Kibble* is fourteen quarts, or thereabouts ; Waggons, calculated for *Six Waggon Shifts*, contain Forty Kibbles, making the *Shifts*, in both cases, equal. The expense of

---

* We presume, that it will not be unacceptable to the reader, to insert the following Table; supposing a cubic foot of pure Galena weighs, on a medium, 7,000 oz. Avoirdupois weight, a Bing will then be equal to 14,336 oz. We shall, according to the above, have as under, viz.—

Inch wide.	Feet high.	Feet long.	Cubic feet.	Bing.	Cwt.	Qrs.	lb.	Oz.
1	6	6	3	1	3	2	24	8
2	6	6	6	2	7	1	21	0
3	6	6	9	4	3	0	17	8
4	6	6	12	5	6	3	14	0
5	6	6	15	7	2	2	10	8
6	6	6	18	8	6	1	7	0
12	6	6	36	17	4	2	14	0
36	6	6	108	52	5	3	14	0

drawing a Shift, in Horse Levels, varies from 3s. 6d. to 8s. including the fiilling, driving, and emptying the Waggons, there being no allowance made for the difference of weight between the Ore and the Stone.

In situations, where it is necessary to use *Whimseys* or Horse Engines, for the purpose of drawing the Ore or Stone up to the surface, the same proportion is followed respecting the Shift, which, in these cases, generally consists of Sixty *Horse Kibbles*, each *Horse Kibble* containing four miner's Kibbles : making the quantity, drawn in a Shift, two hundred and forty Kibbles, as before. The expense of drawing a Shift, including filling, banking, and driving, varies from four to eight shillings, according to the depth of the Shaft.

ON THE

WASHING AND DRESSING

OF

LEAD ORES.

Metals are seldom found in a pure state, Gold, Silver, and sometimes Copper, excepted. The others usually occur in the state of Ores, that is united with

Sulphur, or some other mineralizing substance, and blended with a variety of extraneous matters, so as not to possess the ductility or other qualities of metals. When they are procured in this state, the first operation is, to separate the Ore, of whatever kind it may be, from its bed or matrix. Lead Ore is frequently found in large masses, and may sometimes be dug up pretty free from the matrix, and easily reducible to a state of purity, by the simple operation of breaking off the substances, which adhere to it, by means of a hammer, but as it is often intimately mixed with the matrix, it is generally necessary to try other methods for its reduction.

When it is dug out of the Mine, much mixed with Spar, Lime-stone, and other substances, bulk for bulk, lighter than the Ore itself, it undergoes various Dressings, before it becomes a merchantable commodity, the general tendency of which is to free it, as much as possible, from all heterogeneous impurity.

" Suppose, that a cubic foot of Lead Ore, which contained no Spar, or other extraneous matter, would weigh 7,800 ounces: and that a cubic foot of Spar, which contained no Lead Ore or other foreign substance, would weigh 2,700 ounces: then would a mixture, consisting of a cubic foot of pure Lead Ore, and a cubic foot of pure Spar, weigh 10,500 ounces, and one cubic foot, of such a mixture, would weigh 5,250 ounces. It is obvious, that, according to the different proportions, in which the particular kinds of Spar and Lead Ore, here assumed, are supposed to be mixed together; a cubic foot of the mixture will have different weights, the limits of which are, on the one hand, 7,800, and on the other 2,700 ounces; it never can weigh so little as 2,700 ounces, for then it would consist entirely of Spar without any Lead Ore; nor can it ever weigh so much as 7,800 ounces, for then it would consist entirely of Lead Ore, without any Spar.

" Lead Ore is not always of the same goodness in the same Mine, nor even in the same part of the same Mine; and what is more remarkable, the different parts of the same lump of Ore have, in equal bulks, different weights."

Most of the Spars, met with in *Allendale, Weardale,* and *Alston-moor,* are, either *Rhomboidal* or *Cubical.* They are easily distinguished from each other, by a view of their shape, when their angles can be discovered: and when the shape cannot be easily seen, the nature of the Spar may be ascertained, by touching

it with an acid, the Rhomboidal Spar always effervescing with an acid, and the Cubical resisting its action.

As Lead Ore is very seldom brought out of the
Mine pure, (as we have had occasion to observe before) being frequently intermixed with a variety of
Spars, Vein-stone, &c., it is, in this state, called, by
the *Alston-moor* Miners, *Bouse.* The first Washing
operation, that the *Bouse* generally undergoes, is
either *Grating* or *Buddling*, the former of which is
performed in the following manner:—A pretty strong
Current of Water is allowed to flow upon the Grate,
(figure 1st, plate 9th) on which a quantity of the
Bouse, to be washed, is previously placed. It is then
raked and stirred backwards and forwards, so as to
make the small Ore and *Cuttings* pass through the
Grate, down the Inclined Plane, into a Pit below,
made for its reception. What remains upon the
Grate, consists of Stones, Rider, Spar, &c. and Ore
mixed, and intimately blended with these matrixes,
as also pure pieces of Ore, from the size of a large
walnut to the size of a person's fist, and are of all
imaginable or various forms. These pure lumps are
broken into a proper size for Smelting, and then carried to the *Bing-stead,* a place near the workings, in

x x

which the Dressed Ore is deposited, previous to its
being taken away to the Smelting House. The pieces
of *Bouse,* that are mixed with Stone, Rider, Spar,
&c. are taken to the *Grinder,* or *Crushing Machine,*
where they are reduced to a coarse powder. The operation of *buddling* will be afterwards described, more
at length, in our general description of the Washing
Apparatus; but in it the same methods of picking
out the clean Ore, &c. are practised, as in the process
of *Grating.* After these operations, the small Ore, &c.
which is collected in the Pit, under the Grate, (plate
9th, figure 1st) or left upon the *Buddle,* (figure 2nd)
receives the name of *Dashed Ore* or *Dashed Work,*
from its being *Dashed* or *Crushed* in the *Buddle,* with
a *Bucker,* made of Iron. This last operation is for
the purpose of making, what is called the *Sieve Ore,*
as nearly of an equal size as possible, before it be put
into the *Sieve,* as it greatly facilitates the operation of
Tubbing, and makes the *Sieve* Ore a great deal better; for in the act of *Dashing* or *Crushing* it in the
Buddle, the pure Ore is, in a great degree, separated
from the Stone, Spar, &c. that was attached to it.—
It should be observed, that the operation of *Dashing*
or *Crushing* with the *Bucker,* is only used when
buddling is practised, as, I believe, it has seldom

been done since the Grate superseded the *Buddle;* and this is, the reason why the *Sieve* Ore, when the *Buddle* and *Hand-sieve* are used, is so much better than when the Grate and *Brake-sieve* are used; yet, notwithstanding this, the Grate and *Brake-sieve,* on many accounts, are to be preferred to the *Buddle* and *Hand-sieve,* viz.: first, a man will Grate a greater quantity of *Bouse* in a day than he can *buddle;* secondly, there is more small Ore saved, by *Grating,* as the Pit, below the Grate, catches a great deal of it; whereas, in *buddling,* a considerable quantity of the finest and smallest of the Ore escapes, and goes away amongst the water, as there is no Pit immediately behind the *Buddle.* But some may observe, that there are Pits, at a certain distance from the *Buddles,* called *Slime* Pits, (which will be described hereafter) that collects the *Slime,* that goes away amongst the water in the process of *buddling;* there certainly are such Pits, but it is accounted the best and safest way, to get the most Ore possible, in the first operation.— Thirdly, a man will Tub, at least, four or five times as much in a day, in the *Brake-sieve,* as he can do in the *Hand-sieve;* and, it is owing to this, and other great improvements, in washing, (amongst which the Crushing Mill, I think, stands foremost) that poorer Mines and poorer wastes, &c. can be Worked and

Washed, than could be Worked, &c. before these improvements took place. In Washing very poor *Bouse,*
it frequently happens that there is very little or no
Sieve Ore got out of what goes through the Grate, being intermixed with Spar, Rider, &c. so much, that
no pure Ore can be got out of it until it be put into a
smaller state, which is done either at the Crushing
Mill, or knocking or crushing it with Iron *Buckers.*
There is sometimes a little Ore got out of the *Dashed*
Work or *Gratings,* by the following method :—The
Washer, attending the *Brake-sieve,* takes all that
part, that does not go through the *Sieve,* out promiscuously, and lays it in a heap altogether ; and, after
he has a quantity of it lying, he takes the *Hand-sieve,*
which is a circular one, and puts what he took out of
the *Brake-sieve* into it, and works it amongst the water, in a round Tub, with great agility and dexterity,
till he gets the greatest part of the *Chats* and *Cuttings*
separated from the Ore, which he scrapes off, with an
Iron Scraper, (made of thin sheet iron) or, what,
amongst Washers, is called, a *Limp.* These *Chats,*&c.
cannot be separated from the Ore so well, in the *Brake-*
sieve, as it is always in a horizontal position ; but the
Washer works the *Round* or *Hand-sieve* principally
in an inclined way, and, by this means, gets the re-

fuse out from amongst the Ore. The *Brake-sieve* is made of strong Wire, (figure 3rd, plate 9th) the Apertures of which are about three-eighths of an inch square. The *Sieve* is suspended at the end of a Wooden Lever or Brake, by two Upright Arms, about three feet and a half long, (made of Flat Iron) with Holes through them, for the purpose of coupling them to the two ends of the Lever, with two iron bolts, that go through both the arms of the *Sieve*, and the ends of the Lever; — as may be seen by inspecting the figure. Being thus prepared, and a quantity of the *Gratings* (that was previously taken out of the Pit, below the Grate) being put into the *Sieve*, a boy, at the other end of the Lever, moves up and down, in such a manner, so as to shake and agitate the *Sieve* and what is in it, in such a way, that it causes the small Ore to pass through the openings of the *Sieve*, into a Tub or Cistern, filled with water, and placed below the *Sieve*, for its reception. The Ore, that collects at the bottom of the Tub, is called *Smid-dum*, which is taken out of the Tub, (after there is a certain quantity deposited therein) and *buddled*, in the *Running Buddle*, (figure 2nd) with a quantity of water flowing upon it, and the Washer drawing his *Colrake* through amongst it, from the *Skirts* of the *Smiddum* to the high parts thereof; by this means,

he keeps the purest and best of the Ore at the high
end of the *Buddle,* whilst the *Cuttings* and the lightest of the Ore, which is called *Smiddum Tails,* goes
to the low end of the *Buddle.*   After the *Smiddum*
is put twice or thrice (or as often as is thought necessary) through the *Buddle,* that part next the
Buddle head is put into a *Kibble* or a Barrow, and
taken away to the *Bing-stead.*   The *Smiddum Tails,*
that was carried to the low end of the *Buddle,* by the
water, contains a quantity of Ore, but it is mixed
with so much dirt and tough *Slime,* that it has to undergo two operations before any clean Ore can be got
out of it, which are as follows:—It is taken to the
Trunk Buddle, (figure 4th, plate 9th) and placed in
the square Box, *a,* at the upper part of the *Buddle,*
into which a large stream of water is made to run,
the *Tails* are then worked about with a Shovel, and
the largest particles of Ore and *Cuttings,* which are
mixed together, are continually taken out, the water
carrying along with it the smaller Ore and refuse, into
the flat and broad part of the *Buddle,* towards the
upper end of which is deposited, that part that has
the most Ore in it, (called *Sludge* or *Slime)* in consequence of its superior specific gravity ; and the part
that has a very small portion of Ore in it, is carried to
the low end of the *Buddle,* by the water.   After the

Buddle is filled with this mixed consistence, the water, at the high end of the *Trough*, above the *Trunk Box*, is turned off the *Buddles* into a race or gutter, and the contents of the *Buddle* is taken out, the part that lay at the high end is laid by itself, that in the middle in like manner, and that which was at the low end, and contains a very small quantity of Ore, is hurled to the *Cutting* Washers, to be worked or washed over again, till all the Ore is got out of it, that will pay the Washers for their trouble; but there is still a minute quantity left in the *wastes*, after all these operations have been performed. The two parts which lay at the high end and middle of the *Buddle*, are worked over again in the same *Buddle*, or in one similar, as follows :—The Washer, having a Shovel in his hand, and one foot on each side of the *Buddle*, (which may be called *striding it)* takes it up, and draws it against the *breast-board* of the *Buddle*, cross way, from side to side, the contents of his Shovel being carried down into the flat part of the *Buddle*, by a small stream of water, that flows gently and regularly on all parts of the *breast-board*, and at the same time, a boy or a girl, sitting at the low end of the *Buddle*, rubs the surface of the contents thereof, from about the middle to the high end, with a Wooden

Colrake, to prevent the Ore escaping, and for the purpose of keeping the surface of the *Slime,* &c. in the *Buddle* firm and smooth, which makes the operation go on regularly. It should be observed, that the Wooden *Colrake* is always rubbed in one direction, which is, from the low to the high end of the *Buddle.* This operation is repeated once or twice, or as often as is thought necessary, until the Washer gets the *Slime* into a fit state to be *Dollied* at the *Dolly Tub,* which operation will be described afterwards. The part which was taken out of the *Trunk Box,* in the operation of *Trunking* the *Smiddum Tails,* consists of the roundest particles of the Ore that was amongst the whole mass at first, but is now mixed with particles of Stone, Black Jack, Sulphur, &c. of nearly the same size; and the following method is used to separate the Ore from these combinations :—The Washers put, what they call, *a Bedding** upon the bottom of the

---

* *Bedding* consists of a quantity of the smallest of the *Sieve* Ore, laid in the bottom of the *Sieve,* in the form of a Layer, about two inches thick, and when the *Sieve* is working, the shaking of it, by the boy at the end of the Lever, or Brake, causes the particles of Ore, that is among the *Tails,* to pass through the above-named Bedding and openings of the *Sieve* into the Tub, the Bedding not being that close to prevent the small Ore from passing through; but the tilting or shaking of the Brake must be done very gently, in the operation of *letting in,* or letting the Ore through the Bedding and *Sieve,* into the Tub.

Sieve, in order to prevent the *Smiddum* from passing too quickly through. It must be observed, that owing to the superior specific gravity of the particles of Ore contained in this mass, they pass through the *Bedding* and *Sieve,* while the operation of *braking* or *tilting* is going on, and the particles of Stone, Spar, &c. remain above the *Bedding,* which are scraped off with the *Limp,* and carried to the *Cutting* Washers.— In this operation, which is called *letting in,** there will very little go through the *Sieve* but Ore, (except any thing that is nearly as heavy as Ore) if the Washer has a good *bedding,* and his *Sieve* works true, and when it is taken out of the Tub, it is seldom put above once through the *Running Buddle,* which is to clear it of the *slack* and *slimy* parts, from whence it is taken to the *Bing-stead.*

We shall attempt to detail, rather more at length, the process of Cleaning the *Sieve* Ore, which is from the size of a large Pea to that of a large Bean, and sometimes larger :—It is necessary to observe, that after every *braking* or *tilting,* which is performed by

---

* From the Ore being *let* into the Tub, through the *Bedding* and *Sieve.*

the boy at the end of the Lever, standing upright, and jumping a little up and down, the contents of the *Sieve* are altered, in position, by the jirking and suddenness of the motion, and the heavier and purer parts of the *Sieve* Ore settle to the bottom of the *Sieve;* what are called *Chats,* which are Ore, Stone, Spar, &c. combined together, lay next above the good Ore, and the *Cuttings* and lightest parts, at the top of the *Sieve.* The *Cuttings* are first removed by the *Limp,* then the *Chats,* and lastly the Ore. The *Cuttings,* as observed before, are taken to the *Cutting* Washers, but the *Chats* are taken to the Crushing Mill, and ground betwixt the *Chat Rollers,* as small as the *Rollers* are capable of grinding, the produce of which, is put into the *Sieve,* and the *Smiddum,* &c. separated and cleaned, as before described. There are, in this operation, a quantity of gritty or small *Chats* got out of the *Sieve,* which contain a quantity of Ore, but being too small for the *Rollers* to take hold of, they are put under the *Stampers,* v, w, x, y, (plate 8th, figure 1st) and there reduced to the state of *Smiddum* and *Slime.*

We may observe, that the very large lumps of pure Ore, which are sometimes extracted from a Mine, are taken to the *Bing-stead,* and broken to pieces with a small hammer, without undergoing any of these operations; and that large heterogeneous lumps, called *knockings,* are broken into pieces, about the size of a goose's egg, reduced to a powder in the *Grinder,* and immediately undergo the operation of the *Brake-sieve.* It is obvious, that the fewer processes, used in Washing, the better, as it prevents a great deal of waste, and will consequently increase the profits of the proprietors.

We shall now endeavour to describe the method of Extracting the Ore from the *Cuttings,* which were produced by the former operations :—That part of the *Cuttings,* called *Sieve-toppings,* are placed in the *Brake-sieve,* exactly in the manner we have before described, and the Ore, which subsides to the bottom of the *Sieve,* is removed by means of the *Limp.* The *Smiddum,* which has passed through the *Sieve,* is taken out of the Tub, *trunked, buddled,* and *let in,* as before noticed, respecting the *Bouse Smiddum;* but the *Cutting Smiddum* being so much poorer, takes far more labour, before the Ore can be got out of it, and which is quite inferior to the *Bouse* Ore, being commonly sold for twenty shillings per Bing less, The *hinder-ends*, collected at the low end of the *Running Buddle*, when *buddling* the *Smiddum*, are carried to the *Trunk Buddle*, and *trunked* in the Box, the small *slimy* part going into the *Trunk*, and the rounder part staying in the *Trunk* Box, till the washer throws it out with his Shovel, to the Tub side, in order to be *let in*, and the Ore got out of it. The *Sludge*, produced in the last operation, is now exceedingly fine, and is taken to what is called a *Stirring Buddle*, (plate 9th, figure 5th) where it is mixed with water until it assumes the consistency of *Slime*, much of the impure matter being washed out at the end of the *Buddle;* it is then carried to the *Nicking Buddle*, figure 6th.

In the operation of the *Nicking Buddle*, the *Slime* is spread out upon a sort of Inclined Plane, and a very minute quantity of water made to trickle in small streams down its surface, against the small ridges of the *Slime* made by the Washer's Shovel. The whole compound is taken down this Inclined Plane, by the water, into the *trunk*, over the floor of which it spreads regularly, and the Washer, at certain intervals, (when he is not *nicking* the *Slime*, upon the Inclined Plane) rubs the surface of the *Slime*, from side

to side of the *trunk*, with his Shovel, and sometimes
with his wooden shoes, in order to make the surface
of the *slime* firm and regular, and to prevent the Ore
from escaping. This rubbing the *Nicking Buddle*, is
something similar to that with the wooden *Colrake*, in
the *trunk*, where the *Bouse slime* is dressed, as before
described. The process of *Nicking* is repeated as
often as is necessary, to make it fit for *dollying*, when
it is taken to the *Dolly* Tub, and there made fit for
Smelting. The whole of these processes will be better understood, by referring to the general description
of the Washing Apparatus, where all the figures are
perfectly explained.

In the operations of Grinding the *Bouse* Ore,
buddling the *Bouse, Smiddum*, &c. a stream of running water is always employed; and it is impossible to
prevent a portion of the minutest and finest part of
the Ore, from being carried along with it, as they are
so intimately mixed together. In order to save this
part of the Ore, there are reservoirs, or *slime* pits, prepared, into which the water runs, at a little distance
from the place where the former operations are conducted. These reservoirs, or *slime* pits, are sometimes made of an oval form, and sometimes round,

about three yards in diameter, and generally from two to three feet in depth. They are perfectly close all round, except at one place where there is an opening of about a foot wide, and two or three inches deep from the top, through which the water is discharged. It will be easily understood, that when the *buddling* water, mill water, &c. first flows into these *slime* pits, the Ore gradually subsides to the bottom of the pit, and the water, freed of the principal part of the Ore it contained, escapes at the opening, named above. After the *slime* pit is nearly filled with the Ore, *slack*, &c. that was contained in the water, the water is turned off into another reservoir, and the contents of the former taken to the *Stirring Buddles*, *Nicking Buddles*, *Dolly* Tubs, &c. where it is prepared for the Smelting House, in the manner before described.

It may be observed, that the contents of these *slime* pits are so glutinous and tough, that there would be no chance of doing any thing with it at the *Nicking Buddle*, before stirring it at the *Stirring Buddle* with clean water, which partly destroys that very close adhesion of the parts that it possessed when it was first taken out of the *slime* pit, at the same time it takes

a considerable quantity of the light spungy dirt
out of it.

A Cornish Miner, named Richard Trathan, was
the first who introduced these *slime* pits into *Alston-
moor*, and, since that time, the quantity of Ore saved,
by that means, has been very considerable.

Another mode of Washing *Cutting Slime* has lately
been introduced, which some prefer to the method already described, viz. of *Stirring*, *Nicking*, &c. We
shall endeavour to describe this new method, which is
as follows :—Fig. 10, pl. 9, is a representation of it, *a, a,*
two *slime* Pits, *b, b,* the *outlets* out of said pits, *c, c,*
pieces of flat narrow boards, put crosswise, before the
outlets of the pits, to prevent the *slime* escaping, and they
are put in one after another, till one of the pits is full ;
after which the *buddle* water, &c. is turned into the
other pit, and the *slime* washer proceeds to empty the
full pit, as follows :—having set a stream of clean water into it, he takes out the highest piece of board
that was put into the *outlet* of the pit, while it was
filling, to allow the *slime* to go out amongst the water
into the gutters, *d, d,* after which it arrives at the
heads of three narrow wood troughs, *e, e, e,* where it

divides into three streams, and runs into the three
wooden boxes, *f, f, f,* which are about two feet long,
fifteen inches deep, and twelve wide.   The Washer
with his shovel, works and stirs the *slime* in these
boxes, so as to separate the rounder part from the fine
small part, the former of which he throws out of the
boxes with his shovel, while the latter part goes out of
the boxes amongst the water, into the three gutters,
g, g, g, the low ends of which are stopped with narrow pieces, *h, h, h,* of boards, the same as the outlets
of the *slime* pits, until they are full ; after which the
water is turned off some way above the pits, and the
Washer proceeds to empty his gutters, *g, g, g,* of
what they contain.   The high ends of these gutters
contain the most Ore, which he takes out and lays by
itself ; as also that part contained in the middle of the
gutter, which has a small portion of Ore in it ; but
the Ore contained in that part of the gutters, betwixt
the middle and the low end, being so very minute and
small, that he casts it away.   The parts, taken out
of the high end and middle of the gutters, he draws
against the *breast board* of a *Trunk Buddle,* with a
small stream of water running along with it, which
carries away the refuse to the low end of the *Buddle,*
the Ore lodging at the high end of it, which is taken

out and carried to the *Dolly* Tub, and there made fit
for Smelting.

The Washing of old heaps of *Cuttings*, &c. by
means of what is called *Hushing*, is the last branch of
Washing we have to notice. It very often happens,
that there is a syke or rivulet below all the Washing
places, above described, into which the *Cutting*
Washers put all the refuse and wastes, the quantity
of which is, sometimes, very considerable. Ore,
as was observed before, by its superior specific gravity,
descends to the bottom of the syke or rivulet, whilst
the *Cuttings* and lighter parts are driven away, by the
force of the water, when it is increased to a given
bulk and strength, by rain. If there be a number of
great stones in the syke, the Ore is generally found
lying round about such stones, and in holes at the bottom. If the syke has a Clay bottom, it is a favourable circumstance for *Hushing*. After there has been
a sufficient quantity of *Cuttings*, &c. put into the
syke, the Husher then builds a Dam, or reservoir, at
the high end of it, to collect water to *hush* with. His
first step is, to remove all the great stones that are lying in the middle of the *hush* gutter, to one side, and
there make a wall with them. After this, he sets off

3 A

his *hush*, by lifting up the door of the Dam, which slides in grooves, in a wooden frame. When the door is lifted up the water rushes out with great force, and tears loose the *Cuttings*, &c. in the syke, to a certain depth, and drives them before it down the *hush* gutter. If the *hush* has bared and discovered any great stones in the middle of the syke, they are broken and removed to one side, as they retard the force and action of the water when in the middle. After these impediments are removed, the water is again, and again, let out of the reservoir, until the *Cuttings*, gravel, &c. are *hushed* off the Ore, which is found lying in holes, and about earth-fast stones, at the bottom of the syke, and which the Husher takes and carries to the *Brake-sieve*, there to undergo the operation of *braking*, &c. as before described. If any round pieces, resembling *knockings*, are found in the *hush* gutter, after the *hushes* have been let off, they are broke up in the same manner (to be ground) as the *knockings* that come out of the *Bouse*. As soon as the *hushes* work down as deep as the Clay (if there be any) the process is then greatly accelerated, as the water has then a good sound bottom to work upon.— The syke is *hushed* as far below the Washing places as will pay for the labour and trouble; but the most Ore is generally found not far below the Washing convenience. After the syke is Washed or *hushed*, and all the Ore got out of it that can be got out, at that time, it is then let alone till it again fills up, when *hushing* is a second time, commenced and continued till the Ore is got out; and as often as it will pay for *hushing*.

A considerable quantity of Ore is procured out of *old heaps*, so called, which cannot be discovered till it is well washed with water; but the quantity of Ore is generally too small to pay the expense of washing it, as the first *Cuttings* are Washed, so recourse is had to *hushing*, in order to get the Ore out of the second *Cuttings*, and other poor wastes; which is an excellent plan, when water can be got, and a syke with a proper descent.

Upon the whole, the Washing of Lead Ore, &c. has received great improvements during the last twenty-five years, by the introduction of Crushing Machines, *Brake-sieves*, *Slime* Pits, Stamping Mills, &c. and has enabled many Miners to try and work very poor Mines, which could not have been worked, without these improvements.

EXPLANATION

OF

THE WASHING APPARATUS.

◆

The *Crushing Machine* and *Stampers,* represented in plates 7 and 8, are very essential to every Mine where the quantity of Ore produced is tolerably large. Plate 7th, figure 1st, is a side elevation of the Machine; D is the great Pit Wheel, attached to the axle of the Water Wheel, whose circumference is represented in the figure: the Wheel, D, turns an Iron Cog Wheel, e, on the spindle of which is fixed one of the Iron Rollers, for Crushing the Bouse Ore.— Concentric with the Pit Wheel, D, and upon the axle of the great Water Wheel, is fixed a *Fluted* Roller, which moves another, parallel to it, of the same description. The Bouse Ore, to be grinded, is brought in the Waggon, A, and let out by a door, which opens outwards in its bottom, into the Hopper, S. After passing through the fluted Rollers, immediately below the Hopper, it descends by the two Inclined Planes (represented in the figure) to the two

Plate 7.

Fig. 1.

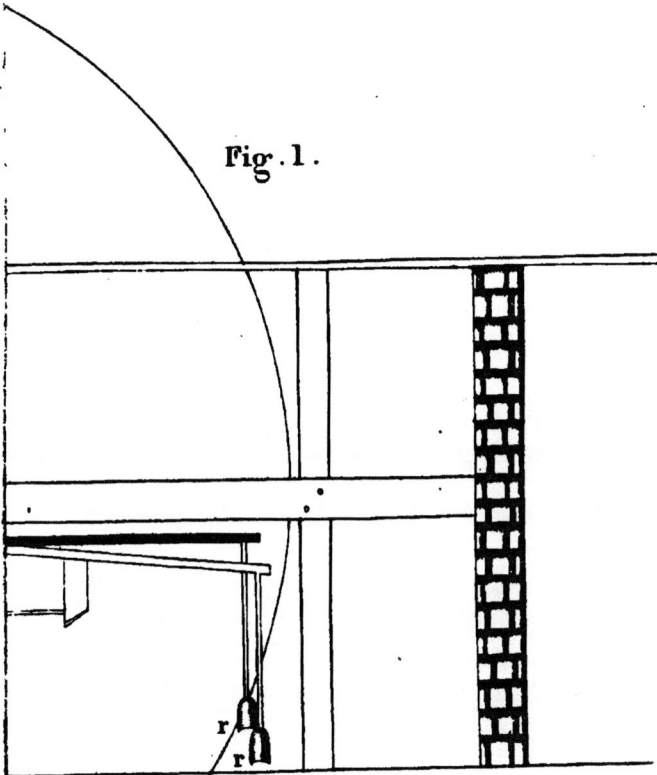

r
r

Scale of 24 feet

smooth Rollers, turned by the Iron Cog Wheel, e, before mentioned. The Rollers are made of cast iron and truly turned, they are represented more distinctly in figures 2nd and 3rd ; the spindles of these Rollers turn in brass bushes, fixed in two iron frames, k, k, bolted down to the wood work; these iron frames have long mortices in them, in one end of which the two bushes, for the pivots of the Roller, f, are firmly fixed. The bushes of the Roller, g, slide in the mortices in such a manner as to allow the two Rollers to be placed, either in contact or at a short distance from each other, as circumstances may require. The Rollers are, however, generally pressed towards each other, by the Weights, r, r, suspended at the ends of the Levers, whose fulcrums are at X, figure 1st. The operation of these Levers, in pushing up the moveable Rollers, will be easily understood, by inspecting the figure. By this contrivance, if a large and hard lump is introduced, between any of the Rollers, they are allowed to recede from each other, and suffer it to pass through without doing any material injury to the Machine.

The two Cog Wheels, m, m, figure 2nd, are attached to the axles of the two Rollers, and cause them both to move round together. The Hopper, h, figure 3rd, is supported at some distance above the Rollers, and the *Bouse*, to be grinded, runs out at an opening in its bottom, into a Trough, i, called the *Shoe*. This Trough, or *Shoe*, is continually shaken, by means of a piece of wood attached to it, one end of which rests upon the teeth of the Cog Wheel, m, and by this means, a small quantity of *Bouse* is made constantly to fall upon the Rollers, without any danger of choaking them up.

Instead of this contrivance, it is sometimes thought necessary to employ a boy, for the purpose of feeding the Machine, who sits in a small cabin near the Rollers, and rakes in the *Bouse*, out of the *Shoe*, as fast as the Machinery can perform the operation of grinding.

It is always necessary to have a small quantity of water running into the *Shoe*, in order to keep the Rollers cool, which would otherwise grow warm by the friction, and greatly retard the process.

The *Stampers*, plate 8th, figure 1st, are used for crushing, and breaking to pieces, the harder and more

Plate 8

Fig 1

A

B

refractory parts of the *Bouse*, which the Rollers, in
the *Crushing Machine*, cannot effect.   In plate 8th,
the *Stamp Mill* is represented entirely distinct from
the *Crushing Machine*, but in many instances they are
carried by the same Water Wheel, the *Stampers* being
placed on one side and the Rollers on the other.

The plate alluded to, figure 1st, shows a longitudinal elevation, of the *Stamp Mill*.   A, is the Water Wheel, framed on a strong octagonal shaft, B, B.
turning on two gudgeons, fixed in its ends.   D, is the
Pit Wheel, or great Cog Wheel, of eighty teeth,
made of cast iron, and turning the Wheel E, of thir-
ty-seven teeth, which is fixed on a horizontal shaft,
F, called the *tumbling shaft*.   The Beams, T, T,
have cross pieces attached to them, between which the
stampers, V, W, X, Y, slide up and down.   They
are lifted up by the *nippers*, n, m, fig. 2, fixed upon
the shaft, F.   These *nippers* take hold of the *tap-
pets*, w, attached to the *stampers*, raise them up to the
proper height, and then allow them to fall down upon
the *Bouse* or Ore, to be *stamped*, which is placed
upon an Inclined Plane, behind the *stampers*, and
gradually slides down below them, as the operation
proceeds.   The descent of the *Bouse*, down the In-

clined Plane, is promoted by a small stream of water, which flows in at its top, as in the process of Grinding.

Plate 9th, figure 1st, is a ground plan of the *Grate;* the operation is performed, by allowing a stream of water to flow upon the *Bouse* Ore, previously laid upon the *Grate.* The Ore is then raked backwards and forwards, so that the smaller parts pass through the *Grate,* down the Inclined Plane, into the Pit below, prepared for their reception.

Figure 2nd, is a ground plan of the *Running Buddle;* the operation is performed, by placing the *Bouse,* to be Washed, upon the floor of the *Buddle, b.* A stream of water is allowed to flow in, at the *eye* of the *Buddle, a,* and the *Bouse* is then turned over and over, with a Shovel or *Colrake,* until it is sufficiently cleaned.

Figure 3rd, is a ground plan, and figure 9th an elevation of the *Brake-sieve,* where *a* is the end of the *brake,* or lever, *s* the wire *sieve,* and *e, e,* the cistern or tub; the method of operation has been already sufficiently described.

Figure 4th, is a ground plan of the *Trunk Bud-dle; a,* is the Hole or Box, where the Ore is put in to be *trunked.* The operation is performed thus :— the workman takes a Shovel, bent at the sides for the purpose, with which he stirs the Ore in the Pit, taking out, occasionally, the rounder parts, called *tails,* with the Shovel ; the minuter parts of the Ore are car-ried out by the water, and deposited in the broad part of the *Buddle,* marked *b,* in the manner we have al-ready explained.

Figure 5, is a ground plan of the *Stirring Buddle; a,* is the Plug Hole, through which the water is in-troduced ; *x,* is the Stirring Box, in which the *sludge* is thoroughly mixed with the water; and *m,* the *trunk,* where the purer part of the Ore subsides near the top.

Figure 6, is a ground plan of the *Nicking Buddle; a,* is the Plug Hole, and *x* the *Nicking Board,* which is a little inclined. The operation is performed by spreading a thin layer of *sludge* upon the board, and allowing a slight quantity of water to percolate in small streams down over its surface, as represented in the figure.

Figures 7 and 8, represent the *Dolly Tub* and *Dolly*,* in making use of which, the workmen proceed in the following manner :—the Tub (figure 7) is first filled, to a certain height, with water, and the *Dolly* (figure 8) introduced, and turned quickly round, which communicates a circular motion to the water; in the mean time, the *slime* Ore, to be washed, is put in slowly, with a Shovel, until a sufficient quantity is placed in the Tub. As soon as the Ore is thoroughly mixed with the water, the *Dolly* is withdrawn, and the workmen beat the sides of the Tub, for a considerable time, with a hammer, or heavy piece of wood, in order to make the Ore subside to the bottom; the lighter part of the *slime*, consisting principally of refuse, is still suspended in the water, (which subsides after the beating the sides of the Tub ceases) and the water is taken out, and the *slime*, with little or no Ore in it, next, which is thrown away, and the pure Ore, at the bottom of the Tub, is then taken away, and placed in the *Bing-stead*, the workmen proceeding to perform the same operation on another portion of the *slime*.

---

* The operation of *Dollying* the *slime* Ore is a most excellent method, as the Ore is both made purer, and more of it saved, than by any other means.

Plate 9.

Fig.5.

a

x

Fig.6.

a

X

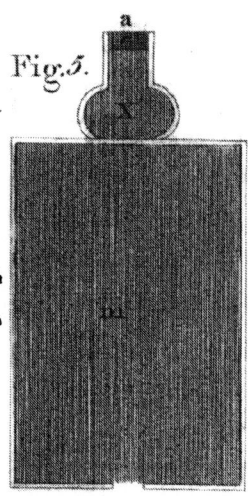

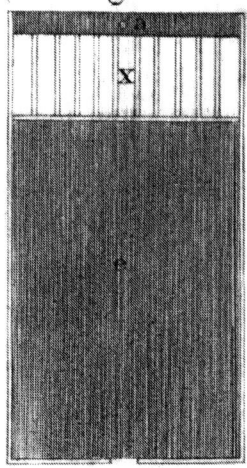

Scale

5 . O

m

c

Fig. 8.

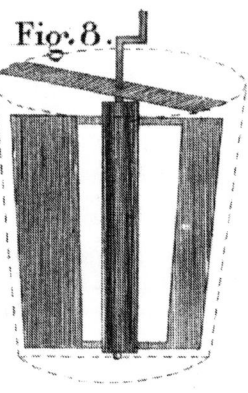

Dolly

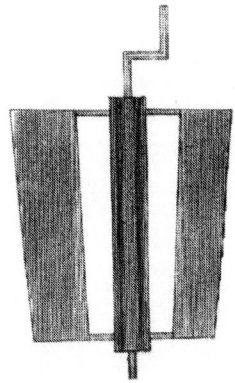

Having gone through the different operations of Washing Lead Ore, we shall now endeavour to state the price that is usually given for performing the process. It is customary, in *Alston-moor*, and the places adjacent, to *let* the Washers a parcel of *Bouse*, to wash, at so much per Bing, and the price depends much upon the richness of the *Bouse* or the quantity of Ore it is estimated to contain in the *Shift*. Some parcels of *Bouse* may be washed for 2*s*. 6*d*. or 3*s*. per Bing or even less, while other parcels will require from 4*s*. to 8*s*. per Bing. *Bouse*, which contains 20 Bings in the *Shift*, consists almost entirely of pure Ore, but the quantity fluctuates, from two or three Bings, to the maximum we have stated, and the price of Washing is regulated accordingly.

SMELTING OF LEAD ORES.

It appears, from the numerous *Boles* or *Bayls* Hills, that are to be found in the Mining Districts of the counties of Northumberland, Cumberland, and Durham, and also, as I am told, in Derbyshire, that the Smelting of Lead Ore, to which I intend to confine myself, was conducted in the following manner :— Piles of stones were placed round a fire, on the western brow of an eminence, (as that is the most prevalent wind of the north) as near as possible to the mouth of the Mine; these stones were so placed, as to leave certain holes or openings, to answer both the purpose of *flues* and the admission of the air; the fuel was supplied from the neighbouring woods, which, on that account, have obtained the name of *Hag-hill*, or *Hag-bank*. It is unnecessary to spend much time in describing, more minutely, these rude and imperfect modes of Smelting, as it is obvious, that, from the variableness of the wind, the workmen could have very little command over the fire, a thing most essentially necessary in every process, conducted by heat; this method may, however, be considered as the first essay of Smelting Lead Ore.

The next mode of Smelting, was the blast *Hearth*, known in various parts of Europe, by the name of the Scotch *Hearth*, something similar, no doubt, to the present one; but, that it was greatly inferior in energy, may be proved, from its not doing one-third of the work; however, considerable allowances ought to be made, for the superior means and method of conducting the present one.

I shall now endeavour to describe this *Hearth*, with the manual operations in directing it; but it is necessary, in the first place, to explain the theory, upon which it operates, and to compare it with the third mode of Smelting, generally known by the name of the Derbyshire *Cupola*, or Reverberatory Furnace, a description of which, I shall extract from Mr. Farey's Derbyshire Report.

The Ores, from which the Lead of commerce is most entirely obtained, are varieties of Galena (Sulphuret of Lead) white Ore of Lead, which is a carbonate, and the earthy Ore, or oxide of Lead, the latter seldom occurs in the Mines of the counties heretofore named; and when it does, is intermixed very minutely, with indurated clay; however, I thought it necessary to mention it, as were it more common, to show, that these two last modes of Smelting are fully adapted for the extraction of its Lead. These three sorts of Lead Ore, exhibit numerous characteristics, or habits, in the fire, owing, principally, to the variable proportions of the Lead and mineralizing substance or substances; and also, a good deal to the extraneous matter, from which they are scarcely ever completely separated, in the Washing, and other processes, connected with the Dressing of Ore. The first of these, viz. *Galena, or Sulphuret of Lead*, when pure, break into smooth right-angled fractures, it is generally known by the name of Cubical Lead Ore; its composition is about eighty-seven of Lead, and thirteen of Sulphur; the other sorts of Galena exhibiting a waving cubical fracture, when broke, always contain more or less Antimony, as is evident from the white sublimed oxide, that attaches itself to the doors and sides of the Roasting Furnace; and as the Sulphuret of Antimony is mineralized with about double the quantity of Sulphur that Galena is, it is evident that a small compound of it mineralized with the Lead in that Ore, may increase the Sulphur to fourteen, fifteen, or sixteen per cent, which has been proved to be the case, by direct analysis; but, it ought further to be observed, that Sulphur, or rather its oxide, exists in Galena, in an uncombined state, so as that a certain portion of it may be volatilized, by combustion, until it is reduced to the mineralizing ratio; and it is chiefly this excess of Sulphur, together with the sulphurated Antimony, that is dissipated in Roasting, and which is the principal cause that Roasted Ore makes a greater produce in the blast, or Ore Hearth, than the raw Ore, because it not only lies more porous in the Hearth, but works, what the Smelters call dryer, and allows the current of atmospheric air, from the bellows, to disseminate itself more perfectly through the contents of the Hearth.

It is true, that the extraneous matter, consisting principally of Argillaceous and Siliceous substances, as well as Pyrites and the Ores of Zinc and Riders of different compositions, containing more or less of the

Calx of Iron, may effect its habits in Smelting, when not sufficiently freed from the Ore, but it is the additional Sulphur, or its oxide, above alluded to, that chiefly alters its constitution.

The next of the Ores of Lead, viz. white Lead Ore, or Carbonated Lead, is the second of importance, as it has been produced in considerable quantities in the Lead Mines of these counties, but most abundantly in the manor of *Alston-moor*, in the county of Cumberland, where, in the amorphous state, it has been found massive, to a considerable extent, particularly at *Fair Hill Flow Edge*, and at the opening of *Hudgill Burn* Mines, the Crystallized, or Dogtoothed Ore, frequently makes its appearance, but always sparingly.

The third, or earthy Ore of Lead, has only, I believe, occurred in these mining districts, at *Greengill West End*, in the manor of *Alston-moor;* the Lead it contains is in the oxide state; this, as well as the former sort of Lead Ore, is intermixed with extraneous substances, but Argillaceous impurities, containing Calces of Iron, are more prevalent in the carbonates than the Sulphurets; as to the oxide, it seems to be intimately mixed with this Argillaceous matter.

The three preceding sorts of Lead Ore, are all that occur in the foregoing counties, but, owing to the different proportions of the extraneous matter, I have already pointed out, that they are combined and intermixed with, the treatment, in Smelting, must be adapted to every peculiarity; but, as the Lead, in the whole of them, can only be in an intimate state of incorporation with the mineralizing substance or substances: viz. with Sulphur in the cubical or right-angled Galena, sulphurated Antimony in that of the waving-fractured, carbonic acid in the white Ore, and Spar of Lead, and oxygen in the earthy (the other substances are supposed to be only in a state of mixture, as before observed); it is clear before the Lead can be separated or extricated from them, that something must be presented to these mineralizing agents, to which they have a greater tendency to unite, than they have with Lead. Oxygen, with the aid of heat, decomposes Galena, by uniting to the Sulphur, and forming the sulphureous and sulphuric acids, dissipated in the gazeous state, along with nearly all the

Antimony, which escapes in a volatilized oxide, wherever it occurs. Heat alone will expel the carbonic acid from the carbonates, and Coal or Charcoal, &c. will abstract the oxygen from the earthy Ore of Lead. Lime is used to render soft or clammy, the Siliceous, Argillaceous, and Ferrigeneous impurities of the Ore, which causes them to unite into balls or lumps, in which state they can be separated from the contents of the blast Hearth; and it promotes their fusion at a high temperature in the reverberatory Furnace, so that they swim upon the surface of the Lead, and an additional quantity of it thrown upon the fused slag, dries it up in a state of mixture of lime and slag, which can be raked from off the surface of the Lead; it only now remains to observe, that Galena may be Smelted with a sufficient quantity of grey or black slag; the separation of the Lead and Sulphur takes place in consequence of the oxide of the Iron of the slag uniting itself with the Sulphur of Galena; hence less quantity of such slag will be necessary where it contains most of the said oxide, and may be known according as the slag is blacker; it is scarce necessary to observe, that this operation must be performed in the Slag Hearth, which I shall describe in due order.

I now extract, from Mr. Farey's Derbyshire Report, an Account and Description of the Reverberatory, or Cupola, Smelting Furnace :—

"The Cupola consists of a Reverberatory Furnace, about ten feet long * and six wide, in the middle, inside, and two feet high in the centre, the flame being supplied from a fire-place at the end, over a wall of fire-bricks, called the *fire-bridge*, one foot high, and reaching within one foot and a half of the roof, † which descends gradually to the end opposite the fire-place, where it is only six inches high, where are two openings, separated by a triangular block of Firestone, which meet in the passage, or flue, 1½ foot wide, which flue curves upwards through a length of ten feet or more, and is covered by flat stones, closely jointed in fire-clay, that can be removed when the flue-glass, or melted flue dust, requires cleansing; the flues, above described, join, by an easy curve, into a tall chimney, whose top is fifty-five feet above

---

* This dimension must surely take in the Fire-bridge, which will reduce the length upwards of two feet.

† I believe, it has been found, that fourteen inches, betwixt the top of the Fire-bridge and roof, answers better.

the ground. One side of the Furnace, or Cupola, is
called the Labourer's side : here the door is situate
for supplying coals to the fire, and also three small
openings, about six inches square, into the Furnace,
stopped by iron plates, that can be removed, when a
free current of air is required, or the Furnace needs
stirring. On the other side, called the Working side,
are three similar openings, stopped in like manner, by
moveable iron plates, and two others below them, for
tapping the slag and the Lead, as mentioned below,
the ash-hole also opens on this side, and has conveniences for raking and opening the grate-bars from below,
in case of their slagging up, so as to impede the draft
to the fire. The floor of the Furnace, which is composed of old Furnace-slag, roughly pounded, and
brought to the proper form by rakes (or strong iron
hoes) when in a semi-fluid state, from the first heat-
ing of the furnace, and is made up nearly to the level
of the small doors on the labourer's side, but declines
so as to be eighteen inches below the middle door on
the opposite or working side ; and here the tap-hole is
situate for letting out the Lead into a large cast-iron
pan, called the Lead Pan, placed under it in a niche
in the lower part of the Furnace. From the Lead
tap-hole, the bottom rises all ways, thereby forming a
receptacle, of the proper size, for the Lead contained

in a charge of Ore; level with the usual surface of
which, another tap-hole is made, under the door
which is furthest from the fire-place; this is for tapping or letting off the slag.* In the centre of the top
of the Furnace, there is a small opening, called the
crown-hole, covered by a thick iron plate, when the
Furnace is at work; above this crown-hole is a large
hopper of wood, with an iron tube below it, reaching
down almost to the plate which covers the crown-hole:
above the iron tube, the hopper is furnished with a
shuttle or sliding valve, and the whole is suspended by
framing from the roof of the large building, like an
immense barn, in which four of the Cupolas, I am
describing, are contained. Into the hopper, above
described, a charge of Ore is put, at leisure times
during the working of the Furnace, ready to be instantly discharged into it, by removing the crown-
plate and drawing the hopper-shuttle, as soon as all

---

* When these sort of Furnaces were first erected, by the
London Lead Company, at Whitfield Mill, in the county of
Northumberland, they were constructed with two taps, as
here detailed; but as the bottom of the Furnace declines, both
from the Fire-bridge to the flue, and from the labourer's to the
foreman's or tapping side, it was found necessary to discontinue the slag tap, as it was so close to the Lead tap, that the
workmen were very much burnt in casting the Lead; instead
of running the slag off in that sort of way, they added a
quantity of lime to the fluid slag, until it was sufficiently
dried up, to be removed higher up the Furnace bottom, from
off the surface of the Lead which, before charging, was raked
out at one of the doors.

the Lead of the previous charge has been drawn off, and the tapping-holes are stopped up by quick lime, tempered as mortar ; so that no time or heat is lost between the charges.

" In the Cupola, or Furnace, thus constructed, the process of Roasting the Ore, in a moderate heat, to expel or sublime the Sulphur, Arsenic, &c. can be performed, and afterwards an intense heat can be applied, for expelling the oxygen or reducing the metal. The Ore, which is here shot down into the Furnace at once, usually consists of five or six or even seven or eight sorts of Ore from different Mines, or dressed in a different manner ; on which mixtures, in due proportion, determined by experiment, the perfection of the process much depends. Sixteen hundred weight (of one hundred and twenty pounds each) is the usual charge : * which is first raked or spread over the floor of the furnace, and then the doors are closed to bring it to a red heat, when the doors are again opened, and the Ore is raked and stirred about, first from one

---

* At Whitfield Mill they found it more eligible to charge with twelve hundred weight of Ore, which they thought answered a better purpose, it was generally worked off in about six hours.

side of the furnace and then from the other, so as to
expose repeatedly every part of the Ore to the action
of the heat and the air, during several hours: at the
end of which time, the doors are again closed, and
the fire increased to an intense degree; by which the
reduction of the metal is effected, the same is collected in the bottom of the Furnace, and the slag swims
on the top of it to the depth of two or three inches.—
The tapping of the slag is then performed, by poking
out the stopping of lime, and the slag flows out like
melted glass, in appearance, and soon cools on the
stone floor of the building, in which state it is opake,
of a whitish grey colour, and moderately heavy: this
tapped or white slag, unknown here until the Cupolas
were introduced, received then the name of Macaroni slag, and used at first to be applied to the repair
of roads, and now is so at most Cupolas; but of late
years, Mr. Milnes has reserved all this kind of slag,
in vast heaps, in his Cupola Yard, thinking, that
either the improved processes of Metallurgy, or the
high price of Lead, may, at a future time, render it
advisable, to submit the same to some further process.
The Macaroni slag is no sooner run off, than the
smelter scatters in, upon the melted Lead, two or
three shovels full of quick-lime, in powder, which

has the effect of stiffening the remaining slag, which floats on the metal, by means of a rake (or hoe, rather); this slag is then drawn carefully off the metal, and raked out on to the floor, in a semi-fluid state, this is called Drawn-Slag, and is, when cold, of a very dark or black colour, and very heavy.

"The Lead-pan is then cleared out, if necessary, and the stopping of Lime being removed, the Lead is suffered to run clean out of the Furnace into the pan, which is then skimmed, and the dross is thrown back into the Furnace, where it exhibits the most vivid and beautiful changes of colours imaginable; the Lead is then taken out by ladles, and poured into seven or more cast iron moulds with round ends, of the proper size for pieces of Lead, which are placed in a row, and are then left to cool. A new charge of Ore is now let down into the Furnace, through the crown-hole, and the same operations repeated, by means of two sets of workmen, during every seven or eight hours, for the whole week."

The Smelting, or Ore Hearth, is of a rectangular form, it is about twenty-four inches long and twelve broad, inside measure, (see figure 1st, plate 10th) at the top; the depth is twenty-two or twenty-three inches, its bottom and sides are made of cast iron, the inside breadth of the said bottom is twenty-two inches and twenty in length; it is one casting, and is surrounded with a ledge, two inches and a half thick and four and a half high, on every side, but that facing the Work-stone, which latter is two feet ten inches in breadth, and one foot six inches in length; it also has a ledge of an inch thick, and the same in height on every side, but that opposite to the Hearth-bottom; it is placed at a slope of about four inches fall in its whole length of one foot six inches; the space betwixt its higher side and the Hearth-bottom, is generally four or five inches, which is made lead-tight by filling it up with a mixture of bone ashes and slime ore, lavigated with water, so that the length of the Hearth-bottom (twenty inches) added to this space, makes the whole inside measure of the Hearth, at the bottom twenty-four or twenty-five inches. The back ledge of the said bottom, is raised with a piece of cast iron, called a Back-stone, twenty-eight inches long and six and a half high, upon which rests the muzzle of the bellows pipe, over which is placed another piece of cast-iron, called a Pipe-stone, of the same length as the Back-stone, and eight inches high;

in its middle is a receptacle for the said bellows pipe, and it projects into the Hearth about two inches; the back part of the Hearth is further heightened, with another Back-stone, of the same length as the former one, of four or five inches in height, which completes the back part of the Hearth. Upon, or along, the two end ledges of the Hearth-bottom, are placed two castings, called Bearers, they are each twenty-six inches long and five inches square, of course, they project an inch or two over the ridge, or highest part of the Work-stone, which greatly tend to fix it firm in its place; then, at the elevation of five inches above these bearers, suported upon fire-brick, at the inside distance of twelve inches from the upper back of the Hearth, is placed the Fore-stone, which is of cast-iron, and is of the same form and dimensions as the lower back, upon which the bellows pipe rests; this Fore-stone is closed in at each end, with a piece of cast-iron, called a Key-stone, being an exact cube of ten inches the side, and these are supported by Masonry; and the intervening space on each end, betwixt these Key-stones and the back part of the Hearth, is filled up with other two castings, similar, and of the same dimensions, as the Key-stones which complete the Hearth, excepting a melting pot to re-

ceive the Lead, as it issues from the Hearth, in a
channel of nearly an inch in depth, formed obliquely
along the Work-stone.

From the above description it will be seen, that the
blast acts the length way of the Hearth, and that the
bottom, or, as it is called, pan, of the same, forms a
reservoir, twelve inches long, twenty-two broad,
and about five deep, which is capable of containing
five or six hundred weight of Lead, that is altogether
below the action of the heat, consequently, as the
Lead in Smelting oozes down in ignited drops, this reservoir of cooler Lead, must greatly tend to lessen the
waste of volatilization as it is formed; it will further
appear, that the fore part of the Hearth is open from
the under side of the Fore-stone to the upper side of
the Work-stone, a space of about twelve inches.—
I shall now enter upon the manual part of the process
of Smelting.

At the termination of every Smelting shift, there is
a part of the Ore, called *Browse*, that remains in a
semi-reduced state, intermixed with cinder and slag,
which is found to answer better to begin the succeed-
ing operation with, than raw or even roasted Ore; the

mode of commencing the working of this Hearth, is
as follows:—the internal part of it is filled with
peats, (a sort of decayed vegetable matter) these peats
are cast about twelve inches long and three square,
such of them as are put into the inner part of the
Hearth, are loosely thrown into it, but the front part
of them, next the Work-stone, are carefully walled
up; one of these peats being set on fire, and placed
before the muzzle of the bellows, which, being set a
blowing, rapidly communicates the conflagration
through the whole mass; to increase the heat, and to
give the fire more durability and firmness, a few
shovels full of coals are cast over these peats; after
these mixed substances are in a proper state of combustion, a quantity of the *Browse*, already mentioned,
is thrown over the top of them; then (and sometimes
before) the whole of the *Browse* is got into the Hearth,
the greatest part of its contents are brought upon the
Work-stone, before described, by the help of a large
iron poker, called a Gavelock, the refuse part of the Ore
designated grey slag, known to the practical smelter,
by its superior brightness to the *Browse*, is picked out
with a shovel, and thrown into the right hand corner
of the outside of the Hearth; the *Browse* is then returned back with a little coal, if heat be wanting;

and lime, if the *Browse* is not sufficiently disengaged
from the Slag, which is known by the whole of the
mass exhibiting a soft appearance, or tendency to
fusion, which the lime prevents from its affinity to the
Argillaceous, Siliceous, and Ferrigenous matter, in
forming them into lumps or balls, it is said, by the
smelter, to dry it up, but though the contents of the
Hearth is rendered thereby dryer and more porous,
yet it is effected by the agency of the lime in conso-
lidating these substances ; these lumps, called grey
slags, contain from one-tenth to one-fiftieth of the
Lead in the Ore, and is obtained at a higher heat
where the whole is fused in the Slag-Hearth (to be
described afterwards:) the heat, used in the Ore-
Hearth, may be said to be such as only to sweat the
Lead out, since the other matter is in a solid or fixed
state, which is one of the great reasons that this
Hearth produces the finest Lead, because it has, at
this low heat, the least affinity to, and, of course,
must be most completely disengaged from, its mineralizing agent, Sulphur. The *Browse* being returned
into the Hearth, as before described, a few shovels full
of Ore is then spread over the top of it; but, previous
to the *Browse* being put into the Hearth, after taking

out the slag, there is always about half a peat put
before the muzzle of the bellows, and being both extremely porous and combustible, not only preventing
any thing from getting into the pipe of the bellows,
but partially resisting the blast itself, yet suffering it
to pass, by that means it is forced to spread and per-
vade the whole contents of the Hearth ; as the orifice,
or muzzle of the bellows pipe, is only about two
inches diameter ; without something of this kind the
blast would only pass in a stream: this being done in
about ten to fifteen minutes, as the smelter must
judge upon, the contents are again brought upon the
Work-stone, the peat put before the muzzle of the
bellows, the grey slag picked out, coal and lime, in
proportions necessary, used, the *Browse* returned,
and a fresh supply or charging of Ore thrown over it,
and the above lapse of time suffered to pass ; the same
operation repeated for fourteen or fifteen hours, forms
a smelting shift ; in which time there is from twenty to
upwards of forty hundred weight of Lead produced.

In this manner the best of the Lead with the Silver,
is, as it were, sweat out, without the fusion of any
thing but these metals, in a complete state of
union.

The Slag-Hearth, with considerable modifications, has been used in this country upwards of one hundred years: its inner cavity is a parallelopipedon of twenty-six inches long,. twenty-two broad, and thirty-three in height; the bottom is composed of a plate, two inches thick, of cast iron, with a slight declination from the back to the fore-part; upon this bottom is placed, longitudinally on each side, the bearers, being castings similar to those of the Ore Hearth, already described, upon which the fore-part of the Hearth is placed, consisting of two pieces of cast iron, of about twelve inches in breadth, and twenty-six in length, so that there is an opening left betwixt the Hearth bottom and these Fore-stones of about seven inches, the additional height of two inches is got by placing a course of fire-brick betwixt these metal stones; the sides of the Hearth, above the bearers, are made of an open-grained Free-stone, and the back above the bellows pipe of the same material, but the back below being twenty inches in height is of cast iron.

Prior to the last twenty years, the Slag, in a state of liquefaction, was run off in cakes that fixed over the top of a pot, placed on the outside of the Hearth to receive the Lead, which were reduced by Stampers, to prepare them for washing; but is now run over the ledge of a pot, of a particular construction, into a walled cistern, six feet long, four deep, and four in breadth, filled by a stream of water constantly flowing through it, in order to keep the water in the cistern as cool as possible, which makes the fluid Slag fly to pieces. To adapt it for the operation of washing, and to make it better for that purpose, the stream of water and that of Slag should fall into the cistern, as nigh as may be, into the same place. It is necessary to state, that the internal part of this Hearth, above the bellows pipe, stands more or less need of repairs every shift, the fore-part excepted, and also the hind-part below the bellows pipe.

The mode of beginning to work this Slag-Hearth is, to fill it up from the bottom with small ashey cinders, beat pretty close to a height of seventeen inches, which is two or three inches below the muzzle of the bellows pipe, the orifice of which somewhat exceeds two inches diameter: the pot, for the reception of the Lead, is also filled with these sort of cinders, which, in both cases, are to answer the purpose of a filter. Upon this filter of cinders, in the inside of the

Hearth are put peats, similar to what is used in the Ore-Hearth, one of which, on fire, is placed before the bellows pipe, and the bellows set to work, which communicates the flame to the rest; then a covering of coal coke is thrown over the ignited peats, which upon arriving at a proper heat, a Stratum of grey Slag, or whatever matter else to be worked, is diffused over them, and, from time to time, as occasion requires, the grey Slag and coke is added *Stratum super Stratum.* In this process the Slag is made perfectly fluid as well as the Lead; but the latter separates from the former, by finding its way through the filter of ashey cinders, which the former cannot do from its viscidity. The moment the Slag becomes melted upon the filter, (which is soon after the commencement of the shift) the workman makes a hole through it, of about an inch wide, with a crooked poker through which it flows, in a red hot stream, into the cistern of water, (before described) passing over the pot, for the reception of the Lead, placed betwixt the] Hearth and cistern.

The Lead, obtained by Slag-Hearth Smelting, is always more impure than from the blast or Ore-Hearth, it never being so entirely freed from the

3 E

mineralizing substance, and the coke hardens it by imparting carbon; of course, it should never be used but in cases where the other Hearth fails, or is extremely slow in Smelting the Carbonates or Oxide of Lead.—See page 370.

THE REFINING OF LEAD

Was introduced into this country in the reign of *William* and *Mary,* but how far it was similar to the present mode of proceeding I do not know, though most probably it was partly the same; however, the speed of performing the work has been nearly doubled within the last fifty years.

Refining is performed in a Reverberatory Furnace, the Fire-place of which is twenty-two inches square, separated from the Furnace by a partition, called the Fire-bridge, fourteen inches broad; so that nothing but the flame enters the Furnace itself, and passes over the surface of the Lead in the Cupel, or Test, to the two flues on the opposite side of the Furnace, which terminates in a chimney near forty feet high.—

The Cupel, Test, or Vessel, in which this operation is conducted, consists of an oval iron frame, surrounded with a ledge three inches and three-quarters deep; its greater diameter is four feet, the lesser two and a half: it has four cross-bars at the bottom, of three inches and three-quarters in breadth and half an inch in thickness, as are the other parts of the frame; the first of these bars is nine inches from the fore-part of its rim or ledge, and the other three are placed at nearly equal distances from this bar to the back end of the rim. The Test-frame, as it is called, being so constructed, is beat full of a mixture of bone and fern ashes, with flat headed iron cakers, the said head being about one inch and an eighth in diameter. The proportion of the former of these ashes (by measure) to that of the latter is from one-eighth to one-sixteenth, according to the purity of the fern ashes, which are used on account of the vegetable alkali that they contain, as it has the property of semi-vitrifying the bone ashes or destroying their friability, and making them more durable. These ashes are levigated with water, mixed up together, and beat, as before described ; they are then scooped out with a small spade, made for that purpose, until they are left about three-quarters of an inch thick

upon the Test-frame bars, the sides are left two
inches broad at the top and two and a half at the
bottom all round the rim, excepting the fore-part,
called the Breast, which is five inches ; a hole is cut
out in this Breast of one inch and a quarter in width,
from the inner side of the frame, and six inches long,
with which the passage, or *gateway*, for the Litharge
communicates.

The Vessel, or Test, so formed, is put into the
Refining Furnace, (in fact it may be called its bottom) propped up at its proper height against, or
close to, an iron ring, fixed in the masonry of
the Furnace ; the height of the Furnace roof, from
this ring, is twelve inches at the fire-bridge side, and
nine at the flue.

The fire must be applied very carefully for drying
the Test, as too much heat will evaporate the water,
with which the ashes were moistened, too quickly, and
occasion the Test to fly in pieces: but being got perfectly dry and brought to a reddish heat, it is nearly
filled with melted Lead, previously fused in a cast-
iron pot, which takes about five hundred weight for
that purpose; but at the temperature the Lead is put

into the test; it becomes covered with a grey pellicle, called Dross, which is a mixture of the first Oxide of Metallic Lead; but, after increasing the heat of the Furnace, the Lead becomes of a whitish-red colour, and its whole surface is covered with the Litharge of Commerce, composed of about ninety-one of Lead and nine of Oxygen: the bellows are then set a blowing, from the bind-part of the Test, which forces the Litharge up to the Breast, and over the Gateway, (already detailed) where it falls upon a cast iron plate, level with the Refinery-floor, in clods, in which state it is taken to the Reducing Furnace to be re-converted into Lead.

The blast of atmospheric air, issuing through a muzzle, put over the bellows pipe, of a certain construction, not only mechanically sweeps off the Litharge from the surface of the Lead, but it also furnishes Oxygen for its formation, the refiner taking care to command the proper heat. As the surface of the Lead must necessarily depress, by its oxydizement to, or below, the level of the Gateway, more Lead is ladled in from the melting pot, to raise it to the proper height as often as that occurs; in this manner the operation is continued until eighty-four hundred

weight, or four Newcastle fodders of Lead is introduced into the Test; and the whole of the Silver in
that quantity is left in combination of about one
hundred weight of Lead: this is called rich Lead,
and is taken out of the Test. After a sufficient number of these pieces of rich Lead is got, as, by assay,
are found will make a cake of Silver, from one to two
thousand ounces, they are re-melted down again, and
the Silver is obtained in a Test, differently formed in
the bottom than the working Test, being hollowed so
as to receive the Silver, and leave a margin of the
bottom uncovered, that the Slag may be raked from
off the edges of the Silver. Thus the Lead, Copper,
Tin, &c. may be separated from the Silver, by the aid
of the Oxygen of the atmosphere, guided with proper care, and continued under a proper heat, until
the Silver only remains. Copper is not so easily separated from the Silver as the Lead, owing to its
great affinity to the former, and is found frequently
to occur in minute portions. Tin has only in one
Mine been found in the Refining of Silver, and is extremely difficult to extricate from it, on account of
its small affinity to Oxygen.

I only now have to observe, that the time of working off a Refiner's Test, of eighty-four hundred weight of Lead, is from sixteen to eighteen hours, if the muzzle (before alluded to) is properly made and put upon the bellows pipe.—The next Process is called

REDUCING,

And is opposite to REFINING, since it is restoring Litharge to its reguline state, or converting it into Lead. This operation has been sometimes performed in a Blast-Hearth, similar to that used in Ore-Smelting, but somewhat larger; but now done chiefly in the Reverberating Furnace, which is six feet long and near six broad, at the middle doors, inside measure; the Fire-place is twenty-five inches square, divided from the Furnace by a partition, or Fire-bridge; and it sometimes has only one and sometimes two flues, through which the flame enters the upright chimney.

In the Refining Furnace, as has been observed, nothing but the flame is permitted to act upon the Lead, because, any combustible, in a state of ignition, suffered to come in contact with that metal, would not only (by its superior affinity for Oxygen) prevent the conversion of Lead into Litharge, but would abstract the Oxygen from the Litharge that had been formed.   Upon this account the Litharge for the Reducing Furnace is carefully mingled with small coal, and the bottom of the Furnace previously covered, about two inches thick, with coals; the flame from the Fire-place very soon sets the coals on fire, and in a little time they are burnt to red hot cinders: the above mixture of Litharge and coal is then thrown upon them, and, by the proper management of the heat or flame in the Fire-place, the necessary temperature is kept in the Furnace, to enable the combustible matter to take the Oxygen from the Litharge and set the Lead at liberty; which, as that is done, is received into a cast iron pot, and then cast into pieces of one hundred weight and a half, and is called refined Lead. It is superior to other Lead, and gives the highest price in the market. Care should be taken, that something short of the necessary quantity of coal is intermixed with the Litharge, previous to its admission into the Furnace, because the workmen, upon seeing the want of them as the process goes on, can mingle (in such parts of the Furnace where they are wanted) a fresh supply of

them: this is a point that should be always particularly
attended to, since a redundancy of coal would necessarily increase the quantity of Slag, at the termination
of the shift, which is to be drawn out, and another
charging of Litharge put into the Furnace, intermixed with coal as before. In this Furnace six fodders of Lead may be run in nine or ten hours. There
is always fresh Litharge thrown into the Furnace during the first six hours of the shift.

It may appear, from the principles thus detailed,
upon which the Process of Reducing is conducted,
that the combustible matter, mixed with the Litharge, should be brought, as much as possible, in
contact with it ; but however specious that may be, it
is a known fact, that the work is neither done so well
nor so quickly, when these two substances are reduced very small ; because the operation is altogether,
or nearly so, confined to the surface, for want of the
admission of the air, for the proper combustion of the
coal mixed with the Litharge. On the contrary,
when a part of the Litharge is left cloddy, or about
the size of a hen's egg, the charge of the Furnace
may be said to work more in a mass, and the bitumin-

ous part of the coal becomes volatilized, pervading
the interstices of the Litharge, and promoting its reduction, by the abstraction of its Oxygen in various
points where the coal itself is not present : and this,
I conceive, is the reason, why a bituminous coal, in
the great work, is preferable to charcoal, since the
latter can only be effective in this Furnace : but,
where it is in immediate contact with the Litharge,
there is no doubt, but charcoal would do better,
were a heat applied to fuse the Litharge ; but that
ought never to be the case in a large Furnace, because
a part of the Litharge, I am afraid, would be un-
avoidably vitrified or run into glass, which, in that
state, is more tenacious of its Oxygen, than in the friable state.

THE ROASTING FURNACE

Has been used little more than twenty-five years, and
has undergone considerable alterations; those the
most approved are nearly of the same dimensions as
the Reducing Furnace, excepting the Fire-place,
which is about half as large again, and instead of a

door on each side, this Furnace has two additional
ones, for the more complete stirring of the Ore, &c.
that it is charged with; it also has two doors at the
flue end, admitting a passage through each of them,
so that the Ore can be raked from the Fire-bridge to
the flues, when the workmen observe much variation of the heat at the different ends of the Furnace.
It is always necessary to keep the heat as equal in
every part of the Furnace as possible, a thing which,
in a Furnace having to act upon Ores that require a
very different temperature for roasting, (say, at least,
as two is to one) is very difficult.   Now, a Furnace
constructed for the higher temperature, if used for
Ores requiring the lower, would act extremely un-
equally in similar distances, or spaces, from the Fire-
bridge to the flue, to what it would do in the case for
which it was adapted, because the flame, in the former
case, would play lambently over the whole surface of
its contents;   and in the latter, could perhaps be
barely permitted to hover over the Fire-bridge : hence
the reason of these end doors, I have alluded to, for
changing the Ore, as above described.

From nine to eleven hundred weight of Galena, or

other Ores of Lead, is thrown into this Furnace for a
charge, without any mixture whatever; three of these
chargings are usually worked off in eight hours. The
fire is introduced in such a manner as to produce a
copious smoke from the top of the Ore, and if any
part of it becomes soft or clammy, a fresh surface of
the Ore is presented to the flame and the Oxygen of
the atmosphere, by stirring or raking it transversely
or longitudinally, as occasion requires, the workmen
taking care to raise as much heat as the operation can
be conducted with, to keep the Ore from slagging or
having the least tendency to vitrifying; because,
whenever these occur, the oxydizement of the Sulphur,
Antimony, &c. or the expulsion of the fixed air, is
very much or entirely retarded; which, to get quit
of, is the principal object of this process. The other
object is to bake or cake the Slime Ore, and the
small metallic particles of the Horizontal Chimneys,
in which they are deposited or condensed, as they
pass from the Blast Hearth, Furnaces, &c.

These Horizontal Chimneys are, in some places,
carried in nearly a horizontal position, upwards of a
hundred yards, ending in an upright stalk; the gene-

ral dimensions of each of them (inside measure) are five feet in height and three in breadth: the plans are various, to suit different situations. But they collect the sublimates of Ore from the Blast Hearth, and the Oxides of Lead, &c. from the Refining Furnaces, the former of which, after washing that part deposited nearest the Blast Hearth, may be Smelted with the other part furthest from it, in the state it is got in the Chimneys, and the Lead obtained is frequently refined for Silver.

The other deposit, or Oxide of Lead, called Refiner's Fume, may be made into common Lead, or Lead nearly without Silver, and without washing; or is frequently grinded in oil for paint, which is a very durable pigment for out-door painting: when these two substances are Smelted, it is generally done in the Slag-Hearth.

The profit arising from them, generally remunerates for the expense of erecting these Chimneys; and, at the same time, the adjoining ground is, to a considerable extent, freed from the pernicious effects that these sublimates of Ore and Oxide of Lead (especially the latter) have upon the herbage, as well as upon the cattle which graze upon it.

It is obvious, that the Roasting Furnace operates upon the same principles, with whatever is subjected to its influence, as that of the Blast Hearth and Reverberatory Smelting Furnace (see pages 366 and 371): in fact, it is precisely the same as the latter as far as it goes; but the Ore, or whatever it is charged with, is drawn out in as friable a state as possible, without bringing it to Lead; which, to obtain, would require from two and a half to three times the hours allotted for Roasting: this Furnace is similar to the Cupola, excepting the bottom, which is perfectly level, (as it is not intended for the reception of Lead) and has, on that account, been considered by some as only an imperfect copy of it; but a little reflection will show the fallacy of that sort of reasoning, since, as an appendage to the Ore or Blast Hearth, the mode of Smelting, by their united means, undoubtedly possesses many decided advantages: first, the work is done at less expense by the saving of coal, and is also generally swifter, the Lead in every case much purer,

so much so, that where it has to be Refined, the loss
of Lead, I am told, is about one-ninth instead of
one-twelfth or one-thirteenth of the whole; as is the
case with Ore Hearth Smelting.

A more convincing proof of this fact cannot be
given, than that from the Ore of the same Mines
producing Lead which would make a profit by Refining; the Blast Hearth Lead only sunk about five
ounces of Silver per fodder, to compensate the
amount of workmen's wages, value of fuel, &c.
whereas the other took ten ounces for that purpose;
at least this was the standing order of the principles
of the Cupola Smelting, not to refine any Lead
containing less than that quantity.

The reason is very short, why it is and must be so,
(with a few modifications dependant on the habits of
the Ore in the fire) viz. if I exemplify in Galena,
that in the Cupola the Sulphur from the first to the
last stage of the shift is volatilized, under the simple
pressure of the atmosphere, by uniting to its Oxygen
(see page 369) ; whereas, in the Blast Hearth, the

pressure from the bellows is much greater, and thereby makes a much more complete separation of the Lead from the Sulphur, Antimony, &c. than can be done in the Cupola Furnace; and the reason of the greater waste of Refining the Lead must be, that these substances are not so completely liberated in the Smelting by the latter method as by the former; but when they have to undergo the action of the Refiner's Blast they are set free, and occasions the greater loss of Lead, I have before observed.

I am aware it has been thought, that, because the heat in the Furnace may be kept more equal than in the Blast Hearth, the Smelting might be conducted to a better purpose; but though there may, and certainly is, a greater diversity of temperature in the contents of the latter, yet that circumstance has little weight with it, since, wherever there is an active heat in it, the stream of air from the bellows must occasion the decomposition of the Ore and fuel, at the same moment and in the same ratio, which certainly will not be the case in the Furnace Smelting.

Having now gone through the different operations, as they are practised in this neighbourhood, in the Smelting of Lead Ore and other Processes appertaining thereunto, I shall now make a few observations upon Assaying for Lead and Silver:

Furnaces for that purpose are variously constructed; the simplest of which, consists of a rectangular Fireplace thirteen inches long eight broad and eleven in depth, with a Fire-bridge of the thickness of a brick, dividing it from the Furnace; the dimensions of which, when properly adapted to the Fire-place, must be about twelve inches square upon the bottom, which bottom must be perfectly level and about six inches distant from the under side of the roof: the flue ought to be an area of seven or eight inches, through which the fire passes into a chimney, fifteen or sixteen feet high from the floor. A Furnace of this sort, will admit two half-pound Assays of Lead for Silver, to go forward at the same time, conducted in circular Cupels of five inches and a half in diameter, made of the same materials as the Refiner's Test, surrounded with an iron ring; the depth of the rim ought to be near one inch and a half, in that case the Cupel may be scooped out on both sides for the reception of the Lead to be acted upon, and, of course, will answer twice.

The most eligible mode of placing these Cupels is, to put the one before the other, as they work off nearer at the same time. But when this Furnace is used for the Assaying of Ores of Lead, the Crucible is put into the Fire-place amongst the ignited cinders, so that it is possible, though not advisable, to have these two operations going on at the same time.

There are various methods of Assaying Galena and the other Ores of Lead; the most common for Galena is performed, either by Metallic Iron Filings or its grey Oxide, in scales. The Black Flux is another of the most general methods used; all of these methods are objectionable; as to the two first, they are no criterion for either the Lead or Silver; one exception is only to be made, with respect to the Lead obtained, where the Ore is perfectly free from Antimony, since the decomposition of the Ore is obtained by the union of the Iron, or its Oxide, with the Sulphur of the Galena, so that, where Antimony is present, it forms a compound with the Lead; whereas, in the great work, it is almost entirely dissipated;

the Silver also, to a considerable extent, unites with the scoria of these substances and the Sulphur, from its great affinity to Iron, and its Oxide; which scoria, in the fluid state, swims upon the surface of the Lead in the Crucible, and, by mingling a few small coals upon it, they become caked, which forms a sort of lid, and hinders the scoria, but not the Lead, from running out, when the Crucible is inclined to one side for that purpose: the Lead, thus got, must be put into a Melting Pan, and the lowest heat, or little more, at which pure Lead will fuse, applied, with a little small coal or charcoal diffused over it, for the reduction of the pellicle upon its surface: if this is carefully done, there will nothing remain but metallic Lead and its Silver, provided the Iron, or its Oxide, has been used in proper quantities for the engagement of the whole of the Sulphur, which, for nice Assaying, ought to be used as sparingly as can be done, to obtain all the Silver possible. But, as Sulphur exists in the Ore in question, (see page 367) in different proportions, it is the safest way not to use above a quarter of the weight of Iron to the Ore, (the proportion for pure Galena) and if, after the re-melting of the Lead from the Crucible, already described, any scoria remains unacted upon by the coal or charcoal, this scoria will be Sulphuretted Lead, and must be returned back again to the Crucible, from whence it was taken, with the addition of more Iron, &c. by which means the Lead and Antimony, with a great part of the Silver, will be obtained.

The other method of Assaying, viz. by the Black Flux, is not so objectionable, though, it is well known the vegetable alkali it contains, acts upon the Lead; but neither of them are to be depended upon, as they do not operate upon the same principles as that of the great work, and therefore cannot be used as a guide to the Practical Smelter, any more than by the humid modes of analysis; on which account, I prefer the Assaying of Galena, with or without Antimony, by the following method.

Pound the Ore very fine, in a mortar, give it a partial calcination upon a Fire-brick, scooped out like a table plate, placed in the body of the Assay Furnace; stir it repeatedly, for the oxydizement of the Sulphur and Antimony, for the space of three hours, then introduce this Roasted Ore into a black or grey Crucible, putting one of the legs of a small porcelain tube, bent at a right angle, to the bottom of the Crucible; the other leg must be attached to a pair of small bellows, the Crucible, with its contents, being placed in the Fire-place of the Assay Furnace, and the Ore brought to a red heat, avoiding indications of fusion: then strew over the matter, to be acted upon, a covering of small coal, upon which, when formed into a cake, place a piece of stone, or any thing to keep this lid of coal close down, the blast being made to issue from the bellows in a gentle manner; keeping up a due management of heat, the Lead and Silver will, in the course of three-quarters of an hour, be disengaged from the Ore, perfectly analagous to that of the great work.

As to the Assaying of the Carbonates and Oxides of Lead, it is only necessary in the former, to put it into a Crucible, placed as the foregoing one, and apply a sufficient heat to expel the carbonic acid gas, generally known by the name of fixed air, but it is better in most cases to add a little lime. The latter, viz. the Oxide, must be mixed with combustible matter, say coal or charcoal, which, indeed, is similar to the Process of Reducing, I would also add lime or chalk, where the principles of Sand or Clay are suspected.

The Lead, thus obtained, to be Assayed for Silver, must be treated as follows:

The Cupel (before described) being brought to a red heat in the Furnace, from a quarter to half a pound of Lead is put upon it, which soon melts, and becomes covered with Litharge; a part of this Litharge is volatilized, but the greater part is absorbed by the Cupel, and the Silver left behind in a globular form. It scarcely needs to be remarked, that the Ores and their produces must be accurately weighed, and the necessary calculations made.

As to the Assaying by the Muffle, it is conducted in the same manner as by the naked fire; the use of it is to hinder the circulation of air, in the Furnace, from taking off small particles of the metal; but it is more inconvenient for common practice, since it obviously must screen the Lead from the heat of the flame, which requires a longer time to start the Furnace; though, when it has once begun to operate, it is quicker, since the smoke of the naked flame (when it comes in contact with the Lead) reduces the Oxide of the Lead in the Cupel.

Where it is necessary to Assay Lead for Silver from the Ores of different Mines, a Furnace may be constructed to take off four of such Assays at one operation, by enlarging the Fire-place and Furnace about one-fourth; and, instead of placing one of its sides against a wall, as is commonly the case, let that end contiguous to the flue stand against such wall, so that access may be had to both sides of the Furnace, which is furnished on each side with a sliding door and valve, or two doors without a valve, and a moveable flue between it and the chimney. The Cupels being arranged in a square, (two in length and two in breadth) the operator carefully adjusts the flue and admission of external air through the valves, in such a manner, as to make the Process go equally forward in each Cupel. Allowing three hours for starting, a dexterous hand will take off sixteen Assays, of half-a-pound of Lead each, in less than six hours, which will be equally as well done as if only one was going forward.

GENERAL SUMMARY.

I shall now recapitulate the various Processes that Lead Ore and its products undergo in the order they take place, from the commencement to the termination of the Smelting-house operations; with an account of the marketable commodities resulting therefrom.

A certain weight of Ore being Roasted and taken to the Blast-Hearth, the greatest part of the Lead and Silver, in a state of union, is obtained, and the remainder is contained in the refuse matter called Grey Slag. (See page 380.) If the mixture of Lead and Silver contains too little of the latter to compensate for the trouble of Refining, then the Pieces or Bars are made one hundred weight and a half each, and marked O, to show that they are from Ore unrefined: but, if the Silver is more than will pay the expenses for separating it from the Lead, by Refining, these pieces, to make them more portable, are cast one hundred weight each, and taken to the Refining Furnace. The Grey Slag is taken to the Slag-Hearth, and if the Lead contained in it is refinable, it is also made into pieces of one hundred weight each: and the Slag Lead that will not pay the expense of Refining, is cast into pieces one hundred weight and a half each, and marked S, signifying that they are directly produced from Slag. This, and the before-mentioned Lead, marked O, is in the marketable state.

After Refining, the Lead is made into Pieces, one hundred weight and a half each; and that produced from Slag Lead, termed Refined Slag Lead, marked R. S. and the other, termed Refined Lead, marked L.

The Refiner's Test, or Vessel, that the Process of Refining is performed in, (see page 388) absorbs a considerable quantity of Litharge, or Oxide of Lead, which is Smelted in the Slag-Hearth, with the aid of Coal Coke and Black Slag, along with the refuse of the Reducing Furnace, being a mixture of Cinder and Oxide of Iron, more or less impregnated with Litharge. (See Reducing Furnace.) The Lead, so obtained, is generally whiter and harder than any other, being, as is the case with all that is got at the Slag-Hearth, partly carburetted. This Lead is not refinable, and is cast into Pieces of one hundred weight and a half each, marked S, the same as the unrefinable Slag Lead from Ore. It may be necessary to remark, that the Black Slag, above-mentioned, is the Fluid Slag got by the Smelting of Grey Slag,

3 H

(see page 385) which, when used as a Flux, is run off into cakes and broke into small pieces; this Flux is also used for working the deposits from the Horizontal Chimnies, after Roasting, in the Slag-Hearth.

REFERENCES TO PLATES.

PLATE 10.

Figure 1, is a horizontal section of the Ore-Hearth bottom and Work-stone; *b*, *c*, *a*, is the bottom and *r* the Work-stone, of cast iron; the space betwixt them, *W*, is made lead-tight, with Bone Ashes and Slime Ore, as described in page 377; *x*, is the Pot for receiving the Lead.

Note.—In this Figure, as well as the following, the Orifice of the Bellows Pipe ought to have been advanced to the inside of the Hearth-Bottom and Back.

Figure 2, is a perpendicular section of an Ore-Hearth, taken longitudinally in the middle, or line of Bellows Pipe; *g*, is the solid part of the Hearth-Bottom; and, by mistake, is here drawn too thick, as it should be about two inches and a half; the space betwixt *g* and *a* is its ledge, of four inches and a half, which is here made too little; the dotted space, *W*, is five inches wide and is stopped with Bone Ashes, &c. as observed in Figure 1; *c*, *d*, is the Work-stone, its thickness is about four inches and a half, but is here made too little; *a*, *b*, is one of the Bearers; *g*, *h*, is the Back-stone, which the Bellows Pipe rests upon, and ought (in the figure)

to have been placed on the same level with the Bearers, it is six inches and a half high and is one inch and a half above them at the top, since their height is only five inches; h, k, is the Pipe-stone eight inches high, upon it is another back of five inches in height; e, is the top of the back part of the Hearth; f, the floor of the House; m, is the Fore-stone, and the cavity below the Work-stone, at d, the Pot for receiving the Lead; the height, from the end of the Work-stone, at d, to the floor, is, in this figure, only about one half of what it should be, namely fifteen inches, though the whole height of the Hearth is correct, as is the application or order of placing the various castings, excepting the Back, at h, (before pointed out) which alone makes an error of five inches, together with a little inaccuracy in the other dimensions. See pages 376, 377, 378, and 379.

Figure 3, is a horizontal section of the bottom of the Slag-Hearth and appendages; m, m, the sides, the space a, b, f, c, the Pot, P the Reservoir, and W the Pipe for supplying the water; the line or partition, b, c, stands a little higher than the top of the Pot, but does not go within three inches of the bottom; through this space the Lead, after passing through the Filter of Cinder, (described in page 384) flows into the triangular part of the Pot, b, f, c, from whence it is ladled into Pieces.

Note.—There is a mistake in this drawing: the sides, m, ought to have been continued up to the line, b, f, so that the wide part of the Pot, which is six inches more than the line, b, c, might enter the inside of the Hearth, to admit the Slag, when in its highest state of fluidity, to fall upon the Filter of Ashes in the Pot, that the Lead may more completely make its escape through the Filter, which penetrates with more facility as it is hotter.

Figure 4, is a sketch, or foreside view of a Slag-Hearth, when off work, a is the top, in which the matter, to be

3 H 3

Smelted, and the fuel is put; b, b, Fore-stones, of cast iron; c, c, the Cheeks or Sides, of Free-stone; d, d, cast iron Bearers; the inner curved line in front of the Fore-stones b, b, represents the side of the Slag-Hearth Pot, and the outer one its ledge or lip, over which the Slag falls into the space before it, being a Reservoir of water.

Figure 5, is a sketch of the same when at work. See pages 383 and 384.

Figure 6, is a perpendicular section of a Slag-Hearth; a, a, are the Fore-stones; e, the Pipe-stone or Back, of Free-stone; f, the Back, of cast iron, below the Bellows Pipe; s, the line of Blast.

Figure 7, is a perpendicular section of an Assay Furnace, see page 407, where a, is the Fire-place; b, the Fire-bridge; c, c, two bricks for covers to the Fire-place, to be taken off for the admission of fuel; d, the Cupel; f, a Flue or Chimney to take off the smoke that escapes from the covers c, c; e, the Flue of the Furnace, which communicates, as well as the former one, f, with the Chimney.

Figure 8, is a horizontal section of an Assay Furnace; a, is the Fire-place, with Grate-bars; b, the Fire-bridge; c, the Cupel in the Furnace; and d, the Flue.

PLATE 12.

Figure 1, is a perpendicular section of a Roasting Furnace; A, the inside of the Furnace; B, the Fire-bridge, over which the flame passes from the Fire-place, C; D, one of the Grate-bar Supporters,—there is always two or three of them, upon which the Bars rest; E, the Ash Pit; F, the Teas-hole, where the coals are introduced into the Fire-place, C; G, one of the Flues; H, one of the Door-ways, through which the Ore is raked and stirred longitudinally; J, J, J, Doors, for raking and stirring the Ore transversely, the middle one, being larger, is also used for charging and drawing; the other side

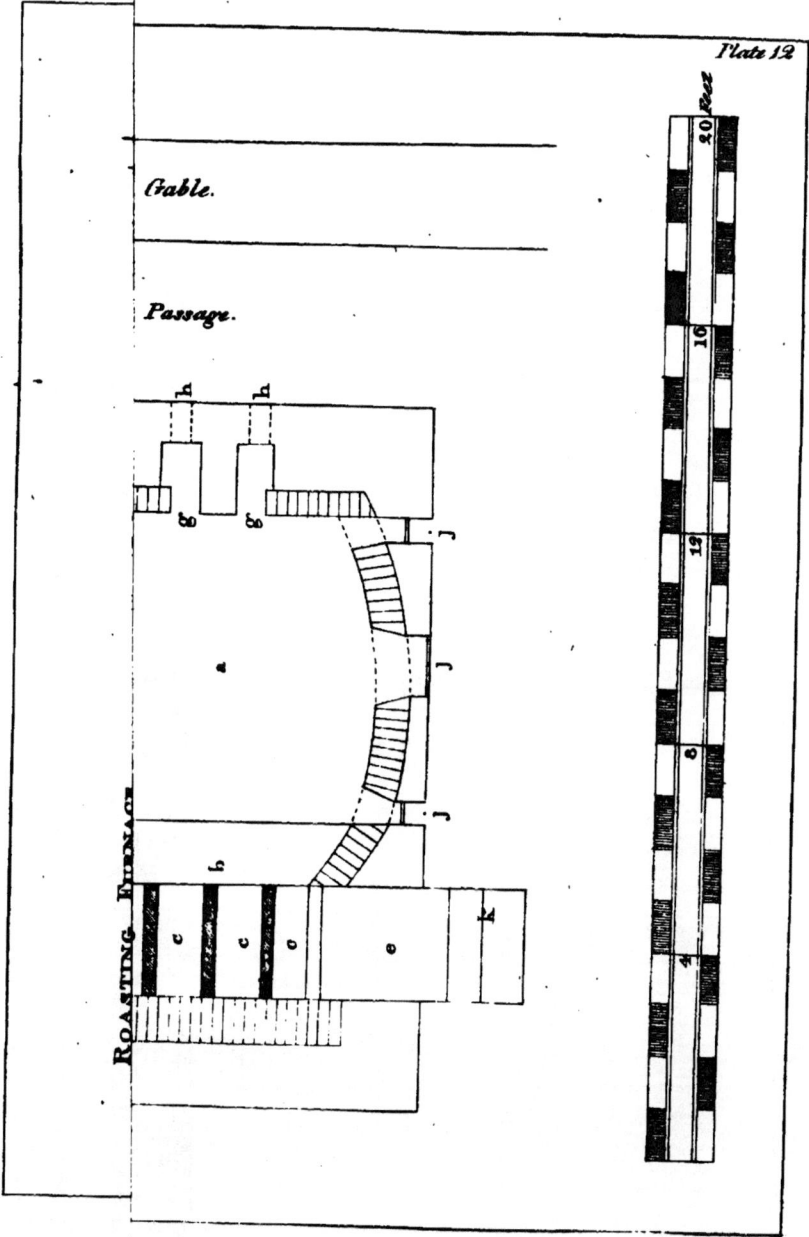

Plate 12

Plate 13

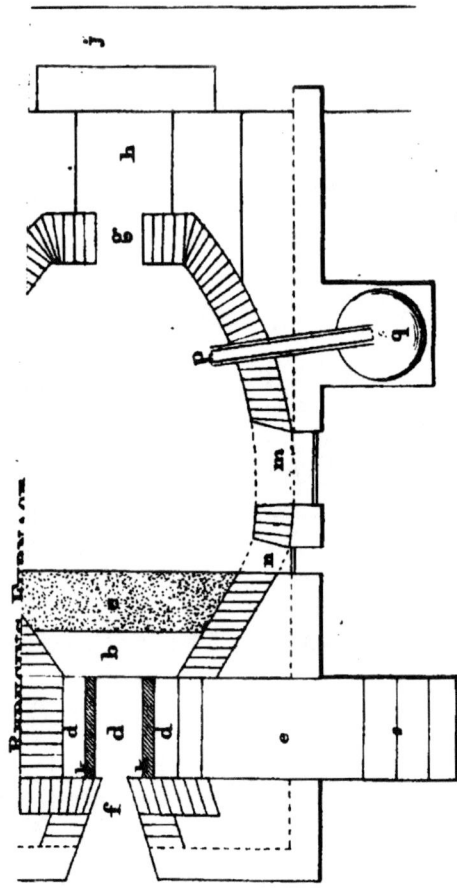

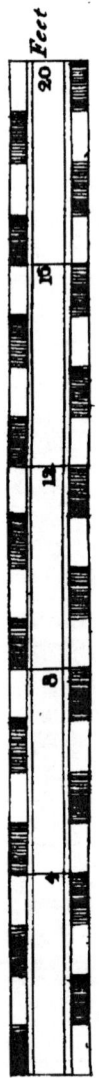

of the Furnace has similar ones; attached to the middle doors is a Flue, on the outside of the Furnace, communicating with the Chimney, for taking off the smoke; K, is an opening, to which is affixed two doors, for taking the Coal Slag out of the Fire-place; L, is a hole for cleansing the Chimney, which is closed when the Furnace is at work; M, ends of the Grate-bars; N, roof of the Furnace, being a nine-inch brick thick; O, passage for the smoke and flame to the chimney, P; Q, passage round the Furnace; R, is the Gable Wall of the House.

Figure 2, is a horizontal section of the Roasting Furnace, a, is the Furnace bottom, composed of Fire-brick set edge-wise, upon cast iron plates; the whole thickness of the bottom is six inches, the space below being hollow; b, the Fire-bridge; c, c, c, c, the Fire-place; d, d, d, supporters of the Grate-bars; e, the Ash-pit; f, the Teas-hole, or entrance of coal into the Fire-place; g, g, the Flues; h, h, Doors, through which the Ore is raked and stirred; j, j, j, j, j, j, Doors of the Furnace; k, Steps into the Ash-pit.

Note.—The space betwixt the external and middle line, is the Casing of the Furnace, and is made of Stone, bound, longitudinally and transversely, with Iron; and the space between the middle and internal line, is the Lining of the Furnace, made of Fire-brick.

PLATE 13.

Figure 1, is a perpendicular section of the Reducing Furnace; A, is the inside of the Furnace; B, C, the Fire-bridge, the part B is of Fire-brick, and the other part, C, is made of Bone Ashes, prepared with a mixture of Fern Ashes, in the same manner as for making a Refiner's Test, beat with small headed pokers; D, the Fire-place; E, the Ash-pit; F, the Teas-hole, where the Coals are introduced; G, the Flue; H, the Chimney; J, the Gable Wall of the

House; K, one of the Grate-bar Supporters; L, ends of the Grate-bars; M, the drawing Door, opposite to which on the other side is that for charging; N, Door to take the Slag from the Fire-bridge, opposite to it on the other side, is a similar one, by which means the Fire-bridge may be kept to a proper size, as the Slag that attaches to it can be taken off, as it occurs in a hot state, without injuring the Furnace bottom, which is the case when done cold; O, Roof of the Furnace, which is a nine-inch brick in thickness; P, a Hole for cleansing the chimney, which is closed when the Furnace is at work.

Figure 2, is a horizontal section of the Reducing Furnace; a, the Furnace bottom, is made of Black Slag, run about four inches thick, supported by common brick edgewise upon cast iron plates of one inch thick; but the safest way for turning the Lead is to beat a layer, of the Ashes the Refiners use for making Tests, an inch thick, upon the plates; the said Slag bottom declines a little on all sides to the Tap-stone, to allow the Lead to run off; the part below the plates is hollow; b, c, the Fire-bridge, made of Fire-brick and Refiner's Ashes, as before described; d, d, d, the Fire-place; e, the Ash-pit, f, the Teas-hole; g, the Flue; h, the bottom of the chimney; j, Gable Wall of the House; k, k, Grate-bar Supporters; m, the Drawing Door; n, n, Doors, for cleansing the Fire-bridge of Slag; o, the Charging Door; p, the Tap-stone, along which the Lead issues to q, the Pot for receiving it.

Note.—The inside of the Furnace is made of Fire-brick, and the outside of Stone bound, like the Roasting Furnace, with Iron.

PLATE 14.

Figure 1, is a Test-frame, see page 387, where it is described as having only four Cross-bars, which is the present mode of making them, only putting the bars a little more separate, that the fourth one may be about three inches farther back than it is here drawn, which supersedes the use of the fifth in this figure.

Fig. 1. Fig. 2.

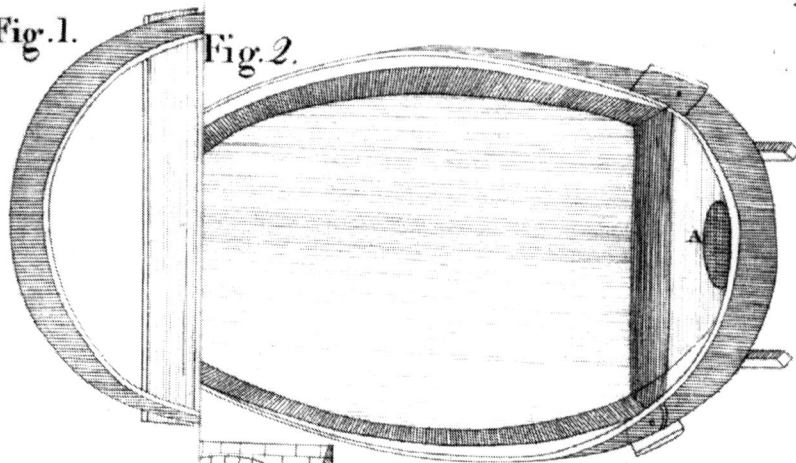

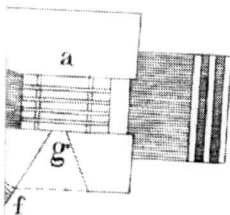

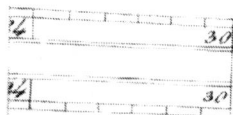

Figure 2, is the representation of a Test-frame, lined with ashes, called a Test fit for work, see pages 387 and 388, where A is the gateway of the Litharge.

Figure 3, is a perpendicular section of two Refining Furnaces, with part of the Chimnies; a, a, the Fire-places; b, b, the Fire-bridges; c. c, tops of the same, where the flame passes over to the Test in the Furnaces d, d; e, e, the Flues; f, f, the inside of the Chimnies; g, g, Holes, on the back part of the Chimnies, to take out the fume deposited, which are closed up when the Furnace is working; h, h, the Ash-pits.

Note.—This figure is the back representation on the bellows side of the Furnace.

Figure 4, is a horizontal section of two Refining Furnaces, showing the Test in the one full of Lead, as when at work, and the other, with a Test also in it, with the common position of a cake of Silver, represented by the internal oval; a, a, the Fire-place of each Furnace; b, b, Fire-bridges; c, the Test at work, full of Lead; d, that with a cake of Silver in it; e, e, e, e, passage from the Flues to the Chimney; f, f, f, f, Feeding Holes, through which the Pieces of Lead were formerly introduced, as wanted, into the Test: but they are now generally discontinued, as these Pieces were melted by the heat of the Furnace, which was, on that account, to be made greater than when put in melted (see page 388); the waste of Lead, by volatilization, being considerably lessened by working at this lower heat; g, g, Teas-holes or entrance of the fuel into the Fire-places, a, a; h, h, h, h, Holes, to take out the fume on each side of the Furnace chimnies, i, i; at present the two holes in the front are left off as the Chimnies may be cleaned without them; and in, or adjoining, that part of the Chimney betwixt the two Furnaces, are placed two Melting Pots, the flues from which enter each of the Furnaces at the two inside holes, f, f, at which the Lead used to be put; k, is the Litharge falling from the Test, and forming into clods.

LIST OF SMELTING HOUSES,

In the Counties of

NORTHUMBERLAND, CUMBERLAND, WESTMORLAND,

AND DURHAM.

◆

Allen Mill. : : : :	2 Roasting Furnaces,
	5 Ore Hearths,
	2 Refining Furnaces,
	1 Reducing ditto.
Allenheads Mill. : :	1 Roasting ditto,
	3 Ore Hearths,
	1 Slag ditto.
Blaydon Mill. : : :	4 Refining Furnaces,
	2 Reducing ditto,
	1 Slag Hearth.
Dukesfield Mill. : :	2 Roasting Furnaces,
	5 Ore Hearths,
	2 Slag ditto,
	2 Refining Furnaces,
	1 Reducing ditto.

In the county of Northumberland, the property of Colonel and Mrs. Beaumont, and occupied by the same.

Rookhope Mill. : :	1 Roasting Furnace,	
	3 Ore Hearths,	In the county of Durham, the property of Colonel & Mrs. Beaumont, and occupied by the same.
	1 Slag ditto.	
Eggleston High Mill.	1 Roasting Furnace,	
	1 Smelting ditto,	
	2 Ore Hearths,	In the county of Durham occupied by the London Lead Company
	2 Refining Furnaces,	
	1 Reducing ditto.	
Ditto Middle Mill. :	3 Ore Hearths,	At present much out of repair.
	1 Smelting Furnace,	
	2 Refining Furnaces.	
Ditto Low Mill. : :	1 Roasting Furnace,	
	1 Smelting ditto,	
	2 Ore Hearths.	
Gandless Mill. : :	1 Roasting Furnace,	
	2 Smelting ditto,	
	2 Refining ditto,	In the county of Durham the property of the Earl of Darlington, and occupied by the same.
	1 Reducing ditto,	
	3 Ore Hearths,	
	1 Bone Ash Mill.	

3 I

Dufton Mill. : : : 4 Ore Hearths.

In the county of Westmorland, the property of the Earl of Thanet, & occupied by the London Lead Company.

Hilton Mill. : : : 1 Roasting Furnace,

1 Refining ditto,

4 Ore Hearths.

In the county of Westmorland, occupied by J. Bland, Esq.

Langley Mill. : : 5 Roasting Furnaces,

10 Blast Hearths, for

Smelting Ores

and Slags,

4 Refining Furnaces,

2 Reducing ditto,

1 Zinc Furnace,

1 Laboratory.

In Northumberland, the property of the Commissioners and Governors of Greenwich Hospital.

Nenthead Mill. : : 4 Roasting Furnaces,

2 Refining ditto,

1 Reducing ditto,

4 Ore Hearths,

1 Slag ditto.

In Cumberland, the property of the London Lead Company, and occupied by the same.

Tyne-head Mill. : : 2 Ore Hearths,

1 Slag ditto,

1 Refining Furnace,

1 Reducing Hearth.

In Cumberland, occupied by John Lowry, Esq.

Cross Fell Mill. : : 2 Ore Hearths,

Occupied by the Cross Fell Lead Mine Company.

Stanhope Mill. : : 3 Ore Hearths,

1 Slag ditto,

9 Furnaces.

In the county of Durham, occupied by the London Lead Company.

Bolyhope Mill. In the county of Durham, occupied by Thomas Hopper, Esq.

Whitfield Furnaces. Now in Ruins. In the county of Northumberland; the property of William Ord, Esq.

Edmond-byers Mill. 2 Ore Hearths.

1 Roasting Furnace,

1 Slag Hearth,

1 Refinery.

In the county of Durham, occupied by John Cresswell Jopling, Esq.

Jefferies Mill. In the county of Durham, occupied by the Derwent Lead Company.

Healy Field Mill. : 1 Roasting Furnace,
2 Ore Hearths,
1 Refining Furnace,
1 Reducing Hearth.
} In the county of Durham, occupied by the Healy Field Mine Company.

Before we leave this subject, I presume, it will not be improper to give an estimate of the Average Produce of the Mines in Weardale, Teesdale, and Alston-moor; including the Mines at Cross Fell, along with some other Mines, in Westmorland; from the year 1800, down to 1821 :

	Bings, per annum.
Teesdale Mines, in the county of Durham, :	8000
Weardale Mines, Ditto,	17000
Allendale Mines, in Northumberland, : : :	8000
Alston-moor and Cross Fell, in Cumberland, :	19000
Dufton Fell, Dun Fell, Silver Band, and Hilton Mines, in the county of Westmorland,	1500
Total : : :	53500

By stating the Ore to take, upon an average, four Bings and a half, to make a ton of Lead, the produce will be nearly Eleven Thousand Eight Hundred and Eighty-nine Tons of Lead.

It is supposed, that there were Sixty-three Thousand Six Hundred and Eighty-six Ounces of Silver made at Langley Mills, in 1820.

◆

The following is the quantity of Lead Shipped at the Port of Newcastle. Average, per annum, for six years, previous to the year 1776,—7072½ Tons.

In 1804 : : : : : : : : :	10352 tons.
1805 : : : : : : : : :	9162 ,,
1806 : : : : : : : : :	3911 ,,
1807 : : : : : : : : :	6809 ,,
1808 : : : : : : : : :	8155 ,,
1809 : : : : : : : : :	4972 ,,
1810 : : : : : : : : :	5670 ,,
1811 : : : : : : : : :	4553 ,,
1813 : : : : : : : : :	6470 ,,*

---

* Price of common Lead, April, 1814, £30 per fother, of 21 cwt.; of refined Lead, £31 per fother; of fine Silver, 7s. 5d. per ounce.

N. B.—The fother, on the Tyne, is 21 cwt.; on the Tees, 22 cwt.

Having now, in the preceding pages, gone through the Operations of DRESSING and SMELTING LEAD ORES, as practised in the Northern Counties of England, it only remains to state, that the Author hopes the subject will be interesting, and, at the same time, of utility to Practical Men and Mining Adventurers; although he does not doubt, but there may be many Improvements and Discoveries yet made in Mining concerns, &c.: and no one, whoever the discoverer may be, will more gladly hail the signal of improvement than the Author.

APPENDIX.

ADDITIONAL NOTES.

Note to Pages 73 and 112.

THE Strata, on the north side of the Great Stublick Dyke, has a great acclivity or rise to the north or north-west, from the vale of *South Tyne*, at *Haydon* Bridge and *Newbrugh*, which causes the Lead Measures to crop out, or basset, from beneath the lower series of the Newcastle Coal Measures. Some Lead Mines have been opened at *Settling-stones*, (see page 112) and also at a place called *Whiteley Well*, in the parish of *Haydon*, about one mile and a half north-west of *Haydon* Bridge; this Mine appears to be in a Lime-stone, denominated the Great Lime-stone, (No. 153 in the engraved Section) and has been worked by Messrs. Coats and Johnson, of *Haydon* Bridge.

Note on Page 108.

The Acqueduct Level of *Nent-force*, which is now driving down from *Old Haggs* Engine Shaft, (sunk by the Commissioners and Governors of Greenwich Hospital, for the double purpose of an Air Shaft, and forwarding this Stupendous Work) will, very probably, be Holed through to a Drift in the course of two years, and will then exceed four miles in length. There is also another Level driving, from the above Shaft, to the southward, under the Scar Lime-stone, being at a higher level, or not so deep from the surface; it will answer the purpose of a double Drift, and will be a means of greatly facilitating the future operations of the work. The above Shaft is the largest that has been sunk in *Alston-moor;* and the machinery is admirably adapted for the purpose, there being a Water-wheel for pumping the water from the works, and a double-bucketted Water-wheel for drawing the Stone, &c.

Strangers, who are wishful to view this Stupendous Level, may be accommodated with Boats and Guides, by application at the Lowbyer Inn, near *Alston;* and, I make no doubt, but those who have the curiosity of taking a subterraneous sail or passage, will be highly gratified, especially when accompanied with Music, which is grand beyond description.

Note to Page 260.

In note, bottom of the above page, I have stated the firm of the *Langley* Zinc Works to be Mr. Thos. Shaw and Co. but the true firm is Whaly, Mulcaster and Co.

Note to Pages 264 and 265.

By mistake, Whetstone Mea Vein, or Dyke, is stated to intersect with the Great Stublick Dyke, between *Cupola* Bridge and *Langley* Smelt Mills; which ought to be between *Cupola* Bridge (a little below the conflux of *East* and *West Allen* Rivers, in *Whitfield*, in the county of Northumberland) and *Eals* Bridge, over the *South Tyne* River, about four miles below *Alston*, in Cumberland. It is the Great *Burtree-ford* Dyke that will probably intersect with the Great Stublick Dyke, between *Cupola* Bridge

and *Langley* Smelt Mills. There is another strong
Vein, or Dyke, known by the name of *Fallow Field*,
which crosses the *North Tyne* River, about two miles
and a half south-west of *Hexham*, in Northumberland,
bearing a south-east and north-west direction, which
has formerly raised great quantities of Lead Ore: its
throw is considerably down to the north, as the Coal
Measures are found on that side.

Note to Page 308.

It may be observed here, that the bearings and
distances of the Mines in *Weardale*, &c. are only *estimated*, and I doubt they will be found inaccurate in
many instances ; but I hope the List will be interesting and useful to Mineralogists, who may visit these
Mining Districts.

A LIST OF THE COLLIERIES,

NEAR CHILCOMPTON,

In the county of Somersetshire, about twelve miles
S. W. of the city of Bath;

*With the Depth of each Colliery in yards, commencing
at the Mountain Lime-stone or Lead Measures,
near Nettle Bridge.   April 12, 1821.*

		Yards.
1. Embrow : : : : : : Colliery : :		45
2. Moor Wood : : : : : : *ditto* : :		140
3. Bentar Works : : : : : *ditto* : :		120
4. Nettle Bridge : : : : : *ditto* : :		50
5. Adford Works : : : · : *ditto* : :		120
6. Edford Marsh : : : : : *ditto* : :		100
7. Leacham : : : : : : *ditto* : :		100
8. Bobstar : : : : : : : *ditto* : :		100
9. Breach : : : : : : : *ditto* : :		70
10. Vobstar : : : : : : : *ditto* : :		80
11. Tor : : : : : : : : *ditto* : :		45

The above abut against the Mountain Lime-
stone to the westward, near *Nettle* Bridge, the
Coal Measures turning up nearly vertical in
the basset.

Yards.

36. Tening Work : : : : : :	Colliery	: :	300
37. New Grove : : : : : :	ditto	: :	250
38. Hay's Wood : : : : : :	ditto	: :	290
39. Puilton Works : : : : :	ditto	: :	300
40. Buttons : : : : : : :	ditto	: :	250
41. Hamwork : : : : : :	ditto	: :	150
42. Upper Hamwork : : : : :	ditto	: :	150
43. Radford, near the Canal : :	ditto	: :	400
44. Withy Mills : : : : : :	ditto	: :	120
45. Clandown : : : : : : :	ditto	: :	403

(The deepest Colliery in England.)

46. Radstock, Old Pit : : : :	ditto	: :	300
47. ————, Middle Pit : : :	ditto	: :	250
48. Ludlow : : : : : : :	ditto	: :	200
49. Withlay : : : : : : :	ditto	: :	250
50. Camerton : : : : : : :	ditto	: :	270

(Six miles south-west of Bath.)

51. Dunkerton : : : : : :	ditto	: :	230

HEIGHT

Of some of the most Remarkable

MOUNTAINS AND HILLS

IN ENGLAND AND WALES.

The following admeasurements of the English and Welsh Mountains, are extracted from the valuable "TRIGONOMETRICAL SURVEY," begun by Major-General Roy, and completed by Lieutenant-Colonel Mudge; which I have copied from Mr. Bakewell's "INTRODUCTION TO GEOLOGY," 2nd Edition.

	Feet.
Allington Knoll, Kent : : : : : : :	329
Arbury Hill, Northamptonshire : : : :	804
Arran, Fowddy, Merionethshire : : : :	2955
Arrenig, Ditto : : : : :	2809
Axedge, Derbyshire : : : : : : : :	1751
Bagshot Heath, Surrey : : : : : : :	463
Banstead, Surrey : : : : : : : :	576
Bar Beacon, Staffordshire : : : : : :	653

	Feet.
Beacon Hill, Wiltshire : : : : : : :	690
Beacons, Brecknockshire : : : : : :	2862
Bardon Hill, Leicestershire : : : : : :	853
Beachy Head, Sussex : : : : : : :	564
Beeston Castle, (top of) Cheshire : : : :	556
Black Comb, Cumberland : : : : : :	1919
Black Down, Dorsetshire : : : : : :	817
Black Hambleton Down, Yorkshire : : :	1246
Bleasdale Forest, Lancashire : : : : :	1709
Boulsworth Hill, Ditto : : : : :	1689
Botley Hill, Surrey : : : : : : : :	880
Bow Fell, Cumberland : : : : : : :	2911
Bow Hill, Sussex : : : : : : : :	702
Bradley Knoll, Somersetshire : : : : :	973
Broadway Beacon, Gloucestershire : : : :	1086
Brown Clee Hill, Shropshire : : : : :	1805
Cader Ferwyn, Merionethshire : : : :	2563
Cader Idris, Ditto : : : : :	2914
Caermarthan Vau, Caermarthanshire : : :	2596
Calf Hill, Westmorland : : : : : : :	2188
Cam Fell, Yorkshire : : : : : : : :	2245
Capellante, Brecknockshire : : : : : :	2394
Carnedd David, Caernarvonshire : : : :	3427

4 B

	Feet.
Carnedd Llewellyn, Caernarvonshire : : :	3469
Carraton Hill, Cornwall : : : : : : :	1208
Castle Ring, Staffordshire : : : : : :	715
Cheviot, Northumberland : : : : : :	2658
Collier Law, Durham : : : : : : :	1678
Coniston Fell : : : : : : : : : :	2577
Cradle Mountain, Brecknockshire : : :	2545
Cross Fell, Cumberland : : : : : : :	2901
Crowborough Beacon, Sussex : : : : :	804
Dean Hill, Hampshire : : : : : : :	539
Ditchling Beacon, Sussex : : : : : :	858
Dover Castle, Kent : : : : : : : :	469
Dundry Beacon, Somersetshire : : : :	1668
Dunnose, Isle of Wight : : : : : : :	792
Dwggan, near Builth, Brecknockshire : : :	2071
Epwell Hill, Oxford : : : : : : : :	836
Fairlight Down, Sussex : : : : : : :	599
Farley Down, near Bath, Gloucestershire : :	700
Firle Beacon, Sussex : : : : : : : :	820
Folkstone Turnpike, Kent : : : : : :	575

Feet.

Landinan Mountain, Montgomery : : : : 1898

Llanelian Mountain, Denbighshire : : : : 1110

Llangeinor Mountain, Glamorganshire : : : 1859

Leith Hill, Surrey : : : : : : : : 993

Lillyhoe, Hertfordshire : : : : : : : 664

Long Mount Forest, Shropshire : : : : : 1674

Long Mountain, Montgomery : : : : : 1330

Lord's Seat, Derbyshire : : : : : : : 1715

Malvern Hill, Worcestershire : : : : : 1444

Moel Fammau, Denbighshire : : : : : 1845

Moel Morwith,   Ditto   : : : : : 1767

Mow Copt, Cheshire : : : : : : : 1091

Nine Standards, Westmorland : : : : : 2136

Orpit Heights, Derbyshire : : : : : : 980

Pendle Hill, Lancashire : : : : : : 1803

Pengaen, Merionethshire : : : : : : 1510

Penmaen Maur, Caernarvonshire : : : : 1540

Pennigent Hill, Yorkshire : : : : : : 2270

Pillar, Cumberland : : : : : : : 2893

Plynlimmon Mountain, Cardiganshire : : : 2463

	Feet.
Radnor Forest, Radnorshire : : : : :	2163
Rivel Mountain, Caernarvonshire : : : : :	1866
Rivington Hill, Lancashire : : : : : :	1545
Rodney's Pillar, (base of) Montgomery : :	1199
Rook's Hill, Sussex : : : : : : : :	702
Roseberry Topping, Yorkshire : : : :	1022
Rumble's Moor, Yorkshire : : : : : :	1308
Saddleback, Cumberland : : : : :	2787
Sea Fell, (low point) Ditto : : : : :	3092
Sea Fell, (high point) Ditto : : : : :	3166
Sherwood Forest, Nottinghamshire : : :	600
Shooter's Hill, Kent : : : : : : : :	446
Shunnor Fell, Yorkshire : : : : : : :	2329
Skiddaw, Cumberland : : : : : : :	3022
Snea Fell, Isle of Man : : : : : : :	2004
Snowden, Caernarvonshire : : : : : :	3571
Stow Hill, Herefordshire : : : : : : :	1417
Stow on the Wold, Gloucestershire : : : :	883
Tregarron Down, Cardiganshire : : : : :	1747
Trelleg Beacon, Monmouthshire : : : : :	1011

	Feet.
Water Cragg, Yorkshire : : : : : : :	2186
Weaver Hill, Staffordshire : : : : : :	1154
Wendover Down, Buckinghamshire : : :	905
Wernside, (in Ingleton Fells) Yorkshire : :	2384
Whernside, (in Kettlewell Dale) Ditto : :	2263
White Horse Hill, Berkshire : : : : : :	893
Wittle Hill, Lancashire : : : : : : :	1614
Wrekin, Shropshire : : : : : : : :	1320

MOUNTAINS IN SCOTLAND.

	Feet.
Arthur's Seat, Edinburgh : : : : : : :	810
Salisbury Craigs : : : : : : : : :	550
Hart-fell, Dumfriesshire : : : : :	3304 or 2800

(Supposed, by Mr. Jameson, the highest in the south of Scotland.)

	Feet.
Goatfield, Island of Arran : : : : : :	2945
Ben Lomond, Stirlingshire : : : : : :	3262
Ben Lawers, Perthshire : : : : : : :	4051
Ben Mere, Ditto : : : : : : :	3870
Schehalien : : : : : : : : :	3281 or 3564
The most southern of the Paps of Jura : : :	2359

Feet.

Mount Battock, Kincardineshire : : : : :	3450
Ben Nevis, Invernesshire : : : : : :	4380

(The highest Mountain in Great Britain.)

Cairngorum : : : : : : : : : : :	4050

REMARKABLE MOUNTAINS,

IN VARIOUS PARTS OF THE WORLD.

◆

IN THE ALPS.

Feet.

Mont Blanc : : : : : : : : : :	15680
Mont Rosa : : : : : : : : : :	15555
Buet : : : : : : : : : : : :	10112
St. Gothard : : : : : : : : : : :	9075
Hospice of Great St. Bernard : : : : :	8040
Ortler Spitze, Tyrol : : : : : : : :	15430

ITALY & SICILY.

Mount Etna : : : : *(doubtful)* : : :	10963
Vesuvius : : : : : : : : : : : :	3900

Feet.

Peak of Teneriffe : : : : : : : : : 12236

Gross Morne, Isle of Bourbon : : : : : 9600

Volcano,   Ditto   : : : : : 7680

ASIA.

The Mountains of Thibet are estimated to

    rise : : : : : : : : : : : 25000

SOUTH AMERICA.

Chimborazo, Quito : : : : : : : : : 22700

Cotopaxi,   Ditto : : : : : : : : : 20325

Pic d'Oriziba : : : : : : : : : : 17368

Many other Mountains in the Andes equal or exceed the height of Mont Blanc.

(lime)	40
(lime)	30
(sand)	100
(clay)	200
y lime)	10
w-	
(lime)	30
(lime)	30
(sand)	
dstone)	400
(lime)	140
	.
(clay)	140
(lime)	40
(sand)	100
(clay)	893

e.

anuscript List, given by the late Herr

July 1816.

	Localities.
· ·	Mont Martre, near Paris
⁝ ·	Dresden
· ·	Pirna
· ·	Weimar
· ·	Jena
· ·	Thuriugia
· ·	Near Cracow
· ·	Eisleben, Ilmenau
· ·	Eisleben, Ilmenau
· ·	Foot of the Hartz

ot included in this list.

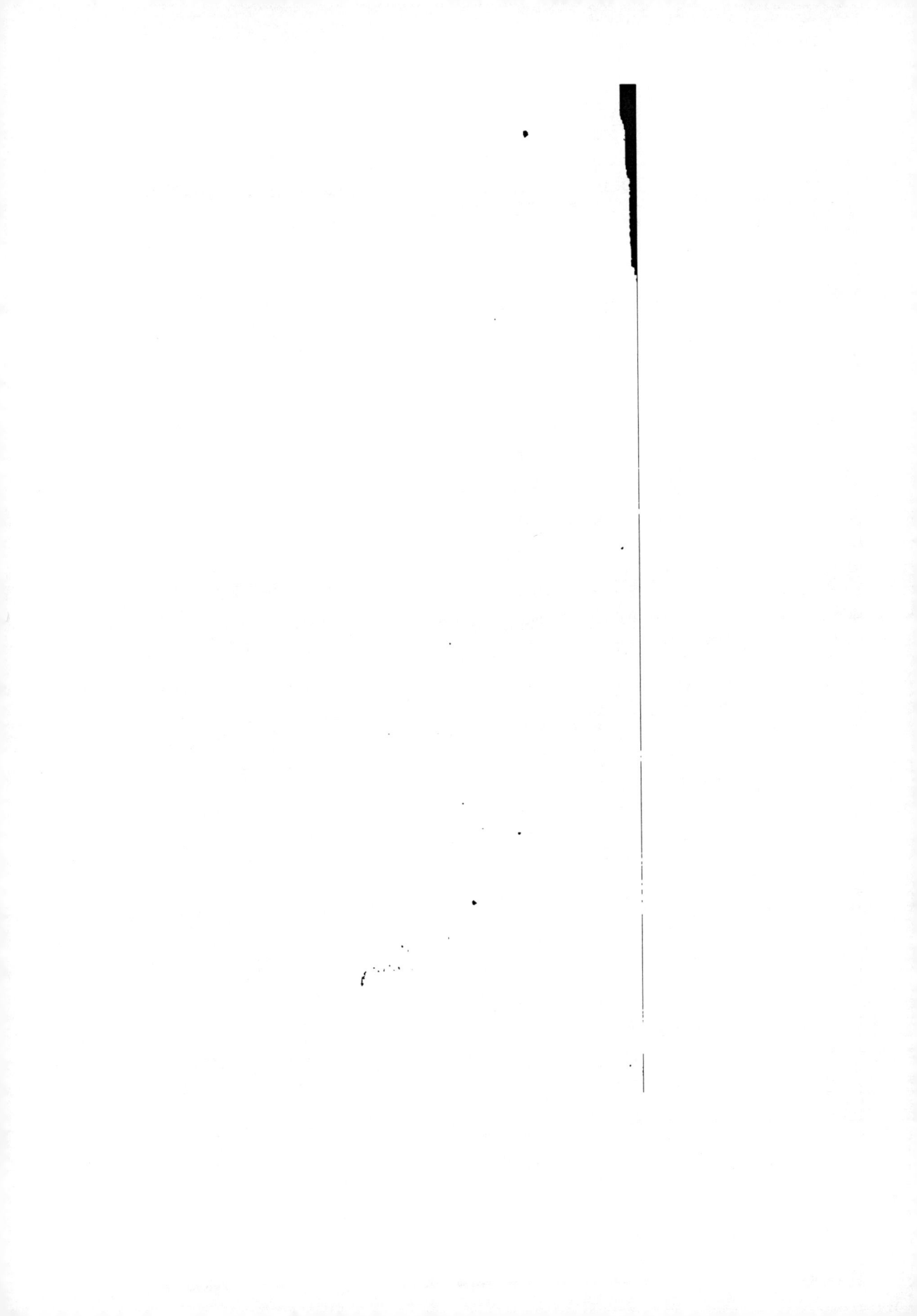

INDEX & GLOSSARY.

A

B

C

4 C 3

INDEX AND GLOSSARY.

LIST OF SUBSCRIBERS.

A

Mr. Thomas Ainsley, Swaledale, Yorkshire.
Reverend Mr. Adshead, Alston.
Thos. Anstey, Esq. Old Bond-street, London—*fine.*
Mr. John Arkless, Tantovy—*2 copies.*
Mr. George Arnison, Selah.
G. W. Aylmer, Esq. London.
Mr. John Akenhead, Newcastle.

B

Count Breunner, Vienna—10 *copies.*
Colonel Beaumont—4 *copies, fine.*
Sir Joseph Banks, Bart. late President of the Royal
    Society.
Henry Banks, Esq. M. P.
Rev. William Buckland, Corpus Christi College,
    Oxford.
Mr. Thomas Bell, Bookseller, Newcastle—3 *copies.*
Mr. Edward Blenk, Blanchland.
Dr. Beaven, M. D.   Ditto
Mr. Thomas Bowden, Grassington.
Monsieur Berthollet, College, Edinburgh.
Mr. Robert Bell, Hexham.

Mr. Robert Bainbridge, Alston.

Mr. William Bainbridge, Alston.

Mr. George Bainbridge, Eastgate.

Mr. John Barnes, Jun. Eggleston.

Mr. Joseph Bowman, Alston.

Mr. Charlton Benson.

Mr. William Bell, Gilsland.

Mr. Edmund Bulman, Alston.

Mr. John Barnes, Sen. Eggleston.

Mr. Joseph Bell, Stublick Colliery.

Mr. Thomas Burdass, Colpits, Blanchland.

John Buddle, Esq. Wall's End.

Mr. William Bolam, Newcastle.

John Bland, Esq. Ormside Lodge—2 *copies, fine.*

Nicholas Burnet, Esq. Black Hedley.

Mr. George Burnet, Ovington.

Mr. James Burnet,   Ditto

Mr. Robert Burnet,·   Ditto

C

Mr. Isaac Crawhall, Allenheads.

Mr. William Crawhall, Allenheads—2 *copies,* 1 *fine.*

Mr. Thomas Crawhall, Newcastle.

Albany Crawhall, Esq.

W. B. Chandler, Esq.

Mr. Thomas Cant, Penrith.

Mr. Thomas Carr, Dotland.

Matthew Cully, Esq. Akeld.

Mr. John Charlton, Dotland.

Mr. Thomas Coultard, Dufton.

Mr. John Cowper, Alston.

Andrew Clark, Esq. Bear Garden, Southwark, London—*fine*.

William Chisholm, Esq. Solicitor, London—*fine*.

Joseph Craig, Esq. Holborn, London.

P. R. Crawford, Esq. Warden Paper Mill.

Mr. Adam Craig, Dufton.

Anthony Clapham, Esq. Newcastle—*fine*.

William Clapman, Esq. Engineer, Newcastle.

William Crackenthorpe, Esq. Newbiggin Hall.

John Crosby, Esq. Kirby Thore.

Mr. William Coats, Haydon Bridge—2 *copies*.

Mr. Thomas Cain, Nenthead.

Mr. John Calvert, Cald Beck.

Mr. Thomas Colpits, Blanchland.

D

The Honourable and Right Reverend the Lord Bishop of Durham—*fine*.

His Grace the Duke of Devonshire.

The Right Honourable the Earl of Darlington.

John Dyer, Esq. London—*fine*.

Mr. John Dickinson, Lowbyer, Alston—*fine*.

Mr. John Dickinson, Newcastle—*fine*.

Mr. Thomas Dickinson, Spency Croft.

Mr. Joseph Dickinson, Lowbyer, Alston.

Joseph Dickinson, Esq. Lovelady Shield.

Mr. Thomas Dickinson, Stone Hall.

Hubert Day, Esq. Chilcompton, near Bath.

Richard Dobson, Esq. Streatlam.

Henry Dixon, Esq. Solicitor, Penrith.

Mr. Thomas Dixon, Dukesfield Mill.

Mr. John Dixon, Jun. Allenheads.

William Donkin, Esq. Sandoe—2 *copies*, 1 *fine*.
—— Dyonly, Esq. Hilton, near Skipton.
Mr. Joseph Dodds, Kirkoswald.
Mr. Thomas Dodd, Middleton.
Mr. Joseph Davison, Blagill.
Mr. James Davidson, Middle Houses.
Mr. Thomas Dowson, Manchester.
Mr. John Dolphin, Ruff-side.
Mr. Thomas Donkin, Bishop Burton.
Mr. Jacob Dawson, Allenheads.

E

Thomas Eddington, Esq. Glasgow.
George Elstob, Esq. Hexham Brewery.
Mr. John Elliot, Middleton.
Mr. Robert Elliot, Silly Hole.
Mr. Michael Elliot, Hexham.
Mr. Thomas Elliot, Washington Wood.
Mr. William Edger, Blagill.
Mr. Thomas Eddy, Alston.
Mr. William Errington, Alston.
Mr. James Easton, Gateshead.
Mr. Thomas Easton, Birtley.
Mr. Thomas Emmerson, Weardale.

F

Mr. John Farey, Mineral Surveyor and Engineer, of
    Howland-street, London.
Mr. Thomas Fenwick, Dipton—2 *copies*.
Mr. Matthew Forster   Ditto

Joseph Forster, Esq.—*fine.*
Mr. George Forster, Hebburn Hall.
Mr. Thomas E. Forster, Ditto
Mr. John Forster, Acomb.
Mr. Richard Featherstonhaugh, Alston.
Mr. Thomas Featherstone, Grocer, Newcastle.
Mr. John Fairlamb, Summer Rods.
Mr. William Forbes, Gateshead.

G

The Commissioners and Governors of the Royal
     Hospital for Seamen, at Greenwich, in the
     county of Kent—30 *copies, fine.*
Mr. Joseph Gray, Dipton.
Mr. Green, Peck Riding.
Mr. William Glendening, Carlisle.

H

Cooper Haffield, Esq. Treasury, Dublin.
John H. Hunt, Esq. Compton, Pauncefoot, near
     Sherborn, Dorset—*fine.*
George Hicks, Esq. Nelson-square, London.
Thomas Harrison, Esq. Saerthaelwyd, near Holy-
     well, North Wales.
Mr. Thomas Hoyle, Manchester.
Mr. John Hall, Gamblesby—*fine.*
Mr. Farbridge Hall.
Mr. Teasdale Hall, Nenthead.
Mr. Michael Hall, Gateshead.
Mr. Thomas Hall, Haltwhistle.

L

D. Lloyd, Esq. Bank-side, Southwark, London—*fine.*

E. H. Locker, Esq.——*fine.*

John Lowry, Esq. Bunker's Hill, near Carlisle.

John Little, Esq. Raise-house, near Alston.

Mr. William Little, Alston.

Mr. William Little, Stanhope.

Mr. John Litell, Blacksmith, Alston.

Mr. William Lee, Burnfoot.

Mr. George Lee, Allendale Town.

Mr. William Laws, Prudoe Castle.

Mr. John Langstaff, Cald Beck.

Mr. C. L. Lawson, Hilton.

M

Professor Millington, Royal Institution of Great Britain, Albermarle-street, London.

Mr. Charles Measton, Engineer, New Bridge-street, London.

Martin Morrison, Esq. Newcastle.

Miles Moukhouse, Esq. Newcastle——*2 copies.*

Mr. James Mulcaster, Langley—*3 copies, fine.*

Mr. Joshua Mulcaster, Grey Southing.

Mr. Thomas Morris, Carlisle—*2 copies.*

Mr. John Millican, Nenthead.

Mr. Ralph March, Middleton.

Mr. James M'Hean, Glasgow.

Mr. Thomas Milburn, Alston.

Mr. Joe Millican, Cald Beck.

Mr. Joseph Mason, Grassington.

Mr. Medcalf, Ravensworth.

Mr. William Makepeace, Bardon Mill.

N

Reverend George Newby, Witton Le Wear.
Mr. Edward Nicholson, Hexham.
Mr. Nathan Newbold, Grassington.

P

Colonel Prowse, London——6 *copies, fine.*
Mr. John Pattinson, Bookseller, Alston——10 *copies.*
Mr. Nicholas Phillipson, Allenheads——*fine.*
Mr. George Pearson, Kingswood.
Mr. John Pearson, Brampton, near Dufton.
Mr. William Price, Allen Shields.
Mr. John Pears, Coalcleugh.
Mr. Richard Pattinson, Alston.
Mr. Jonathan Pattinson, Mine Agent.
Mr. William Pearson, Hexham.
Mr. Hugh Lee Pattinson.
Mr. Peacock, Sunderland.
Captain Thomas Patterson, Shields.
Mr. William Patterson, London.

R

Nicholas Ruddock, Esq. Hexham.
John Ruddock, Esq.   Ditto
Mr. James Reed, Dowgate Wharf, London.
Mr. Charles Rain, Lonton.
Mr. John Roddam, Land Surveyor.
Mr. John Ritson, Old Dike.
Mr. Jonathan Robinson, Alston.
Mr. John Robinson,   Ditto.
Mr. William Reay, Walker.

SUBSCRIBERS.

Mr. George Rutherford, Cald Beck.
Mr. J. Rewcastle, Gateshead.
Mr. John Ramsey, Wood Hall Mill.
Mr. G. H. Ramsey, Derwent-haugh.
Mr. Robert Rutter, Middleton.
Mr. Thomas Robinson, Glasgow.

S

The Right Honourable the Earl of Strathmore.
Robert Stagg, Esq. Middleton——3 *copies.*
Hugh Singer, Esq. Newcastle——*fine.*
Mr. James Sowerby, Mead-place, Lambeth, London.
Mr. Thomas Shaw, Shield Hill.
Mr. John Stout, Garrigill.
Mr. Mark Sherlock, Middleton.
Mr. Cuth. Shield.
Mr. John Smith, Low Leases.
Mr. Jonathan Sparke, Peas Meadows.
Mr. Edward Steel, Mire Meadows.
Mr. Thomas Simpson, Allendale Town.
Mr. Joseph Skelton, Lowes Water.
Mr. Saunderson, Bridge-master, Carlisle.
Mr. Thomas Seymour, Hebburn Colliery.
Mr. J. P. Spencer, Hilton Wilts.
Mr. James Summervill, Millwright, Morpeth.

T

Hugh Taylor, Esq. Newburn.
Mr. John Tomason, for the Book Club, Garrigill.
Mr. William Todd, Alston.

SUBSCRIBERS.

John Taylor, Esq. Benny Court, St. Mary Axe,
   London——2 *copies.*
Doctor Thompson, Regius, Professor of Chemistry,
   Glasgow.
Mr. Trist. Thampson, Hebburn Colliery.
Mr. William Todhunter, Kendal.
Mr. William Thompson, Alston.
Mr. John Tebay, Whitehaven.

v

Mr. Thomas E. Vipond, Newcastle.

w

Thomas Wailes, Esq. Receiver for Greenwich Hos-
   pital, Newcastle——2 *copies.*
John Wilson, Esq. Nenthall——2 *copies.*
Mr. J. B. Wilson, Solicitor, Brampton.
Mr. Jacob Wilson, Clargill.
Mr. Henry Wilson, Coalcleugh.
Mr. George Walker, Westgate.
Alexander Whaly, Esq. Sandoe.
Mr. George Walton, Alston.
Mr. Jonathan Woodmass, Alston.
Jonathan Walton, Esq.   Ditto—2 *copies*
Mr. Ralph Wanlass,   Ditto
Anthony Wright, Esq.   Ditto Brewery.
Rev. Mr. Joseph Whaly, M. A. Cambridge.
Mr. Jacob Walton, Grass-field.
Mr. F. Whitfield, Dryburn.
Utrick Walton, Esq. Farnberry.

Mr. Joseph Wallace, Dufton.
Mr. Fewster Ward, Healy Field.
Mr. Thomas Walton, Cald Beck.
Mr. John Whinfield, Gateshead.
Mr. Joshua Watson, Cheese-monger, Newcastle.
Mr. William Wilkinson, Middleton.
Mr. Adam Walton, Garrigill.
Robert Watson, Esq. Plumber, Newcastle——*fine.*
Mr. Thomas Ward, Edmond-byers.
Mr. Thomas Walker, Mill-wright, Morpeth.
Mr. Joseph Walton, Alston.

ADDENDA.

John C. Curwen, Esq. M. P. Workington.
John B. Longmire, Esq. Whitehaven.
Mr. Edward Routledge, Surgeon, Alston.
Mr. James Thompson, Kirk-house, agent for the Earl of Carlisle.

Thomas Wailes, Esq. Receiver for Greenwich Hospital, ought to be——2 *copies, fine.*
Mr. Robert Rutter, Middleton, ought to be——3 *copies.*

4 E

ERRATA.

Page 13, last line, for *comitant* read *concomitant*.

Page 34, five lines from the bottom, for *from* read *form*.

Page 37, first line, for *Enerinal* read *Encrinal*.

Page 169, at No. 163 in the Section, for *fourth* read *fifth*.

Ditto,	166	Do.	for *fifth* read *sixth*.
Ditto,	169	Do.	for *sixth* read *seventh*.
Ditto,	181	Do.	for *seventh* read *eighth*.
Page 171,	186	Do.	for *eighth* read *ninth*.
Ditto,	190	Do.	read 10th or Tyne-bottom Lime-stone.
Ditto,	200	Do.	for *ninth* read *eleventh*.
Ditto,	204	Do.	for *tenth* read *twelfth*.

Page 210, nineteen lines from the top, for *course* read *cause*.

Page 290, seven lines from the bottom, for *Birch* read *Birchy Bank*.

Page 291, nine lines from the bottom, for *Cable* read *Caple*.

Page 292, five lines from the bottom, for *Craig Green* read *Crag Greens Sun Vein*.

Page 293, ten lines from the bottom, for *Craig Green* read *Crag Greens Middle Vein*.

Same page, six lines from the bottom, for *Craig Green* read *Crag Greens North Vein*.

Page 294, six lines from the bottom, for *Fairnberry* read *Farnberry*.

Same page, three lines from the bottom, for *Fletchers* read *Fletcheras*.

Page 296, ten lines from the top, for *Holey* read *Holy Field*.

Page 298, first line, for *Nattriss* read *Nattrass*.

Same page, nine lines from the bottom, for *North Grains* read *North Grain*.

Same page, two lines from the bottom, for *Arbestus* read *Asbestus*.

Page 299, No 60, for *Roderhope* read *Roderup*.

Page 300, No. 66, for *Thoughtergill* read *Thortergill*.

Same page, four lines from the bottom, for *Specula* read *Specular*.

Page 306, three lines from the bottom, for *north* read *south*.

Page 316, twelve lines from the top, for *Merton* read *Murton*.

Page 328, eight lines from the top, for *bearing* read *bearings*.

Page xi, in the Appendix, nine lines from the top, for *under* read *upon* the Scar Lime-stone.

CPSIA information can be obtained at www.ICGtesting.com
Printed in the USA
LVOW111725150213

320346LV00012B/583/P